SKY TIME
in Gray's River

---

*Living for Keeps
in a Forgotten Place*

Robert Michael Pyle

HOUGHTON MIFFLIN COMPANY

BOSTON · NEW YORK

2007

For information about permission to reproduce selections from
this book, write to Permissions, Houghton Mifflin Company,
215 Park Avenue South, New York, New York 10003.

Visit our Web site: www.houghtonmifflinbooks.com.

Library of Congress Cataloging-in-Publication Data
Pyle, Robert Michael.
Sky Time in Gray's River : living for keeps in a forgotten
place / Robert Michael Pyle.
p.   cm.
Includes bibliographical references.
ISBN-13: 978-0-395-82821-2
ISBN-10: 0-395-82821-X
1. Natural history — Washington (State) — Grays River.
2. Pyle, Robert Michael. I. Title.
 ⌐ QH105.W2P948 2007
508.797'91 — dc22   200600309

Printed in the United States of America

Book design by Victoria Hartman

QUM 10 9 8 7 6 5 4 3 2 1

For THEA

For the AHLBERG, SORENSON, SWANSON,
and LARSON families, and all the other
pioneers who made this place

And to the memory of ED MAXWELL,
dear friend and great naturalist,
gone too soon

Here, this, is *It*. The world as it is, is Heaven, I'm looking for a Heaven outside what there is, it's only this poor
pitiful world that's Heaven . . . what there is, is ecstasy.

— JACK KEROUAC, *The Dharma Bums*

I would remain where I was and make the most of what
I had. — JOHN HAINES, *The Stars, the Snow, the Fire*

Contents

✦

Sky Time in Gray's River

Beforetimes
Going to Ground in Gray's River

"To go to ground"—an English fox-hunting term, meaning "into a burrow or hole in the ground, 'to earth'"; as in "When a Fox goes to ground, after a long chase . . ." With respect to the digging of Foxes which hounds run to ground.

—*Oxford English Dictionary*

Walking to the compost this morning, I was arrested by the sight of a leaf pinioned on a rush spike. The bunch of rushes grows in a pot in the corner of the heather garden. The leaf was birch, clear yellow spattered with remnant green. It hung there, impaled as it fell from the tall white wand of the birch. Shivering on the light November air, the leaf was like a moment of grace before the fall. The compost heap shone bright with still more leaves of maple, oak, and hornbeam, spattered among bracts of Brussels sprouts, over-the-hill red currants, and the collapsed brainpan of a jack o' lantern—the exuviae of a satisfied autumn and its festivals.

Returning to the house, I paused as always to rinse the white china chamber pot in the spray of a standing spigot. Just before tossing the water onto the heather, I noticed a struggling spider in the chilly swirl. Spiders up spouts suffer a well-known fate, and so it had. But rescued with an oak leaf, it unfolded just fine. When I placed it on the spigot post, I saw a rotund female of another species, a big native orb weaver, hunched up under the handle. The skinnier one crawled back into its shelter, apparently uninjured by the dunking. So the two spiders had been there together at this late date, somehow surviving the harsh frosts and heavy rains of recent mornings.

As I approached the back porch a Steller's jay rocketed off, screaming that the kibbles were all gone from the cat's dish. An elegant Anderson's slug, slender, yellow-rimmed, reticulated, glided away from the bowl too. From the doorway I noticed a flutter in a tall English oak by the drive. The first-year Townsend's warblers that had come for Thanksgiving were still there, flickering through the tawny foliage together while chickadees and kinglets loitered off to the side. The migrant warblers' lemony breasts and faces were as bright as the slug's mantle; their presence was as unexpected as a pair of spiders in late autumn, their gift as sudden and fleeting as a birch leaf on a rush spike.

ONE APRIL DAY in 1970, I drove a wide circle through southwest Washington in search of early-season butterflies to photograph. Very few were yet on the wing, and I came home with only one good shot, a linen-fresh margined white basking next to a new leaf of its host plant, toothwort. I also brought back a vision of the kind of place where I would spend most of my life. My random route took me through several broad, low valleys where streams ran down through green velvet pastures between low evergreen hills to Puget Sound or the Pacific Ocean. To an urban visitor, these valleys looked both bucolic and idyllic. The sun was out that day, giving the rural prospects an uncommon luminosity that intensified their magnetism. I decided then and there that I would someday like to live in such a valley: a place where I could see something new every time I stepped outside.

Now that they are in their fifties, as I am, many of my friends are just beginning to seek a permanent home. Work or adventure has taken them here and there, to this house and that, and at last they hope to find abodes that will see them happily into old age. They may think I settled into my long-term habitation awfully early, though it seemed none too soon to me at the time. I had grown up in a Colorado suburb, gone to college in Washington and Connecticut, lived and worked in California, England, New Guinea, and Oregon, dwelling in some twenty homes along the way. I had long idealized a rural or edge-of-wildland domicile that would serve as a "central repository" for my stuff and a warm retreat from which I could range outward into the world. I knew several biologists and writers who had indeed established such holts, but usually only after retiring from a long academic, bureaucratic, or journalistic career. What right had I, a mere whippersnapper, to a country seat?

My family had once owned several ranches in western Colorado, any one of which might have been a perfect place for me to live. But they had been lost since the Depression or before, so I had no patrimony of land to which I might repair. I would have to find and adopt my own home place. My ideal of a naturalist's abode was Trail Wood, the old New England farmstead where Edwin and Nellie Teale made their final home after Long Island became too populous for them. In his book *A Naturalist Buys an Old Farm,* Teale described the arduous process of finding the right place and the success that finally came through the grace of happenstance. I expected that it would be many years before it was time for me to settle, and I would have to make just such a search. The only similarity between my search and the Teales' was the good luck.

It happened like this. My first long-term job, with the Nature Conservancy in Portland, Oregon, involved a great deal of travel and furnished a ration of stress. The gallery job that my wife at that time, Sally Hughes, held was also stressful. Yet our combined salaries were too small even for the tiny shack under the abutments of the St. John's Bridge in North Portland that we considered buying. We dreamed of retreating to the country. That summer of 1978 I had a field assistant, a teenager from Ithaca, New York, named David Shaw. On weekends David and

I often prowled terra incognita for butterflies within a day's drive of Portland. On August 30 we ferried across the Columbia River to Wahkiakum County, Washington, where no butterflies had been recorded. I didn't know at the time that most days it rains in Wahkiakum County. This day the sun shone hard. We found a few butterflies on pastoral Puget Island, netted a few more up the Elochoman River out of Cathlamet, then drove up into the Willapa Hills and crossed the Gray's River Divide to the west on logging roads.

We came down from the hills not long before sunset into Gray's River Valley. Three years previously, a friend named Denny Gillespie had taken Sally and me here—in the rain—to see a number of historic buildings and to look for butterflies. Remembering a nearby covered bridge from that visit, I proposed that we look for it. "Heck, New York is full of covered bridges," said David. "Let's get back for dinner." I began to turn left on State Route 4 to return to Portland. Then I realized that *I* wanted to see the covered bridge, and I was in charge. I turned west instead.

After we crossed through the bridge and paused on the other side of the river, I beheld a green valley much like the ones I'd fallen in love with eight years before. Then I looked up and saw an old white farmhouse perched among huge hardwood trees. English oaks, red oaks, black walnuts, European beeches and birches, Scots pines, sugar maples, and one great Port Orford cedar all loomed over the place. FOR SALE BY OWNER said the sign by the road.

"That's where I want to live," I told David, and set off to find the owner. Ed Sorenson was away, but his son, Merle, showed me around the place. The next day Sally and I made an offer. We borrowed money for a down payment, closed at Christmas, weekended all winter, and moved in June. I have essentially lived here ever since. Lives change, and after greatly enhancing the fabric and gardens of the place, Sally returned to her native Eng-

land in the early eighties. My old friend Thea joined me here in
1984, and we married the following year.

WHEN I OPEN my eyes in the morning, my vision is framed by
four rectangles of wavy old glass enclosing a field of gray sky
of many possible shades or, occasionally, blue. As I sit up with
my cup of coffee, the sash windows of our bedroom shift perspective, opening onto a view of cake-plate-flat fields of green,
hemmed in by dark hemlock hills. One scrubby meadow away
runs the river, crossed mid-window by the old gray covered
bridge. A scattering of houses breaks up the verdant plain, looking smaller for being so few and spread out. Cattle, the agents of
the short grass sward, roam broad pastures that were created for
producing dairy cows but are now more often occupied by Hereford beef cattle, blackberries, and thistles. Any black-and-white
Holsteins still to be seen are heifers raised to replace dairy cows
elsewhere.

Through it all runs the river, which very gradually wavers
from one side of the valley to the other. The East Fork and the
West Fork of the Gray's converge just three miles upstream from
the house. Breaking out of two canyons, the river long ago laved
the floor to make the valley that runs for some ten miles down to
the marshes of Gray's Bay on the Columbia River. I am looking
out from one of several old river terraces. Broken slices of these
former levels survive at various heights above the present valley
floor, left behind as the river cut deeper into ancient seabed sediments. They support some of the few flat forests in these hills
and most of the sensible home sites, stable and well above the
floodplain.

Down in the valley, Larson's Pond, freckled with ducks, glitters in thin mild sunshine. The river describes a long S into the
west. Heavy rain could set in tomorrow, or even snow, but right
now there is no more congenial place in the world than this little
vale. Come summer, waves of blue timothy and green canary

grass will replace the pond, and the river's S will slink behind a screen of foliage. Next winter high, wild water will pour over the whole bottom, bringing down the silt of the hills and sweeping away any semblance of congeniality. From my vantage on the river terrace, the valley presents a world both contained and expansive, handmade and natural, ancient and hopeful. It is beautiful in a flawed and unspectacular way, and homely, like river-scoured lowlands anywhere.

Nothing appears to be moving but the river. Then the motionlessness is broken by the yellow school bus, delayed by slick roads, making its way around Covered Bridge Road. The mail lady's car appears from the other direction, slowing for our box. At tonight's Grange meeting, the annual Christmas party will be planned, the winter floods predicted.

From my second-story study, I can see that the birch leaf has blown off its pikestaff, to join the thousands of other leaves in the glowing, already rotting carpet. Later, fetching tea, I check on the slug, which has slithered off someplace. Both spiders are gone, too; maybe the jay, deprived of kibbles, found them and saved them from the coming frost. The warblers continue to forage for insects among late leaves, flitting from tree to tree in a loose bunch, siskin-like, packing fat against their inevitable departure.

None of this is high adventure, but it meets my hope for a home where boredom remains at bay. I live where I do so I can look out or walk outside at any time and instantly be within "nature." Of course, one is in nature everywhere, since there is nothing else. But I mean a place where you can actually see all the swallows depart on a certain day in the fall and see the first arrivals in the spring in all their joy and relief and know there is nothing sentimental in saying so. See rufous hummingbirds working the sparse nectaries of blood currants while they wait for the salmonberries to break bud. Watch the early vultures ride the airs just above the treetops, and the bald eagles, whose nest in a cottonwood top was blown away by last winter's winds, start in again to soar, to hunt, to feed their young in a brand-new nest. See the bleeding hearts fan, the trilliums crack, the banana slugs strike out from their cold-weather hideaways for fresh pastures of moss, and the first spring azures appear on what Robert Frost called "Blue Butterfly Day." These things are as important to me as love, and in fact, that's what they are.

As for high adventure, it's here too, if wanted. Out over the valley, one harrier, one kite, and one eagle quarter, flutter, and soar, each hunting after its own fashion; the ravens circle far above as the redtail hunkers and watches, and two westering swans silently merge with low clouds, all against the ever-changing, ever-present sky. More than anything, it is the sky that defines this old homestead in this small valley in this subtle range of hills. Often gray, sometimes blue, always dissected by a canopy of leaves and needles and crisscrossed by birds, and ordinarily the conveyor of dampness in one form or another, the Gray's River sky reflects every story that happens here. It is here, beneath this particular slope of sky, that I have chosen to go to ground.

1 ⋅ The Time of Mew Gulls

These are the hills, these are the woods.

— ROBERT LOUIS STEVENSON, "Story Books"

The first of the year was sunny, as January days surprisingly often are in the rainforest winter. I was cutting English ivy away from the trunks of trees, where it clambers back eternally, and watching with satisfaction the periodic spurt of the saturated soil's floodwater from a new drainage pipe: water that for years had overtaxed the cellar's sump pump and flooded the furnace. I decided to survey the damage from the previous night's storm, which had been so strong that Thea was trancelike with trepidation during our New Year's Eve of reading and playing Chinese checkers.

About half of a splendid Scots pine had fallen between a great beech and the tallest red oak. Something had to give in the freeway-speed winds of midnight, and it was the foot-and-a-half-thick upper trunk of this pine. Pale lichen-dressed twigs and brushy green, needle-bearing branches brought to ground an elfin pinery, laid out on the fern, bramble, ivy, and woodruff floor, where deep purple columbines would bloom in June. I was taken by the trunk of the fallen bole, its bark and underbark deep cinnamon red and many shades of russet, black where the bark was thickest, green where thin scales had peeled away like sunburned kidskin. Soft and soaked, pocked by the sapsucker's bill. When it was standing, I'd mostly noted its Japanese form and wispy brush against the sky. Fallen, it seemed not at all wispy, but solid now in its last stand before rot. I knew I would miss its full form in the southeast treescape, but half was left. So many trees had broken in the hundreds of storms over twenty-some years since I'd landed here.

That night, when I stoked up the blue enamel cookstove that warms our living room, I began with broken shingles of old-growth western red cedar, the fine grain overprinted with the name Knappton Mill, once active on the Columbia, where the shingles had been sawn from great rounds. This perfect kindling came from a previous roof. Instead of hauling the old shingles off to the dump when the roofers tossed them down, we stored them along with our firewood. The supply has lasted fifteen years so far. Atop a bit of paper and the shingles I place lichen-fuzzed sticks, usually from blown-down branches.

After the kindling I toss in chunks of solid oak. Even if we had a fire every night, we would have a hard time keeping up with the good oak that appears on the ground, great thick branches as big as trees, cracked off in winter storms or, more often, dropped when the sap is up and leaves are heavy in the still air of summertime. Bucking and splitting all the wood is another matter. Once dried, the pitchy pine logs will take their turn in the firebox, burning faster than the oak but not as hot. Looking over the remnants of that wind-broken pine, I thought of the Swede who made this place parklike but who never saw his trees get big, let alone grow old, shed giant branches, or break in two.

Living in England for some years, I occupied a series of houses and cottages with wonderful names: Stuart House, Southcot House, Toll Bar Cottage, Owlstone Croft. The British enjoy a long-standing tradition of naming their domiciles rather than merely numbering them. I liked the feel of that habit and often thought I might eventually name my home. Friends sometimes assume that I followed through with this whim here in Gray's River. But in fact I chose a home that already had a name: Swede Park. Even though it comes with liabilities—mail addressed to "Sweet Park," visitors searching for the public park of which we are presumably the caretakers—I have stuck with it. Ed and Lenore Sorenson, who sold me the place, gave me a fancy butter wrapper from the twenties labeled S W E D E P A R K D A I R Y. The Swede was Ed's grandfather.

Hans Peter Ahlberg was born in La Holm, Sweden, in 1842. He spent five years in the Swedish army, which he liked, but because of the small pay he emigrated to the United States in 1869. Trained in horticulture, he went west to a cousin in Batavia, Illinois, and found work as an assistant gardener at the sanitarium where Mary Todd Lincoln resided from May to September of 1875. There he fell in love with Mrs. Lincoln's French companion and nurse, Miss Belle Bouchur, and married her. Ahlberg traveled to Portland, and after a season Belle followed. In Portland he met the Danish immigrants Chris and Antone Sorensen, as well as a man named James who owned land in Gray's River and persuaded the others to go see it. The party crossed the rough, miles-wide Columbia River just above its mouth in a skiff. According to an interview with Maggie Ahlberg by H. Alta Meserve in *The Grays River Builder,* a local newspaper she published, "Ahlberg was immensely pleased with James' place," so when James told Ahlberg he was willing to sell, they promptly struck a deal: Ahlberg gave him one hundred dollars, his gun, and fishing tackle for the title. Belle lived with him there for twelve years before frontier life defeated her. She went one whole year without seeing another woman, then lost her reason in the rain and solitude. Gray skies overwhelmed the blue, and Belle died in Steilacoom State Hospital. By the time Ahlberg married Maggie Olson, another Swede, they had neighbors.

Ahlberg built a cabin and barn just above river level, on the first terrace, in 1875. First he raised garden produce, such as cabbage and cucumbers, which he took to market in Astoria by sailboat. Though a gardener by inclination, he found dairying more profitable, so he built a herd to run on the valley pastures. Right around the turn of the century, with a much bigger barn, his own preemption land claim, and more fields cleared of floodplain cottonwoods and willows, Ahlberg built a bigger, two-story Swedish Victorian house on the second river terrace. Its lines were simple but handsome, and it looked bigger from without than within. One deep gable graced the front, with two windows set into it like eyes over the valley. A photograph taken in 1909 shows the freshly whitewashed house with a gingerbread porch and balcony, a gabled gazebo for a bee house off to the side, an array of outbuildings, and the young trees and shrubs that would eventually make the homestead a horticultural showplace, all carved out of the clear-cut hillsides. Ahlberg, vested, stands by a small oak, ax in hand.

"Pete" Ahlberg, as he was called, played a major role in the early life of the village of Gray's River. A contemporary photograph shows him with a high forehead, combed-back dark hair, intent eyes and mouth, and a long mustache and goatee. With a few other valley pioneers, he erected a cable bridge, moved from its first position downriver, below his house; and then, in 1905, he helped build a substantial truss bridge in the same location. In 1908 the bridge was covered. The Grange movement (the Order of the Patrons of Husbandry) came to southwest Washington early and strong. Ahlberg founded Gray's River Grange, the first in Wahkiakum County, on December 30, 1901, and it was chartered in April 1902, number 124 of several hundred local Granges in Washington. His name appears in the back of the Grange Bible, written, along with those of the other officers, in an earnest farmer's hand: "*1902*: Stuard—Theodore Rhule; Ass't Stuard—Frank Walker; Lady Ass't Stuard—Ella Sorensen; Overseer—Thomas Walker; Master—Hans P. Ahlberg." Grange would prove influential in every arena of county life, including the recruitment of the first county extension officer west of the Mississippi, George A. Nelson, in 1912.

For Ahlberg, every day was Arbor Day. He pursued his green-thumb penchant by planting European and Midwestern trees on his own land and around the valley, from starts and seeds he brought or purchased. The valley flora today owes much of its character to his plantings of birches, maples, oaks, both horse and sweet chestnuts, beeches, hornbeams, lindens, tulip trees, and many others. In 1911 Ahlberg returned to Sweden, long before the trees reached maturity but not before his neighbors had taken to calling his place the Swede's Park. I've never found out why he left. Maybe the arduous life in the rain of southwestern Washington, with more mud than roads and more mildew than sunshine, got to him; maybe he never got over the death of Belle; maybe he just missed his homeland.

It is also possible that the trip was intended to be only a visit. According to Lenore Sorenson, after Pete and Maggie traveled to Småland in Sweden, Ahlberg became crippled with rheumatism. He never returned to Gray's River, though he lived to be ninety years old, dying in 1934. Margaret sailed back to the States in 1935 but settled in South Dakota, where she had been living when Ahlberg advertised for a wife after Belle's death. Ebba, George, and Ed Sorenson journeyed there and fetched her back to Gray's River, which, she said, "was always her home."

Meanwhile the Ahlbergs' daughter, Ebba, had married Chris and Ella Sorensen's son George, and the couple ran Swede Park Dairy, one of the larger of the hundreds of milking farms that sent their butterfat to the Ferndale Creamery. Another was Chris Sorensen's Pond Lilly Dairy downvalley. In 1916, to ensure higher standards, the village blacksmith, C. C. "Pop" Schmand, organized Gray's River Cooperative Creamery. A new riverside depot was built in 1928, and it shipped more than a million pounds of milk products in 1936. The creamery building is still standing despite many floods. Before the highways brought tankers, the co-op's cheese, butter, and dried milk went to Astoria by small tugboat. Between the world wars, most of the row crops in the valley gave way to more milk cows and hay. Both

Gray's River and Skamokawa, a few miles east, became famous for their milk, butter, and cheese, romanced from the nutritious grass of the valleys through the rumination of Holsteins and Jerseys. That rich flow, just a trickle today, began in Ahlberg's time and would last about a century.

George and Ebba's son, George Edwin Jr., changed the spelling of the family name from the Danish Sorensen to the Swedish Sorenson, maybe to match Swede Park, or because he was surrounded by Swedes. He and his wife, Lenore, one of several Swanson sisters from another prominent local Swedish family, continued milking and built a new farm a mile down the valley, now the Joel Fitts family farm. George died in 1952, and Ebba stayed on at Swede Park. Like her father, she served as Grange Master and carried on the gardening that he had begun. She wrote him letters about the now-towering trees he had planted as acorns and shoots. She never visited Sweden, and he never returned to see his park in its glory. Ebba died here in 1975, a hundred years after her father had stepped out of a skiff at the head of tidewater on Gray's River.

Three years later I came to the old Swede's Park, already growing rough with rampant Himalayan blackberries, English ivy, English oaks, and sycamore maples in the absence of blades and grazing animals. I first saw the place in late summer, when these and many other plants give new dimension to the word "rampant." I felt a burden of responsibility, if not to restore Swede Park to its manicured state, at least to respect its history and the effort that went into making it. The challenge never seems greater than in winter, when rain and rot trade places with growth, and life finds other ways to make itself known. Belle, who turned down Mrs. Lincoln's offer of a Grand Tour of Europe and followed her heart to Gray's River instead, must have felt this damp burden too, and even Ahlberg.

SOME VILLAGES IN England still adhere to the ancient practice of "walking the bounds," whereby the people, on the first day of the year, saunter all the way around the parish boundary, usually a distance of a few miles, checking walls and fences and noting what's going on as the fresh year gets under way. Though I am constantly checking this place out from my window and watching as I walk to the mailbox or the compost or through the butterfly garden, taking tally, there are corners and whole sections of Swede Park I seldom visit. Some small nooks of the almost three acres I may never have seen at all. And so, although I have not made it a regular New Year's habit, on some firsts of the year I am drawn to walk the bounds of this pie-shaped piece of ground. I usually begin below the house, where the old cart path meets our driveway at the county route known as Loop Road.

This three-way juncture is situated beside the Tall Oak, a red oak that exceeds 130 feet in height. When I first arrived, its trunk bore a county sign from the 1950s banning "vehicles with lugs on wheels and sharp-shod animals" from traversing Loop Road. Since then the road has been widened and asphalted, there are no sharp-shod animals left, and I have taken the sign indoors. Turning left onto the county road, which still sees very little traffic, I climb a gentle incline to the junction with State Route 4. The two roads meet at an acute angle that encloses the eastern point of Swede Park's pie slice. The tip itself has been graded at least twice by the crashing cars of dozing drivers; the harsh soil is so stripped of humus that the best thing we could grow in that no man's land where county and state rights of way overlap is butterfly bush (*Buddleia*), which loves poor soils. I am trying Douglass-firs, with much water and mulch. But the narrow section of land inward from the apex is one of the wildest sectors. A tangle of Sitka spruce and western hemlock, it encloses the sole big-leaf maple on the property, as well as the biggest birch, some old apple trees, and the massive Eastern Oak, another red. The highway came through in the thirties, defining the pointy end of the Ahlberg place, which holds the only grape ferns we have found here and a few huge trilliums each spring.

Next comes the north-side leg, which lies entirely along the state highway. While not heavily traveled most of the time, the road does carry a motley fleet of log and chip trucks, delivery vans, local pickups, and the automobiles of beachgoers and passers-through. This bound I walk with care, due west. The hillock of the east end, sword-fern-mantled, quickly drops away as the road becomes an embankment above our yard. One great English oak (which has a double a hundred feet farther along), a sugar maple, a tall Port Orford cedar, and clumps of cherry laurel and rhododendron do their best to hold back and screen the stark roadside. English ivy clings to the verge and keeps it from eroding, the only helpful function of our worst botanical adversary. A tattered scrim of small oaks, hornbeams, birches, and maples takes over from the laurels, leafless now and too thin even in summer to muffle the ear-splitting jake brakes of the log trucks slowing for the highway's curve. But the crowns of the trees are alive in winter with feeding flocks of kinglets, chickadees, and siskins working over the buds, seeds, and lichens for whatever slender forage they might hold; in summer, with black-throated gray warblers after aphids.

I see the roof of the old smithy, too mossy for its own good. This white clapboard outbuilding, which stores our wood and the canoe and contains a garage and studio, was here before the highway, and it extends almost to the rim of the road: if a chip truck ever left the wet pavement at this point, our outbuilding would be history as well as historical. A linden and a catalpa guarded this exposure when I came, but both have since fallen down. Now a spindly butternut and a hickory hang over the smithy, dropping their hard little nuts onto the pavement, where cars obligingly crush them for the jays. Dropping to the level of the land, the verge here is lined with thick growth of blackberries, salmonberries, and thimbleberries, which we must cut back every year to keep the Department of Transportation crews from spraying them.

The pie slice broadens out. Big trees punctuate the woods between the two roads: more tall oaks, both red and English, and a sole Douglas-fir of almost old-growth proportions. The forest deepens to my left as I hurry along the highway, past the place across the road that was once the hired hand's house and a view of the peak of another old house of much the same design, materials, and period as ours. If I carried on (as I normally do when I take this walk), I would pass beneath a sword-fern hillside, round the western borders of the original Swede Park, and then drop back down toward the river and Loop Road along steep little Fairview Road. But this crust end of the pie slice was carved off before we were served our piece. Our property line was surveyed from culvert to culvert, along the creek bed between the two roads. The descent is difficult, the slope steep, the ferny ground unstable, but with care I can drop into the little canyon.

When Ed Sorenson showed me the chunk of the old farm he was slicing off to sell, I was especially interested to see the creek. He didn't intend to include it, because it cuts the ravine between the part he was selling and the part he wanted to keep for himself. I told him I really wanted a site with running water, and he offered to compromise. In the end our western bound ran from the culvert on the highway above to the culvert on the county road below, with the stream braiding back and forth across the property line. The very idea of owning a watercourse struck me as absurd, so this arrangement suited me fine. In later years I had reason to wish I had pressed to extend the property line to the far side of the ravine. But at least Swede Park was graced by a creek, and I had lusted to live beside one ever since I first toddled to the classic brook beyond the end of our street in North Denver.

Our creek has no name, and this is satisfactory to me. I have toyed with Skunk Cabbage Creek, Yellow Violet Creek, Salmonberry Creek, Big Spruce Creek, and Licorice Creek, for the licorice ferns that crowd the fallen, mossy cottonwoods and willows. But whenever I actually refer to it, the name just comes out as The Creek. It is, after all, in the contained infinitude of Swede Park, the only creek there is. It comes off the low, nameless mountain and marshy flat to the north, logged now and then, and again as I write. For a long time I intended to walk the stream's full course and find its source in the hills. When I finally set out to do so, I found that the creek, before a sweet, straight run through our neighbors David and Debbie's place, swung past the only silver maple I know in the valley and emerged smack out of a new clear-cut. I don't think dumping a fifteen-foot slash pile right on top of a creek is exactly what the fisheries biologists had in mind when they recommended leaving coarse woody debris in spawning streams. But this stretch crosses a higher river bench, flat and swampy, where the stream spread out and ran partly underground even before the latest logging. It still follows a tiny rill as it drops from the yet-wooded hills above.

I now clamber down from the road beside old fallen alders and muck my way around a shallow pond. Ed told me that George Sorenson once maintained three trout ponds on the premises, and this was the largest. Construction of the highway cut off the inlet, stuffing it into a culvert, and the Public Utility District's water line breached the dam at the lower end. In winter the one remaining pond is a shallow swamp, and in early spring a pool greened by celery-like water parsley and flagged by immense yellow spathes of skunk cabbage. Here plastic soldiers took a beating from BBs at the hands of my stepson, Tom, in his younger days, and countless red-backed salamanders rescued from the basement sump pump have been liberated, also mostly by Tom. Here the first cerise salmonberry blossoms will open, roselike, in another month or two, and the rufous hummingbirds that nectar them will nest in a low alder crotch.

I cross the main east-west trail, which follows the water line. Left goes to the compost and then the house; right runs up through brush to a higher bench, where the Sorensons lived when I first came. I go straight, down another steep and friable slope, past a big culvert installed to carry floodwater over the buried water line. The outflow is a waterfall that merges with another from the west to form the main body of the stream. Three great spruces hold the ravine's west bank. My predecessors had landscaped the ravine into a fairy glen, and rotting sections of cedar water flumes remain, geometric intrusions among the water-side mosses. I step gingerly down through algae and fern, hand-over-handing the moist trunks of alders across the canyon from the spruce wall. Though I haven't yet spotted them, I suspect that it is sewellels (primitive rodents often called mountain beavers or "boomers") whose burrows render every footstep a potential sinkhole.

I pick my way over deadfall, past the little double waterfall on our side of the property line. A tributary comes in from the west, taking a ten-foot plunge down from Ed's old place before doubling the size of the stream. Here, on a sedgy terrace, I could linger to find any number of aquatic insects, amphibians, and early green shoots of plants ready to emerge when the water drops and the days lengthen. Here the yellow stream violets will burst forth in April as the skunk cabbage goes over, and tall willows dip and sometimes fall across the stream.

Before I know it, I have emerged onto Loop Road. A left turn completes the circuit, heading me east once more, and uphill. On my right is the brambly site of a big red barn that was still standing when I came, until Ed tore it down, opening the view to the river and the covered bridge. On my left stands a wall of sycamore maples, beeches, birches, and oaks, with a single native vine maple struggling for the southern exposure. Here the old cart path takes me up past the plum grove, above the county road, along the tangled bank of hazel, cherry, unruly oak, and wisteria, until once more I come to the huge gray trunk of the Tall Oak beside the drive. Across the road towers a monumental European beech, one of two that used to create a portico to a riverside portion of the original homestead. When rot and insect damage began to show in the larboard beech, drawing the pileated woodpecker for the beetle grubs, the county took it down, and the one remaining now guards the driveway to the Petersons' house. But I turn away left, up the drive lined by spruces and by woodruff that snows in May, under the prolific apple, and into my own dooryard. And so I round off the bounds as the short New Year's day closes out, with a better picture of this odd little precinct that is our home. Such as it is, it's all still here.

SITTING UP WITH coffee on a winter morning, I see the first mew gulls and dunlins from my bed. As the fog lifts and condensation evaporates from the windows, the soggy fields light up with silver puddles and packs of pale birds. The gulls swing one way over the water meadows, dunlins the other, as a single swan wings in between. Mews are the smallest of the local gulls, almost petite compared to the glaucous-wings and ring-bills that line the tide on the beach to the west. They too come inland, but mews are the main winter visitors upvalley. Sometimes Fitts's fields host a thousand or more mews after a flood. Walking near them, I can hear how they got their name, as their shortish yellow bills open to emit catlike sounds. When they lift en masse to shift up- or downvalley, mew gulls fly in slow motion, clustered like atomic particles in their fields, until their weak bond of attraction decays and the gullitrons split off, circling in wider and wider orbits and wild, independent arcs to hundreds of feet above the silver meadows. Then they are a galaxy of gulls, expanding and spinning on the valley's damp airs, until gravity or food brings them back to the grass, like so many of their own feathers floating down.

Ornithologists lump gulls and terns together with shorebirds in a single order of birds, the Charadriiformes, a classification I found strange when I learned it. Mew gulls are compact enough, and the black-bellied plovers who come in the same season big enough, that you can accept their relationship. Yet when the dunlins show up, you see a world of difference between even these robust sandpipers and the smallest gulls. While the mew gulls slowly flick and switch on the wing, gliding and flapping just enough to exceed stall speed, the dunlins never slow down until they brake to land in the muddy turf near the cattle trough.

And while a flock of mews in the air suggests the random aftermath of a pillow fight, the dunlins' flight is as tightly woven as a good percale sheet snapping in the wind. Not everyone around here knows what these long-billed sandpipers are, let alone what they are called, but everyone has seen the dunlins change color and direction, wheel and tack, with the fleet cohesion of a buckshot load in an elbow pipe. Then, just as snappily, they'll hit the ground, only to blast off again.

Mew-gull time brings other birds onto the silent ponds left from the winter floods. I always try to remember to carry my binoculars on a trip to the post office or the Rosburg Store, just to scan the ducks on the Lily Pond or Durrah's flooded fields. (These now belong to the Larsons, but they'll always be Norman Durrah's place; just as their pond, sold off to someone else, will always be Larson's Pond.) Each year certain birds return to the same damp declivities in the valley floor. On the Lily Pond most winters we see ring-necked ducks, with their bright white shoulder stripes and blue-tipped bills, green-winged teal, and buffleheads, the dash-faced females and white-puffed drakes popping up and down like bobbers. Hooded mergansers have a similar pattern of black shot with snowy white, but they are sleek compared to the chunky buffs and are often seen in the low swales south of where Hull Creek slips into the river. Durrah's fields-cum-lakes have pintails and widgeons, while Larson's longer-lasting pond across the river from Swede Park is mostly mallards. Wahkiakum County is almost lakeless in summer, but in its winter seepage and pondage, its lowlands look almost Minnesotan, minus the ice. Could this watery condition have something to do with the abundance of Scandinavians in both places?

We have come to expect the mew gulls and the mergansers, but at this time of year many unexpected birds show up as well. A mountain plover was seen recently at the North Jetty of the Columbia River. Driving over for a look at the handsome refugee from high grasslands, related to the dunlin but closer to the dotterel, we found birders from afar lined up with a phalanx of

Swarovskis just shy of the Hubble Telescope. Snowy owls materialized, as they do some winters, across the river mouth at the South Jetty in Oregon. A white ibis appeared among the Holsteins at a tidewater farm where the Palix River empties into Willapa Bay.

In one recent rounding of the loop we actually saw snow on the ground. A few golden-crowned sparrows loafed just inside Doug Larson's cattle barn in the warm fog of calf-breath, as a song sparrow sang like spring on a post outside. A Turner sky lit the west. As the day ran down, a pair of white-tailed kites hovered low and alighted over the snowy old Larson fields. Unlike the pearly white mew gulls, which decorate the valley by the hundreds, the kites are a rarer treat, having moved up from California in recent years. But almost any day early in the year they may appear, like snow.

Not very deep into the year I took a warm winter night's walk at dusk. The elk lay at rest in the field, a musk was on the air, ducks erupted off a stock pond. A barn owl creaked out of an abandoned silo to quarter the field. Later that week I watched a pair of kites doing the same by day, but hunting more from a hover than a glide. On a rise above the river I met Noreen Fitts and Frances Phelan on horseback, clop-clopping toward me. I asked them if they had ever seen live angels on the wing in the sunshine. They said they hadn't, so I pointed out the white-tailed kites hanging over the valley floor. With their heads and tails pointing down, their silvery fluttering wings straight up, the kites look just like christmas-tree angels. The riders were amazed by these seraphim in our midst. Ghost-owls by night, angel-kites by day, both of them white death by beak and talon to the voles that are the valley's main offering.

Frost descends and sticks some nights, and occasionally it snows for a little while. Suchtimes we spread birdseed beneath the umbrella boughs of the capacious Port Orford cedar beside our drive. Until recently we didn't keep feeders. But when the weather is harsh, and snow or interminable cold rain prevents the birds from normal foraging, we break down and buy bags of millet and sunflower seed. In no time the varied thrushes drop down from the hills, the Steller's jays arrive, and the resident rufous-sided towhees tuck in. Later in the season they will be joined by song and fox sparrows, purple finches, and juncoes. The birds at seed create a spectacle, vying and trouncing, retreating and running back in, or just pecking away in relative amity. In this time of depleted colors, we take pleasure in the deep rust of the towhee's side bands, the orange breasts and eye stripes of the Alaska robins, and the bluebottle blue of the massing jays, sometimes twenty or more bolting seed together on the scarified ground beneath the cedar. The sentry jay screeches and puts the rest up when a truck comes by, then all settle again.

One day early in the first year of the third millennium, I was in the kitchen making tea and absently glancing at the sapphire storm of jays, the retiring towhees, and the testy varied thrushes jumping all over one another. A flurry of juncoes swept in and began pecking seed from the driveway gravel. Suddenly I noticed a bird that in no way fit with the rest. Against the puritan juncoes in their black hats and bibs, homespun grays, and sensible browns, this passerine looked outlandish even in its dull winter garb: garishly striped headgear with a bit of a cocky crest, a dandy's mottle of scales and streaks all down its back, and hints of frivolous rusty red along the sides and over the abundant breast. With its conical bill it was doubtless a finch relative like its company, the juncoes, but not one that I knew. I went through the longspurs, finches, sparrows, and buntings in my Roger Tory Peterson and Robbins, and never got close until I checked the "Accidentals" and then my European Peterson. Twenty minutes after first laying eyes on it, I had my bird figured, and eventually confirmed it in my National Geographic, Kaufman, and Sibley. The bird before me was a rustic bunting.

Checking with better birders, I learned that this was but the fourth rustic bunting recorded in Washington. Without a doubt, many would be eager to see this Old World bird, which usually breeds in Siberia and winters in Japan. My first impulse toward other naturalists is to share, and I wanted very much to pass on our good fortune in receiving this unwonted visit. After several days the bunting was still with us, foraging for seed among but not quite with the juncoes, sometimes off to the side under a cut laurel trunk, where a song sparrow hung out. I wanted to trumpet the news to the birding world, but I knew that to do so would be near-suicidal.

A couple of years earlier, our friend Rex Ziak discovered a brambling at his feeder in Naselle. This pretty peach-and-coal European finch has been seen more often than the rustic, yet within days of calling the Tweeters rare bird hotline, Ziak, a busy filmmaker and historian, was besieged by hundreds of birders from all over the continent. He gave himself over to being the bird's protector, interpreter, and booking agent for weeks. Two men came separately from New Jersey to make the brambling their seven hundredth American life bird. I knew that if I called Tweeters, we would have an even worse time. The only good place to view the bird was from our kitchen; its times of appearance were unpredictable; and it fed chiefly in the driveway, so every arriving car put it to flight. Hosting hordes of tickers and twitchers (as the Brits denote the more rabid listers) alongside scores of earnest watchers was more than we were prepared to contemplate. So we kept the bunting under wraps.

We did invite a dozen or so friends to enjoy the handsome oddity, and a discreet (though not blindfolded) party from the Willapa Hills Audubon Society, our local chapter. Otherwise we monopolized our distinguished visitor and tried to figure out its gender, for the sexes look similar in winter.

Often the bird came early, stoking seeds for the chilly day, then took off with the juncoes to the gods knew where and returned in the afternoon for another nosh before roosting in bramble or camellia. We lured it to a pan of seed between the Brussels sprouts and the frost-blackened perennials, within twenty feet of the window. Sometimes the chunky bunting hunkered incognito in a low spot, almost like a nestling, disguised as an oak leaf until it showed its stripes or put its crest up to a cheeky fox sparrow.

If our bunting was a male, that erectile crest would grow as the season advanced. It would serve as an advertisement for a mate he would never find unless he made it all the way home or settled for a junco. One winter when a smew (a small pied merganser with a natural range similar to the bunting's) came to New England, he stuck around in spring and mated with a goldeneye, so perhaps a hybrid bunting–junco arrangement was not out of the question. Thea quipped that the offspring could be called buncoes.

Such birds out of range are anomalies, insignificant from the standpoint of the population, unlikely to leave offspring behind or affect future numbers or the range unless they really are scouts for an advancing species. Biologically speaking, they are unimportant. But by coming to us in the strained season of short, chilly, pearl-gray days and abiding until daylight regained its hours and its warmth, the bunting brought brightness and life and made us glad. And on the morning of the last day of 2001, the rustic bunting returned to Swede Park for a second winter, and remained just as long. We can never know what his adventures were in the interim. But when that small Siberian bird fell out of the sky over Gray's River, not once but twice, he brought with him the sweetness of chance in any place, the certainty of wonder in all places. And if that's not grace, I don't know what is.

2 · Frogsong

Out of these choral frogs would come acclamation
as wild as the wind.

— JOHN HAY, *Mind the Gap*

The spring chorus, frog section, happens in winter here
and has no absolute start or finish. Any day of the year,
any time of day, we might hear the odd emanation, almost disembodied, from the throat of a lonely or hopeful frog. These solo
questions, hoarse, low in register, and slowed down like a record
played at the wrong speed, are croaks, not song. But there comes
a time when more than one gives voice, both the frequency and
pitch pick up, and the calls come from the fields by the river instead of the garden and the woods. There comes a gathering at
dusk when the bassos have all gone countertenor and the falling
dark is a curtain rising on the water meadow. That's when the
spring chorus really takes off.

I've always attended closely to sounds in the dark. Of course
I listen too by day, but in the sight-deprived night, noises count
more. They carry promise and mystery that our eyes cannot con-
firm, that we can only wonder about. Maybe it is the element of
imagination that makes me care more about night noise than
about the voices of the day. As a boy in Colorado, I lay in bed and
listened to eighteen-wheelers rising through the gears as they

left town on U.S. Route 6. I've slept beside many shores with pounding or purling waters and by freeways whose swoosh I've tried to turn into surf. Whether trying to sleep in New York City when striking hotel workers used trash-can lids for cymbals until the garbage trucks came at dawn, or camping on a high ridge with nothing in my ears but the murmurings of night birds on the mountain air, I've always felt that the sounds that enter at night *matter,* as if they affect who I will be by day.

As a teen in Colorado, I bought an LP of amphibian calls from the Cornell Laboratory of Natural Sounds and listened intently, wishing I lived where such sounds rang out. My friends and I tried to mimic the southern toad, and croak (inhaling and going *braaaack!*) for as long as the toads trilled on the record. I found leopard frogs in prairie creeks and western toads in mountain bogs, and heard the occasional vocalization. But I don't think I encountered a real spring chorus until I went to Seattle in 1965. That first March I visited the wild ravine of Carkeek Park, where a creek runs down to Puget Sound. I crossed the railroad tracks to the beach and faced back toward the swamp. Here was the real thing: a blasting, almost deafening concord of sex-driven trills. I couldn't catch the makers, couldn't even see them, and they shut up when I got close. But man, they sang! And they went at it for hours, those frogs.

The frogs in that city glen were the same species we hear in Gray's River Valley. In fact, apart from the hoarsely honking introduced bullfrogs, we have but one kind of full-singing frog in coastal Washington. Red-legged frogs live here, but they call underwater or so quietly that they are all but silent. Elsewhere in Washington, where they survive, western toads may be heard, and some species of frogs dwell in the Cascades. But down here in the frog-friendly lowlands, our chorus (unlike a southeastern or New England polyphony) consists entirely of one part, repeated ad infinitum. The singer, long known as the Pacific tree frog (*Hyla regilla*), is now called the western chorus frog (*Pseudacris regilla*). Closely related to the spring peeper of the

East, it is one or two inches long, ranges from brightest spring green to mottled or rusty brown, and is always graced with a Zorro mask over its brilliant golden eyes.

One night it is cold, and no frogs sing. The next night is milder, and frogsong is suddenly there. It begins weakly, with a few half-hearted voices, and rehearsals may be suspended if the weather turns colder again. But by Saint Valentine's Day, the concert is well under way. It peaks by Saint Pat's, carries on at fever pitch through Easter, encores after May Day, and tails off into early summer. By Midsummer Night we're back to recalcitrant or complacent *c-r-o-o-o-a-a-a-kkk*s from the oak foliage or the oxalis in the dooryard. A given evening mimics the progress of the season. I'll be on the porch working out, to no sounds but birds settling in or cars driving home, the odd dog barking. Then — at what signal? — around six o'clock a single voice rings forth. Another follows. Then a few more take it up, like lights flickering on from tussock to tussock. Then it's only a few minutes until the whole damn Mormon Tabernacle Choir has moved into the marsh. The individual voices are not as high-pitched as spring peepers, not as nasal as leopard frogs, not as staccato as wood frogs: pretty standard tin-clicker frog *ribbets,* with a little vibrato on the uptake.

Two years ago the frog ensemble first swelled on February 5 and was going strong on February 22, with Orion overhead along with Jupiter and Saturn, and Venus brilliant in the west. During the same interval the daffodils burst, as did crocuses and heather, and the first red-bottomed bumblebee appeared, and a bright Milbert's tortoiseshell butterfly that showed up on the front steps and proceeded to nectar on snowdrops. This hibernating butterfly, chocolate with bright slices of orange and lemon, is often the first one we spot as winter trades places with spring. But I'd never seen it visit snowdrops, a plant I didn't even know produced nectar. A fortnight later I saw it probing fruitlessly at crocuses, which do not have nectaries, then sipping from white and purple heathers, which do, below my study window. Rising, it glided by, its broad yellow bands very pale from spending the months since autumn eclosure sheltered in shed or woodpile. Half a dozen species of tortoiseshells and anglewings overwinter here, and if there's a butterfly to be seen in early frog season, it will be one of these.

Not every February comes in so lamblike. My mother was born on February 3, 1916, in the worst snowstorm in Seattle's history. And not many years ago, when I was trying to get away for a trip to the Mexican monarchs in February, I awoke to find the car under two feet of snow and the airport a hundred slick and slushy miles away. The drifts of snowdrops sometimes get snowbound. Other winters distinguish themselves chiefly by being absent, as endless autumn soggily drips into attenuated spring. And still other winters average their rain months into a long, cold season of relentless sog and little color. At such times, looking out through the spattered glass, I feel, deep in some spongy, unignorable organ, that we will have floods, and damage, and losses; we will have gray till the cows come home, and there will be no more cows—they'll all just rot, drown, or simply wash away. We will have rain until the very hills dissolve. And when the dirty cotton swaddling of fog finally falls away, we will all be desperate for vital signs.

Then one mid-Feb afternoon clarifies, shortly before the first sunset visible as such in weeks. A branchful of last fall's oak leaves glimmers robin's-breast red against a robin's-egg sky as actual robins call from the rooftops of the red oaks. Even in the rainforest the rainy season has its limits. As I head out to the Rosburg Store to pick up a video and a quart of milk, still more forgotten color leaps from the fields. Nothing signals the sun's return to the northern sectors as clearly as its reflection in the upstart flags of skunk cabbage in the sodden pastures. Unlike the olive-purple twists of northeastern skunk cabbage, the western species unfurls its spathes into broad, tall ensigns of uncompromising yellow—the yellow of pioneer daffodils, early dandelions, and buttercups. I fancy that even the few remaining turgid, waterlogged Holsteins greet these pennants with pleasure, saluting with raised muddy tails and hot streams of pee, making the water meadows run even yellower. No emblem commands a fonder allegiance from winter survivors than skunk cabbage, bringing the deep relief of early spring, just as frogsong announces winter's flight once again.

WE SELDOM SEE the frogs making their way from our upland precincts down to the river bottoms, and I doubt they follow any particular paths. But many other creatures, not least among them our species, travel by repetitious routes. Edwin Way Teale and his wife, Nellie, chose their rural Connecticut farm partly because of the footpaths that laced its acreage. In fact, they named the place Trail Wood after all the footways. I envied their paths when I came to Swede Park, which lacked them. It is one thing to have major trails or country lanes nearby for ambitious hiking or daylong rambling. It is quite another to have immediate out-the-door access to a network of little paths for spontaneous saunters—the sort of walks you can take between rain showers or chapters, which refresh out of all proportion to their time or distance. I think of Charles Darwin's Sandwalk, out behind Down House in Kent. I have walked there and imagined Darwin ambulating his way out of his current conundrum or ailment, trying out his thoughts, as he rounded the walk again and again while noting the slow shift of the Wormstone, by which he measured the earthworms' reconfiguration of the landscape with their castings. His contemporary Henry Thoreau said that for him it wasn't walking if he couldn't do it for four hours a day. That kind of walk is nice when it happens, but I'll take four minutes now and then over being butt-stapled to a chair all day long.

During H. P. Ahlberg's day and Ebba Sorenson's younger years, when Swede Park was still parklike, there must have been many paths—from fishpond to bee house, garden to barn, house to well, chicken yard to stream, and, certainly, tree to tree. Over the years most of these footways were lost to rampaging brambles, twining ivy, and diminishing tread. The only ones that remained were the driveway up from Loop Road, the old wagon track that would become our mail walk, and the Public Utility District's water line from our house west to the Sorensons' place on the higher river bench. So we brushed out some trails to connect these arteries. My former wife, Sally, intimate with the many public footpaths in her native England, was especially vigorous in doing this. Several of her routes survive today, having become footworn into the soil and foliage.

Nearly every day that I am home, whether I take any other outings or remain mostly within the walls, I walk the path to the compost pile to make the daily deposition. And one or both of us walk down the mail path to Loop Road, over the stream, past Covered Bridge Road, to the mailbox each day. Coming back, I am likely to turn off at the plum grove to take the uphill trail through alders and maples and spruces, past the Western Oak, and up to the pond path, circling around the house from the rear. If I need a Sandwalk airing midday to clear my brain, I'll head out past the heather garden and the Lincoln Oak (which Ahlberg planted from an acorn he brought from Mrs. Lincoln's residence in Illinois), beyond the two compost mounds and into the woods on the pond path. It begins between the horse chestnut and the sweet chestnut and continues past the giant tulip tree, through a witchy wood of elder and alder in various states of dropping, decay, and resprouting, and finally to the pond at the western extremity of the place. Swede Park is no Trail Wood, and our paths are short and familiar. Still, their predictability often gives way to surprise, and these small traces let us range afield without taking to the roads.

The paths made by humans are not the only ones. The ground around me here is impressed with passages that other creatures use to get about these acres. As I walk my own entrenched ways or leave them to examine the untracked wood, I come across the evidence of regular passage over a season or, sometimes, over many years. For example, I see the thoroughfares of western thatch ants, midsized red ants that are known for their truly monumental nests made of soil particles, grass, stems, and twigs. Some of the nests in Thurston County, north of here, reach ten or fifteen feet in width and four or five feet in height. Such architecture requires the transport of vast amounts of vegetation, one bit at a time. Provisioning the nest with animal and plant foodstuffs requires innumerable passages. The perpetual to-and-fro motion of multitudes over an active ant track on a fair day is beyond comprehension. And the impact of their tiny feet, six per ant, millions of steps per day, billions in a season, actually indents the trail like tire tracks in the turf.

For years such a formic freeway crossed the main path midway between the Lincoln Oak and the compost pile, leading down to the ants' modest nest on a warm southern slope, where early daffodils catch the gaze of the sun returning to the northern latitudes. Sometime in February, when those sun flags came out, the ants would begin their convoys, which continued all spring, summer, and fall. But the many small trees that grew up filtered out the direct sunlight necessary to fuel their activity, and the antway diminished, languished, then disappeared. Now we are progressively freeing that slope to increasing radiance, and the old pioneer daffodils are responding to the warmth. I wonder if the ants will return too. I can still see portions of their beaten ground, years after the last thatch ant gridlock. The paths remain, like tiny versions of the Oregon Trail's fossil wagon ruts lingering on windy rims of the high desert for a century and more.

Another well-worn track, a four-inch-wide runway in the mossy lawn from the back porch around the west side of the house to the front porch, is the stylized pathway of cats, or of one cat in particular: Bokis, a male tuxedo shorthair who came to Swede Park with me. I first saw him as a tiny, sodden kitten trying to get out of the rain in Portland. I was conducting a meeting in the old house that served as the Nature Conservancy office. As each person arrived out of the bucketing October night, the kitten would dash inside, only to be tossed out again. Finally I scooped him up and tucked him into my Volkswagen bus. The next day I drove him to Seattle, whereupon he crapped on the brake pedal. I got him shots and he became my cat. People assume he was named for Bacchus, but actually, because he was a compact little animal, I named him Bilak Bokis, New Guinea pidgin for "black box," a contraction of the phrase for "piano": *bilak bokis im gat teeth allasem shark, you straikim, e sing out.*

The following spring, Bokis disappeared from our apartment, and we thought him gone for good. Another cat, a beautiful tortoiseshell tabby named Peatling Parva, brought with us from England, had turned up poisoned, so we were worried. But after a sad catless month had passed, one morning our landlord called out, "Bokis is here!" I couldn't believe it. He had indeed returned, but with a bad burn on his side and a shattered leg. He never told us his story, but we imagine he may have sought warmth up under the hood of some vehicle. For weeks he underwent surgery after surgery, way beyond my capacity to pay. Taped in the middle and splinted on his left hind leg, he looked like a poodle crossed with Peg Leg Pete, and he certainly sang out. Finally, after a painful pin had failed, the vet made him a charity experiment and tried a risky procedure. This worked, and although his kittenhood mangling left him with a steel plate in his leg, arthritis, and a distinctive, loping gait, Bokis became a hiking cat.

When we moved to Swede Park, Bokis took up the habit of pacing a habitual track from porch to porch, depending on the weather, in pursuit of the sunshine, his food, or our company. He walked every path on Swede Park with me, some of them hundreds of times, and he almost always accompanied me to the mail. At first he waited at the lip of the mail path where it drops to the road beside the plum grove. But later he took to coming down to meet me at the edge of the county road, mewling as I approached, then walking the long way back up the road to the driveway instead of the shorter, safer mail path.

Bokis walked the white line—what the highway department calls the fog line—near the edge of the pavement. He strode along with his long black tail in the air as if claiming that stripe as his own—or, rather, as if he were laying it down himself, the way he did the rut alongside the house. Of course I worried about cars, but he always took to the ditch if one approached, while I stood in the middle of the road like a traffic cop. I called his habit "white-lining it." Returning from the mailbox, I'd ask him whether he wanted to take the path or white-line it, and he would decide. He was too slow for me, stopping often to sniff, just like a dog, and sometimes he paused and looked back over his shoulder, as if unsure whether he really was up to the trek or whether something was behind him. If he just would not continue along the road, I'd pop him up the bank beside the hazel tree and onto the mail path. But usually Bokis white-lined it all the way home.

In the country, irresponsible people often drop cats off, maybe supposing that farms can always use another. Every other cat we've had—Brownie McGee, Milkweed, Virga—has been a dropoff, and each has since gone to join the coyotes. Every cat established its own routes; none adopted Bokis's exact path around the house. The only one who has been here long enough (and is heavy enough) to make an impression on the earth is Firkin, an oval, kinky-tailed tortoiseshell. Firkin's ways are more random, though I think she is beginning to lay down her own version of a Bokis Road on the *east* side of the house.

What all the cats have had in common is their devotion to another portion of the Swede Park route map: the trails of the Townsend's voles. The multifold runways of the voles carve through the taller grass and dive into perfectly round holes in the ground. Voles are pretty, blunt-faced, short-tailed meadow mice that nip bulbs and tuck sprouts and generally rework the vegetation of the valley and garden as much as all the cattle, elk, and insects do together. Townsend's voles are the largest members of the genus *Microtus*, commonly reaching six inches and several ounces. They make up the broad foundation of the food pyramid for most of the hunting birds and mammals in the valley. All of our cats have preferred Townsend's voles to any other prey. They are relatively easy to catch and, though not as much fun as the beautiful jumping mice, they deliver much more ounce for the pounce than any other victims except the succulent flying squirrels. (Being so plump and popular, the voles often leave vacant holes, ready for the next queen bumblebee looking for a nest.) Succeeding generations remember their parents' trails, an intricate network of petite trackways in the Swede Park turf.

The vole trails have a subterranean mirror in the mole tunnels. We can't see these, but we know they are there from the periodic humping waves they make in the brown earth. Beyond the mailbox we come across dragways made by beavers—those that haven't been trapped—as they tug saplings from the slope across Loop Road down the bank to the marsh they've made of our stream before it reaches its meadow outlet. Up in the richer forest slopes run the loose, ankle-trapping furrows of the sewellels. The paths of coyotes, decorated by their pointy gray tokens full of felted fur and tiny bones, often follow human routes but diverge across the meadows where the invisible traffic signals of night scents direct them. The deer browse brushways through the woods beyond our own demesne, and the bigger hoof-roads of the elk rival the loggers' Cat trails, breaking the forest tangles and bursting down to the county roads in broad muddy runnels. If human trails are rare here, apart from the thousands of miles of logging roads, there are nonetheless paths all over the place.

THE SMELT ARE in. Bald eagles line the alders along Gray's River below the village; herring gulls join the mew gulls in the silver meadows or wheel over bends in the river to catch the fish as they swap the sea for the rivers on their way to spawn. The six-inch-long smelt (*Thaleichthys pacificus*) are also known as candlefish because their high fat content makes them flammable when dried. That fat is the basis of a rich oil precious to all the coastal Indians of the Pacific Northwest. Traditionally, the oil is prepared in a semicontrolled rot of the fish in a seaweed-covered pit; if the process goes wrong, the resulting fluid, like motor oil in color and consistency, can be toxic. But even when all goes right, the odor of the oil at close range is nearly lethal. Bill Holm, the legendary teacher of Northwest Indian arts at the University of Washington, concluded our class on dance with a Kwakiutl feast, complete with smoked salmon and eulachon oil. The idea was to dip the fish in the thick yellowish grease, then eat it without first smelling it. Though the aroma was appalling, the taste was enigmatically sublime.

Around here, nobody makes eulachon oil anymore. The Wahkiakum Indians wore cloaks of swan and otter skins and built big cedar houses when Lewis and Clark entered Gray's Bay two hundred years ago, but smallpox and such erased their numbers and culture with tsunami-like speed and thoroughness. The people who took their place, Finns and Swedes and Norwegians, came with their own traditions for small, oily fish. They catch them en masse, smoke them, and eat them whole. And this we still do when the smelt come in. Or, rather, others catch them and smoke them over alder, and we eat them. Hordes with long-handled, broad-hooped nets line the banks of the Cowlitz in Kelso and other tidal rivers when the smelt run up, never predictably in a given place. When the eagles again adorn the alders over Gray's River, we know that the smelt have come back to the valley and that hopeful smelters will materialize overnight down by the concrete bridge. Sometimes a fishing boat even rides up the tide, an extraordinarily rare event in the fifty years or so since the channel silted in.

I've never been much good at catching smelt, but when our friends Ed, Cathy, and Gavin Maxwell called and asked me to join them in search of smelt on our own river, I gladly agreed. They drove over from their home above the Naselle River to pick me up at dusk, and we headed out. Cathy, an accomplished botanist, has parsed the flora of these hills. Ed oversaw the whole system of state hatcheries on nearby rivers and knew their fish—salmon and others—as well as anyone. Struck at an early age by a degenerative neurological disease, he was getting in as many experiences with Cathy and Gavin, their son, as he could. Ed and Gavin had tried for a deer the previous autumn, and now they aimed to bring in a mintful of silver smelt.

We hoped to find the nearby spots uncrowded, but the local fishers had also noticed the eagles — it's hard not to, when fifteen or twenty decorate the riparian fringe between Gray's River Grange and the Rosburg Store, a distance of two miles. All the river beaches were occupied by hopefuls wielding lights and nets and, judging by their stoic appearance, not having much action. Finally, we took one last look at the Rosburg boat ramp. There, suspended in Gavin's torchlight, we saw one silver sliver resisting the slack tide. Ed, long a master smelter on the broad Cowlitz, could no longer wield the big net. Gavin decided not to take that singleton, and we all watched it disappear into the dark green water. The next day I bought smelts at the Rosburg Store.

When the smelt come up, we eat the catch from the Naselle, the Gray's, or the Cowlitz for weeks. Smoked at home, they are sweet and salty, just fishy enough. I eat them—head first—like buttered popcorn, and with all those omega-3 lipids they're better for me, though Thea says I smell as if I've been eating cat food. Every time I munch one, I look into its little orange eye and think of the one we saw out there in the river. Though these aren't mighty fish like salmon, they come upriver from the sea just the same. They fueled the great winter Hamatsa ceremonies of the Kwakiutl and lubricated entire cultures with their ribsticking fat and coveted value for trade. They power the very eagles themselves and help keep me going through the viscid days and nights of late winter, when eulachon oil is just the trick. One night I awoke to the light of a lantern down by the covered bridge. I made out three nets swishing in its reflection, like a dream of Wynken, Blynken, and Nod seining the stars. In the morning I wasn't sure I'd actually seen such a picture until Thea came home with a bag of fresh smelts from the Saaris. She breaded and fried them in their own oil for dinner.

ONE MORNING IN late February, I enjoyed some good long looks at a slate-colored junco snatching seeds beneath the Port Orford cedar. This midcontinent variant of the dark-eyed junco has a clean white crissum with nebulous gray between it and the white belly, and a slaty hood reaching halfway to the legs, rather than a third of the way, as the black hoods of our common Oregon juncos do. It also lacks the reddish side bars of the northwestern variety, with several of whom it was hanging in close company. While watching the oddball junco, I spotted the rustic bunting, which had been with us off and on. The raccoon-face mask and head stripes had blackened perceptibly, telling us it was indeed a male. He also seemed even feistier, his testosterone increasing along with the spring plumes. As the mew gulls departed downvalley, the bunting really began to rusticate. He disappeared for longer periods into the boskier precincts, and when he showed, his new plumage had brighter rusty tones.

I had just turned away when W H A M !—a very loud bird-bang rang from the kitchen window. Rushing out, I expected to find a Steller's jay. Instead, there in the ferns and irises struggled a traumatized male varied thrush. I picked it up, and it panted for a minute or two, then expired in my hands. Emmy Lou Harris chose that moment to sing Steve Earle's haunting "Goodbye" on the radio.

Death is a common companion of anyone who lives in the country. Most folks around here hunt, and animals are constantly dying on the highway. Predation takes place daily, and if you are observant, you can't help seeing it now and then. A sharp-shinned hawk has lately taken up residence, and every now and then I catch its swift brown blur past the window, and then a little heap of feathers from a junco or a jay. I have come across a mother possum, savaged by coyotes or, more likely, dogs, with the pink young still fixed to her teats in the pouch, and have been obliged to drown them in the pond. Dogs also ran Lobelia, our big white rabbit, to death by heart attack, and rodents are always meeting their maker around here, thanks to cats, garter snakes, birds, and cellar-set mousetraps. The city insulates us from death; the country rubs our noses in it.

That thrush was not the first creature here to die in my hands. Where moles shove up the surface of the land, plants die off for some time afterward. We're hardly lawn-proud, loving the mosses and forbs that many folks poison in their lawns, but when a mole has taken to turfing up an area we don't really want turfed up, we have succumbed to the temptation of the trap. Mole traps are difficult to use effectively; you have to dig into a hill and bury the device in a two-way tunnel rather than a dead-ender so that if the digger passes through again, it will trip the trigger and the stiff steel jaws will snap shut, squeezing it breathless. When Thea hasn't had much luck with a particularly troublesome mole, I have sometimes planted such a trap, putting Mole from *Wind in the Willows* far from my mind.

One such time not long ago, as I was walking toward the house, I heard the trap snap shut beneath the surface, moments after its planting. I lifted the soil, and in that iron clutch throbbed the soft taupe form of a big boar mole. I released it into my hand and felt the velour of its fine fur and the pulse of its throes as it died. I'll not be setting any more mole traps—which in any case have since been outlawed in Washington.

EVER SINCE THEY were small, my stepchildren, Tom and Dory, have kept frogs now and then as house pets. Now Tom has two children, and he wanted frogs to enjoy with them. Thea cleaned out a spare terrarium and filled it with a marvelous carpet of mosses and ferns, and we began watching for suitable recruits. One night when we were driving home from Naselle in the rain, we noticed the road littered with skittering frogs. We dodged them and turned off onto Loop Road. Beside the Lily

Pond, little frogs bounced across the pavement like water drops on a hot skillet. I pulled over, and in the headlights and rain, we stooped and grabbed, stooped and grabbed, mostly missing, following and stopping like comic robots and laughing at each other. Finally we managed to snatch a couple of small red-leggeds, which will likely have a much longer and easier life than all the ones that got away.

As the climate warms, I wonder whether our frogs will become confused. December before last, Noreen showed us scads of tadpoles in the stock tank behind Fitts's barn. From a half to an inch and a half long, many of them had hind legs already. They lacked the heft and big bull heads of baby bullfrogs, so we wondered if they might not be chorus or red-legged frogs, though neither is known to reproduce in winter this far north. Bullfrog larvae routinely take three years to develop into adults and are therefore around in winter; they get hind legs early, while the pre-eruptive forelegs that make their heads look so big come much later. We concluded that the tadpoles probably were bullfrogs, as our herpetologist friend Bill Leonard also suspected. Too bad, because these aliens are predaceous on native amphibians. We have heard their foghorn calls in the area and found a few roadkills. Thea brought several of the tadpoles home and reared them in a pot on the porch; the two that survived turned out to be chorus frogs after all, the first record in Washington of this species passing the winter as an immature. By June one had all four legs, its tail had shrunk to a point, and it lived mostly in the air instead of water. Then it escaped. A month later the other one was still in the water, not much more developed than its sisters born that spring. Eventually it too became a froglet. And the following winter the stock pond was aswirl with polliwogs again.

Joel Fitts thinks frogs have been around in midwinter in his stock pond for a while, that biologists have just been looking in the wrong places. But what if our native frogs did begin to skip their hibernal shutdown altogether? As freezes become less frequent, will we come to see larval tree frogs—usually a summertime feature—as a winter norm? Recent research has shown that eastern wood frogs and peepers can be frozen solid and then revivified, an adaptation to especially hard winters. Having a second generation in a single summer, with the first brood's offspring passing the winter as tadpoles, would be an opposite adaptation in response to milder conditions. This is already known to occur in California. If the example here in Gray's River Valley should be repeated elsewhere, northwestern chorus frogs may become one more exhibit in the case for pervasive climate change.

As I write, one of two frogs that made it all the way through the second winter with tadpoles at Fitts's farm still sits in a terrarium on the front porch, awaiting its morning spiders and flies. It is very small for a harbinger, but that is what it is.

Last year the amphibian evensong began in earnest on the fourth of January, weeks earlier than ever before. What if it should continue to advance until it overlaps with Christmas music? That would be strange caroling indeed, even in our rainforest version of bleak midwinter. The mildness compensates for long weeks of rain, but I would regret a resetting of the calendar so radical as to bring frogsong forward to the winter solstice. Nothing signals spring's relief more sweetly than batrachian voices raised to fortissimo. These days, with so many places losing their amphibians, their songscapes switching off altogether, I am grateful that we still have ours, and I hope it will remain a vernal refrain.

3 ⋆ When Echo Azures Fly

On a warm April day, a butterfly as dainty as a
Dresden shepherdess emerges and flutters
forth from her dark retreat on china-blue wings.

— L. Hugh Newman, *Butterfly Haunts*

⁂ By its very name, March does not connote soft loveliness, as April and May do, but it has its bright points. This is when our spring azures emerge, a month earlier than Hugh Newman's holly blues or Robert Frost's "sky-flakes" in Vermont. Our West Coast kind has a name as fetching as its looks — *Celastrina echo,* the echo azure. One day they appear in the watery sunshine, to dance over the hoops of spirea, spikes of bluebells, and plumes of cherry laurel for weeks to come. Another fine thing about March is that foliage is still sparse — the line of unobstructed vision goes far. So you can see an azure as it enters the yard on the left and, if nothing tempts it, follow its cerulean sky-scamper right through the pale green scrim of waking leaves and out on the right: a blue doodle looping through the air in exploratory ovals inscribed on the clean slate of early spring.

We too make our loops, again and again. If State Route 4 is sometimes a trial to live near, Loop Road is a constant window on the life of the valley. Like the highway, it was created where people had walked and ridden and carted long before cars came to Gray's River. The section that runs in front of our house (Loop

Road proper) has gone from oil and gravel to asphalt since we've been here, and the connector across the valley (Covered Bridge Road) was completed only thirty years ago. Traffic is light, often nonexistent, and (usually) much slower than on Route 4. The verges have been sprayed less and therefore have a much more interesting flora. The best of it is that the two roads make up a loop of four and one-half miles—just right for a good walk, a bracing run, a short bike ride, a lively bird walk, or a contemplative lookabout drive. By all these modes, I have circumnavigated this green vale hundreds and hundreds of times.

These hills are ringwormed by thousands of miles of logging roads. Except for a few relics of railroad grades, these roads make for mediocre hiking, with steep, rocky ups and downs through uniform doghair forest and recent clear-cuts. The only trails are those made by deer and elk. I love to follow them, but if I do, I'd better not say I'll be home for dinner. So the loop, in its swervy bottomland dance with the river, is where we most often walk. It is also my neighborhood, stuffed with stories of big and little change. Each rounding of the oval byway that has kept me company for countless hours and miles gives its own reply to the question: is it still worth the walk?

I SET OUT in midafternoon, under a sunny haze of maybe sixty degrees, as the cat basks on the stoop. I take a hickory stick as a walking staff, a stout slat I salvaged from a Kentucky tobacco barn where my grandfather worked a hundred years ago. Tiny swarm flies blaze over the base of the disintegrating concrete steps down to the former cart track. A towhee scratches under the wisteria tangle above the road. The mail path swings down past cherries and hazels to the blacktop. Our stream is running high, its bed and banks viridescent with skunk cabbage and licorice fern and the brightest green of a 7-Up bottle washed down from above. At the first of the loop's four curves, which I call the near-near curve, a neighbor lady goes by in a snappy yellow car with a smile and a wave. Farmer Derek passes the opposite way on his tractor, having taken a hay bale to his cattle. Then two pickups full of fishermen—a veritable traffic jam at Loop and Covered Bridge roads, as thick as it gets except on some bridge-visiting weekends in high summer. Last fall's leftover blackberry leaves, as red as any maple's, climb beside a hillside rill between the two big Douglas-firs.

Sixty-some elk loaf across the valley in the middle of Elk Mountain Ranch, as if they could read the sign. They ignore the fences, pushing them aside if they are in the way of fresh grass. Understandably, the farmers appreciate the elk less than the rest of us do. One of the last two Sorenson fields, golf-green pasture in Ed's day but now going to willow and reed canary grass, fronts the river below the bridge on my left. The elk would be welcome to it, but they prefer the short turf of the still-worked fields. Some landowners obtain wildlife-damage permits and actually shoot the animals. Others employ propane cannons to scare them away. Years ago one such noisemaker, placed in a field somewhere in the valley, drove me crazy. I so hated the periodic blasts that I went out with a heavy maul after dark one night with a mind to smash it. But, perhaps fortunately, the valley's mystifying echoes frustrated my search. Soon the cannon was gone, and the elk returned.

The first hill brings me to Fairview Road. Turning up its steep narrow track to the highway would be the short loop, but I'm taking the long loop today. Over my left shoulder, I have a fine view of the mole-gray bridge, and the river purling over the beach that used to be. For the first decades I was here, Ed's field ran down to a broad shingle studded with white and opalescent agates. Many sunny afternoons found us walking that beach with our kids, gathering agates, the eroded tree knots known as riverteeth, and the best of the beaver sticks, throwing driftwood into the chilly flow for Dory's indefatigable Aussie–Border collie, Woody, to chase. As long as we threw, he would swim, snatch the wood from the current, emerge like a soaking sea beast, shake, and ask for more. At low water in late summer, the county routinely harvested gravel from this beach, but the winter floods always restored it. Then one year a private operation dug the gravel and took too much, cutting the toe of the slope. That winter the floodwater took hold of the cut and carved it deeper, whisking away part of the field, scooping out the gravel bar, and depositing it on the opposite shore. So we lost our beach to the river's rebuke, and the kingfishers gained a new bank in which to nest.

Down dale to maples and cedars where a wild bee tree once hummed, before the mites, before the loss of still more maples to river wash and driveway dozing. Here lies the spot known as Torppa's Beach, a grassy bank now, this strand also washed away by the river's changing mind. The agent of change curves off into the middle of the valley below Torppa's old milking barn: long, low, broadly peaked, with a white metal roof and three silos. Bob Torppa Sr. was a dairy farmer who became a county commissioner and remained involved in local politics the rest of his life. A good Democrat, he knew how to make deals and bring home allocations to our oft-neglected district, but he traveled outward as well: he loved to share a photograph of himself taken with Jimmy Carter. Another photograph shows several of the lads of the village in the 1940s, most of them tall and fencepost-thin. Bob stands out, shorter and thicker in his double-breasted suit. When some of the same men made up the American Legion color guard decades later, Bob's uniform strained at the buttons, but his hair was still black. He came to our wedding, and he wasn't put off by environmentalists moving into the valley. A corral and loading ramp on the edge of his former fields are now deep in lichen, moss, and elder, and a long-parked, disco-era Dodge is following suit. Beyond a stream bright with yellow winter willows stand Torppa's two cottages, now homes for other people. Bob has been gone for years, along with two of his sons. The dairy cows are gone too, but barn owls still occupy one silo.

Broad fields open out on the left, some hayed, some fallow, where those pale night-hunters divvy up the voles with coyotes, harriers, and kites. Dachshunds bark from Nelson's house tucked under a bank by the barn, and two rowdy retrievers bound down from Robert Torppa Jr.'s place on the bench above.

Then, as if to remind me that a few newcomers and weekenders aren't likely to alter the basic nature of this place or the work of the world, a log truck crawls down the steep ramp of Chamberlain Road across the valley, going through its gears like a logger hawking lugies.

The second hill, and maples again. The biggest maple has generations of kids' ladder-slats nailed to the mossy side, reaching up to licorice-ferned, moss-padded boughs. A treehouse platform, hanging out over a winter pond, graces another tree. When I was a kid in Colorado, our cottonwoods were grand but fernless, with few low branches for climbing and no club-moss cushions. I wonder what dreamy afternoons were spent up in this tree before the days of PlayStation—and maybe still are. My reverie ends with a wake-up call from a field guide's worth of corvids, all voicing—crows in my face, ravens across the way, Steller's jays behind, scrub jays up ahead. I walk beneath the Saaris' place, with its gardens and greenhouse, where we buy strawberries when we don't grow them. A birch grove shimmers bright in late sun. Birches are not native here, but the Scandinavian settlers planted them all over the area to remind them of home, and the trees settled in just fine. Next is Frida and John Footh's; he gave our house its most recent cedar-shingle roof, and she has kept the Naselle–Grays River School tidy for years. Then comes a private road for a cluster of residents, including former logger Kenny "Buckshot" Wirkkala, once a Sorenson son-in-law, now an early-morning Loop Road fixture on his bicycle. The road is signposted WHISKEY FLATS — POP. 6+1, but five kids get off the school bus there as I pass, so the sign may need revision.

At the highest point, the old Chris Sorensen house perches

over a brambly drop on the left. Bill and Pat Potter saved it from falling into the blackberries, as its dairy house did long ago, and renovating it has been their perpetual project. Below it to the west lie the broad, grazed, deep green pastures of the Fittses' place. Among the last real farmers here, Joel and Noreen came from a farm in Petaluma, California, to take over the last dairy developed by Ed and Lenore Sorenson. Their low white house perches above a line of cedars, with white pickup, white camper, and big white Dutch barn. Their handsome sign, now well adorned with lichen, reads G R A Y'S V A L L E Y H O L - S T E I N S and features two classic carved and painted black-and-white cows with big bags. The black-and-whites are still here, but bagless: now the Fittses raise replacement heifers to sell to other dairies.

Joel is a big man of faith, good cheer, and wit who smiles more than any farmer who has fought fence-busting floods, months of mud, and recalcitrant cows for decades has any obligation to do. He drives the volunteer ambulance, plays the guitar, sings sweetly, and writes and recites fine cowboy poetry. Though sorry to see the cows go, he and Noreen relished the freedom that came from divorcing them; it meant they could travel south in winter and go to town at milking time. And Joel could indulge his passion for flying the small plane he shared, anchored in Astoria. He wanted to fly to and from home, so he laid out a grass runway, put up a windsock, and named the field for a friend he deeply admired, Harold Badger. Entire weeks pass in this valley when you'd scarcely know that we've entered the aviation age. We lie off the main air routes, so apart from the rare, almost invisible airliner and its contrails, the occasional Coast Guard or timber-company helicopter and a local ultralight, we seldom see a plane. But for a few years, small Pipers and Cessnas came and went on fair days, landing in the shadow of a bald eagle's nest that Joel watches with fierce protectiveness. Eventually he gave up flying because of an ankle injury and stopped mowing the field. As I walk down the hill, I make out the line of the road to Badger Airfield, now gone to bramble.

Horsetail cirrus clouds sweep in over Noreen's riding ring and brown horses. The cattle-feeding trough stands in mud— shallow this year—one mile from our house. Some years the floods have carried the trough hundreds of yards, or the rains have left the cows to forage knee-deep in cold, pungent muck. It's easy to see why, when the milk receipts fell below anything that could properly be called profits, a dairy farmer would be glad to get out of the business. But today, crows, starlings, ear tags, and grass blades all shine like glass in the mellow sun. A green-tagged Holstein, handsome in her fluffy winter coat and forehead cowlick, moos low and querulously, as a Hereford bullock scrunches a salad of grass, rich and green after the winter wet.

Here, where the road runs low across the green mead, floodwaters routinely cross and close the way. Firred hills rise to the north behind the Fittses' farm. Next comes a subhamlet known as Badgertown, named for Harold's pioneer parents and their descendants, some of whom have stayed put. Two modular homes arose where Harold's big house sadly burned a few years back; past those is a nice new stick-built house, the Berkshires' place, and the Valley Bible Church, which used to be postmaster Jean Calhoun's place and is now being converted to a home once again. Across the road loom two great Gray's River landmarks: first the square, concrete, rusty roofed potato shed–cum–cattle shelter that still says ED SEZ — L.B.J. FOR THE U.S.A.! in fading white script on the north side. The graffito was probably a dig at Ed Sorenson, one of the valley's foremost Republicans. His grandfather Chris Sorensen's Pond Lilly Dairy and its enormous barn, which once occupied these fields, have vanished except for a big, four-plank wooden sign in our smithy, hand-painted in red and green letters, that reads:

POND LILLY DAIRY
C. SORENSEN, PROP.

The other landmark is the Lily Pond itself, at high water now, but in late summer choked with yellow pond lilies. Eighty or ninety American widgeons graze and chuckle beside a flock of Canada geese on the far shore and one cinnamon-crowned Eurasian widgeon, its bald pate rich cream instead of the skim milk of the Americans. The Lily Pond, which used to be frequented by muskrats, has lately been used more often by nutria. In the winter and early spring its surface is often furrowed by buffleheads, ring-necked ducks, mallards, green-winged teal, and hooded mergansers; in summer a pied-billed grebe submarines among the floppy lily pads. The pond is always an oasis of life, and the Badgers have long since gotten used to my stopping there for a look.

Beyond the pond lies a willow swamp, where hairy woodpeckers pick. There I once heard the rare, quiet call of the red-legged frog, almost more of a gentle whisper in the head than a voice from without. Thea, on her runs, has heard it here too, and the white detritus of red-legged roadkill too often paints the road. Now I put up a red-tailed hawk from the thicket, though sometimes a black merlin hunts from here. Those raptors aside, the swamp is one place where a duck can get some rest out of sight of hunters. When a shotgun is fired twice across the valley, all the widgeons and fifteen brace of crows fly up. The widgeons whirl and whip and break up and recombine almost like shorebirds, and when they fly overhead, I hear their quail-like chirps and the soft bat-flutter of their wings. They circle several times—what a lot of calories expended!—then drop like a throw tossed across an upvalley field. Five great blue herons fly in line toward an upriver roost.

Loop Road turns off to the right toward the village. I continue west on Barr Road. At this junction lies one of several spreads called the Kandoll Place. This one was Gust Kandoll's, although Bill Maloney owns it now, and it has been much fixed up. I miss the old fence, whose uprights were rusty spigots from the stanchions of a dairy. Bill's white geese wheedle and scream as he leads them around to the back. They are one less than last night, and a drift of white feathers near the fence suggests why. A kestrel hangs out here on the wire for much of the year, but a small falcon can't take a goose. A raccoon, a coyote, and dogs running wild all can.

Shaun Matthews, a log-truck driver turned wildlife refuge worker who is building a house down the road, comes by in a small truck, waves and smiles, as do Hank and Linda Nelson. They are beef farmers, and Linda was Dory's favorite teacher at Rosburg School. A Wadsworth Electric van crosses the river on the concrete bridge that was built in 1967, according to the mossy numerals. Its railing was recently cut away by aluminum thieves, a current nemesis of rural road departments. Long ago, another covered bridge spanned the river here.

This crossing is just above the head of tidewater. Below the bridge, Gray's River runs straight and fast on a dropping tide between cottonwoods, alders, and brambles into the hamlet of the same name. Across the bridge, hammer blows emanate from new shingling at Colleen Haley and Dave Henderson's house. They own the Covered Bridge Cafe and an ultralight plane service, and Dave will happily show anyone the valley from an eagle's perspective, if not with its acuity. At a Covered Bridge Festival a few years ago, Dave offered rides in his bright-winged machine. Never at my best in direct conflict with gravity, I nonetheless took a turn. Dave strapped me into the ridiculous buggy on wheels and started the engine. We whined down the field and into the hot, still August air. Wheeling left, then left again, we motored over the ant hive of the revelers in Larson's riverside meadow, then wheeled again to pass directly (and not very high) above the tall oaks of Swede Park. How wonderful it was to see our domain as the vultures, band-tails, and ravens have seen it forever but as I had only imagined it. A green sheen hung over the whole tableau, which I see again now as I glance at the flimsy yet airworthy aircraft in its barn. Here at ground level, the crushed carcasses of slugs and frogs mixing with the Cretaceous carbons of tar give the road an organic glaze.

IF I WERE to carry on straight ahead, Barr Road would take me around the back side of the lower valley to the Altoona Road, which runs out to the confluence of Gray's River with the Columbia in its own broad bay. Instead I veer south onto Covered Bridge Road. This is the near-far curve. My way follows the bench above the river, beside the steep bank, and the smells change from grass and pasture to damp and woodsy humus as sword ferns and a thousand small spring green things thrust out from the wet slope. A sign announces ROAD NARROWS as asphalt becomes chip seal or tar and gravel; Bob Torppa's paving job, when he was commissioner, came only this far. Though not as nice for bicycles, this part feels much more rural. When I first knew it, the loop was all unpaved, and better for it. A song sparrow, our most common companion all year long, roots noisily in the leaves. Over its rustle I hear geese, hammer, faraway trucks, river chuckle, towhee *scree,* wren chip. The sun has slipped behind the ridge, a half moon is overhead, and the air is fifty degrees tops. Gilded clear-cuts stand out where last light hits low mountaintops—the subtle Willapa Hills' best imitation of alpenglow. A lone cormorant flicks upriver toward the far scarps of the Gray's River Divide.

The house that once belonged to Johnny Kapron perches on the high terrace up above; he's long gone now, along with his heavy horses. He and Joel Fitts, who also kept a team, gave wagon rides around the valley on special days. I loved to hear the ponderous clop of eight enormous hooves and the hum of steel-rimmed wagon wheels on the deck of the covered bridge, echoing out of its open mouth—sounds that spoke of a time when work horses undergirded every farm. Other houses have been built up near Johnny's; I can't see them, but a dog from one spots me through the hemlocks and barks until I'm past. Here the river takes a sharp dogleg turn away from northeast, and the water whips around the elbow thick and green; rotted pilings and an ancient school bus show where farmers tried to maintain the much-eroded shoreline. Across the road rises a high cobble and siltstone bank, where one spring my birding friend Fayette spotted a kingfisher's nest secreted behind ferns. We watched the female come in with a fish, the male leave with a fecal sac. Now, with the leaves off, I see two side-by-side burrows, two or three inches across, five feet below the top, forty feet above me. Come summer and a fresh green screen, kingfishers will reclaim these burrows.

In this cool, north-facing reach of the river course, the vegetation thickens into heavy sword fern–red alder–western hemlock woods, moss plush on the trunks. Springs leak out of the whole hillside, and their combined rivulet plays through a culvert. Later in springtime the soft green shamrocks of oxalis spilling down the slope, the tossed salad of toothworts in the ditch, and the drifts of candyflower along the verge, each with its different pinky white blooms, will make this one of the brighter stretches of the circuit. But for now a dank, shadowed chill falls over the dusk. An empty log truck, back wheels stacked, goes home over on Loop Road. Two or three women returning from jobs or errands pass and wave, as does Danny Zimmerman in an old pickup. The road rounds the far-far curve, where a little waterfall drops beneath the road to feed the river.

THE BEND BRINGS me up along the great glory of the valley's remaining agriculture: Zimmerman's organic truck farm. In season Tom Zimmerman's prized carrots travel to the Astoria Cooperative, and other fresh produce goes to restaurants around the region. As I pass, last year's excess root crops rot into mulch between long red and green rows of kale and chard, and slack runners of snow peas slip beneath the soil as new sprouts charge up where winter's greens have gone.

Yellow lights come on in the village and up on Whiskey Flats. In the Zimmerman compound windows brighten too. Three of five brothers live here with their wives, thirteen children, two grandmothers, a grandfather, and a great-grandmother. Along with the old farmhouse and handsome barn, there are a couple of cottages and a fine home literally built around a trailer, which was then moved and recycled as a granny flat while another house went up. Paul, the father of the brothers, recently passed away. Possessed of a long white beard, a prominent bald forehead, a restless intellect, and many beehives, Paul had a passion for books, and his house was filled with them. Now and then when I bought honey, he brought me a book to read. Along the driveway stand stone tablets engraved with Scripture, erected in observance of the strict and sustaining faith that underlies the entire Zimmerman enterprise. If Paul looked the part of an Old Testament patriarch, he also lived it. A few years ago he decided that he was on the way out. Family and friends helped with everything from vitamins to colored-light therapy. From time to time he rallied, and some thought Paul's malady was mostly a matter of attitude. But he really did die, leaving the family to handle the burial and then get on with their lives.

Tom, the farmer, tends his crop rows side by side with the Mexican workers he hires and carts the produce to market in a boxy little white truck. Danny Zimmerman has milked for the Burkhalters, the last dairy farmers in the valley, and he leases and hays the Gudmundsen fields. John is a metalworking wizard whom many in the area rely on to handle tricky jobs, from fixing the canopy of Thea's truck much better than new to fabricating tractor parts in the heat of haying season. At a recent public meeting on the future of the watershed, I learned that John had invented a new type of fish-friendly tide gate for dikes, which has been used to great advantage in salmon restoration projects. The Zimmerman brothers' wives, April, Tee, and Becca, teach their children well at home while maintaining the joint households. Grandmother Elizabeth, with her long silver braids, presides over the whole. This extended family lives about as self-reliantly as anyone can in this country these days. One day, while roofing a compost structure, Tom fell from a ladder and broke a hip. He crawled out to the edge of the road and lay helpless in the cold rain for an hour. A logger passed by once, then came back later to see if he was okay. "I didn't think much about it," said the logger. "I see guys laying by the road all the time." Tom said that was the only funny thing he had heard all day. I saw him back on his tractor just weeks later.

In the gathering dark I can just make out a walnut and a cedar that have grown together in a woody embrace; a skunk cabbage swale; and the coltsfoot verges, where the echo blues and margined whites nectar by day on pale pink composite sprays. Worrell Creek tumbles through, draining salmonberry swamps and rainforest maple slopes. This is the dark, frosty side of the valley, and I speed up, for my hands are already cold at six o'clock. A rise takes me above the river and another stream, which goes through a big new culvert designed for the passage of anadromous fish. At the highest point on this side, the road wants very much to fall into the river, which eats its underpinnings a little more with every flood. On the other shore spreads a white-spackled snowberry savannah. Down then to Badger Beach, made parklike by Kenny Wirkkala after he logged and prepared house lots up above. On one site sits a two-story Victorian trucked in from Devil's Elbow, several miles downriver. The river, swinging in from mid-valley, eddies and riffles at a popular surfing spot for common mergansers; it was a basking, wading, and fishing spot for generations of locals until the banks were swept away in a flood. On the far shore stands a grove of cottonwoods, one of which holds the bald eagles' nest aloft.

A pale mist rises as I pass the Hillsberys' tidy place set among big spruces. Their yard is decorated with Kathy's collection of elephants and, in season, Keith's elaborate Christmas lights, including a gillnetter outlined in blue bulbs and trailing an outstretched net etched in little white lights. Now I pass Chamberlain Road and Creek, just before the old Cook and King places, then Veryl and Barbara Chamberlain's Elk Mountain Ranch. Another erstwhile dairy farmer and an expert horseman, Veryl took long trail rides into his eighties, while Barbara gardened even when arthritis made her sit beside her roses. Veryl, as compact as a jockey and crowned with a white hardhat, loved his horses and cared for them as well as he managed his pastures. He had no patience with anyone who did less. In our earliest years here, he took Sally riding on old logging roads up the side of Elk Mountain. Later he often walked his big horse Beauty around the valley. On days with sufficient snow, Veryl used to hitch up a sleigh for lucky riders, then take them coursing over fields where sleigh rides are about as rare as surfing.

In any season, from horseback or Oldsmobile, Veryl dispensed advice and stories from a life in the Columbia Gorge and Gray's River Valley, with a wry but ever-friendly smile. He'd remove his hardhat, dab his round bald brow, often furrowed with wonderment at the folly of others, and begin: "As the doctor used to tell me," and go from there. For years the Chamberlains lived in the Columbia Gorge east of Washougal, where he ran a farm for a Portland doctor while he and Barbara dwelled in a converted garage on the place. Veryl's employer made a deep impression upon him, leaving a store of aphorisms and anecdotes that seemed to fit most occasions in the years to come, from field management and the care of animals and tack to county roads, gardens, taxes, and the weather. After selling the herd, Veryl and Barbara retired to a manufactured home in the green V of a meadow where Chamberlain Creek's canyon opens out and where he could keep his horses. We wondered what would become of his lovingly managed farm after an ecologist friend of ours came close to buying it to raise alpacas. Just as well he didn't know then what plans lay in store for those lowland acres. Passing by, I look north across Elk Mountain Ranch to the lit-up squares of our own windows, our house perfectly framed above the covered bridge between two tall black cottonwoods.

The stretch of the loop above Elk Mountain Ranch has changed. I failed to interest a conservation group in buying the property, and a friend of mine, a logger from Naselle, purchased Veryl's easternmost acreage to fell its timber—not realizing that the stumpage he'd bought lay smack in the middle of our view. The handsome stand contained mixed alder and second-growth conifers. Lorne left as many trees as he could, but later the new county road foreman, concerned about ice, directed his crew to cut many of the trees that shaded the road and its right of way— including most of those that Lorne had left to screen his logging show! So the southern side of the loop has become less a bowered lane than a savannah—sunnier, but less intimate and mysterious. A new house has been built on that slope for a new family. This is not the first time this corner of the valley has changed. A hundred years ago a logging railroad crossed the valley below this point to the Saldern Company's logging camp on Hjalmar Klint's land, where his daughter, Marie Fauver, still lives, and the hills were bare of timber. Today that picture is hard to imagine.

INSTEAD OF DWELLING on the loss of the bowered lane and the winter wren's seventeen-acre wood, I thank the valley gods for the surviving marshy nook, the haunt of swamp currants and anglewing butterflies. Rounding the far-near curve takes me past the Linquists' steep-roofed but slumping barn and two houses. In one of them lives Virginia Wendelin, who sprang from one of the earliest families on this side of the valley; *her* mother, Helen King, not long gone, lived for almost all of the twentieth century in Gray's River. Helen's granddaughter Bonnie taught school here for many years, and *her* daughter, Mindy, is an aide to Senator Patty Murray in her Vancouver office. The family has gone from the farm chores of Washington Territory to the congressional chores of Washington, D.C., in four generations. Mindy's dad, Mark Linquist, a logger turned county commissioner, has run the Boston Marathon twice, and when we both ran the loop, we'd pause to compare notes on the tedious matter of battling bellies.

Straight and flat runs the road north through the valley bottom; the air is distinctly warmer away from Elk Mountain. Next comes what's left of the Larsons' farm, one of the oldest spreads in this part of the valley. When the milk business soured for Darigold's outermost suppliers and the federal dairy buyout program came along, the Larsons sold their herd and, since then, much of their land. On one of my earliest walks to the bridge, I met a farmer with high, taut red cheeks and a big, rough, warm handshake. Somehow, before long Bobby Larson and I were talking about the Alaska oil pipeline—then just under construction, now running low on supply. Though we disagreed on that subject, Bobby invited me to visit the Grange. I took him up on it, and Bobby and Ila Mae and their sons, Doug and Brian, have been our good friends and neighbors ever since.

The Larson farmhouse was cobbled together from two of the hundred bunkhouses at the Saldern logging camp. Bobby built a new white house and a red metal cow barn across the road from the original home site in the seventies. When the dairy went, he and Ila Mae moved back into the remnants of the old farmstead. Tucked among the fossils of Fords of various eras, beneath a vast big-leaf maple in which blackbirds and starlings mass in winter, the Larson ménage puts me in mind of Stella Gibbons's *Cold Comfort Farm*: a living vestige of yesteryear. Bobby's son Doug still tends a small herd out of a shed that serves as a barn. Now, as I pass by, he is pulling bales for feeding and calling in a cow named Lorraine from the deep dusk. Doug is usually accompanied by his good-natured if crooked little goat, Bukken, and his current cow dog. For years he had a blue heeler named Lucky, whom we found starving, with pups, one winter and gave to the Larsons. Doug's dog now is Spud, a brown rottweiler mix. In the rising mist I shiver at the memory of Spud's former pack and of a Thanksgiving outing that ended badly.

Our traditions include a good, vigorous walk after holiday

feasts. It was on one such Christmas walk that Thea, Dory, and I discovered the heelers in an empty shed. A few Thanksgivings ago, I was strolling across the bridge with our friends Fayette and JoAnne and Dory's new dog, Lucy, a small sheltie–Aussie shepherd. The woman who had bought the Larsons' house and barn, Jackie, kept a clot of rottweilers. Their roar always put an end to any frogsong or sleep and made me thank the gods for strong chains whenever I walked past them. But that Thanksgiving they were unchained, and the pack came at us in a raging fury, aiming especially for Lucy. I had no choice but to fight back with my stout walking stick, as dogs and people screamed. Finally, Jackie's son got the dogs in hand as Jackie and I exchanged heated words. JoAnne and Lucy both went home with bites, and we spent much of the evening relating our story to a sheriff's deputy. When Jackie left the valley with most of the dogs, Doug kept two of them and somehow trained them to be relatively nice (though Spud has to wear an orange "bad dog" collar that says D A N G E R , the product of our so-called dangerous dog ordinance). In the gloaming I surprise Spud, and at first he seems about to eat me, but he ends up licking my hand.

On the left stands an attractive new house, blue-roofed and Swedish red, mirroring Swede Park's gabled roofline. Built on a tract sold off by the Larsons, the house sat uncompleted through years of neglect and decay due to floods and changing ownership, and I doubted it would ever be occupied. But at last a contractor, David Clark, bought and beautifully finished the house, and moved in with his wife, Cathy. Most of the year you'd never imagine the water rising to the Clarks' porch; but anyone who occupies the floor of this valley knows that inundation is always a possibility. The Larsons knew this all too well; several times each winter the river ran through their living room.

Hedges of wild rose and snowberry line the lane past Larson's Pond, the closest thing to a lake around here. A great blue heron rises noiselessly and wheels eastward without the usual crusty complaint. My approach has silenced the frogs as one. The single streetlight on the loop, next to the covered bridge, pops on. I prefer a dark valley and an unlit bridge, especially on Halloween, to the orange sodium vapor glare. But at the moment, chilly night having fully fallen, the light feels friendly. The lamp illuminates one of the Larsons' last fields, the site of picnics and festivals, which abuts the bridge on the southwest. The meadow, sheltered by low-limbed lindens and maples, was deeply rutted by the big tires of fishermen's pickups until spruced up for the Covered Bridge Festival. The picnic tables have long since been carried away by the winter rampage.

Up the bridge ramp. My footsteps echo across the shiny wooden deck spattered with starling lime and barn owl pellets. On the other side a luxuriant band of comfrey leads past a broken-down cattle pen, and the way climbs sharply to Loop Road, back at the near-near curve. In honor of the state's hundredth birthday in 1989, the Centennial Commission awarded special signs to families that had owned a particular farm for a century or more. The Ahlberg-Sorenson one-hundred-year-farm sign is mounted on a robust ornamental gatepost, hand-hewn by Ahlberg with a diamond-shaped top, and planted beneath a trio of his graceful old trees. The weathered post stood for years along Covered Bridge Road, then disappeared in a flood, and I thought it lost. But Joel Fitts had rescued the post and returned it to the Sorensons, and it was resurrected in this eminently suitable role. Bridge tourists often think it marks a grave on the corner knoll. Grazing cows used to keep the turf short, but now Doug, Bobby, and I have to trade off weed-whacking the sycamore maples and brambles that would otherwise overwhelm the site in a single season.

Another, larger sign across the road welcomes visitors to "the only historic covered bridge in Washington," with a handsome portrait of our pride and joy painted by Dan Howard, a local glassblower. And now, the stars out, the frogs on, my loop is complete. As my feet find the familiar grade of the mail path to home and dinner, I conclude that the loop is still worth the walk.

Compared to most places today, here changes have come slowly, and so far we have avoided the worst kinds of change. Overall, enough stays the same that we can keep our bearings. Like this scent that honeys the night air. It flows from our heather garden, where echo azures will nectar tomorrow if the morning is fine.

4 • The Time of Trilliums

On such rare afternoons the most prosaic becomes the most poetic, and months of sodden days are offset by a moment of miracle.

— WILLA CATHER, *Alexander's Bridge*

Walt Whitman, in a poem entitled "There Was a Child Went Forth," described the way "the early lilacs became part of this child." He, like Willa Cather, knew that the bursting of violets, greens, violet-greens, the springing of irises, lilacs, and suchlike from the waterlogged soil, make life worth living all over again.

While I'm equally a captive of lilacs and irises, nothing among the wild flora speaks to me of the redemption of spring like trilliums. And the best place for trilliums has always been a certain knoll across the valley, a knee of Elk Mountain cut off by Covered Bridge Road. The knoll sits just inside the far-near curve of the loop. On a walk or run around the valley in the time of trilliums, it would take real discipline not to pause to sniff, feel, and gaze on the linen tablecloth of blossoms spread beneath the old hemlocks.

Around here and, I suspect, in many rural districts, trilliums are called Easter lilies. Though their scent is lovely, it is softer and subtler than that of the grocery-store lilies. But the pure white petals, the prominent golden anthers, and the trinity of its parts make it a perfect stand-in for the nursery-grown *Lilium longiflorum* of church and festival. This works to its disadvantage when country kids take home big picked bunches of soon-to-wilt "Easter lilies" for their moms or grandmas. Trilliums do not respond well to picking; the loss of the vegetative parts can weaken or even doom a whole plant and prevent future flowering for years to come. So we were saddened when someone plucked a big solo trillium that bloomed each year around Easter time. The species *Trillium ovatum* (the only one in Willapa; the East has several, including a blood-red species) is fairly adaptable and still common hereabouts. But we missed ours just the same and hoped it would come back.

To me the redemptive power of *T. ovatum* has nothing to do with any imagined Christian symbolism. Rather, something about the improbable unfolding of the three great-hearted leaves, followed by the bombast of a big white lily somehow reconstituted from the dark, dank elements of soil and rot, says "Carry on!" When the first trillium appears on a logging road bank, I take hope; it's as simple as that. It seemed right one year when this event—and so much more—happened on the spring equinox.

The day dawned fair. Still abed, catching up on bird notes, I had just written that other than the hummingbird first heard and then seen yesterday nectaring on a tall red huckleberry, and the turkey vulture spotted last week in Skamokawa, we'd had no migrants. Suddenly I caught the flash of small white sickles across the valley that could only mean the swallows had returned. Throughout the morning I saw them. But just as they linger for a while on their departure day on the south side of the valley before finally disappearing over the hills, so these were still hesitating over there and hadn't yet crossed the river. Then Thea called that the rustic bunting was back, after two weeks away.

There he was indeed, among the juncoes, in full spring plumage, a complex mix of dun and rust stripes and patches. As Fayette Krause wrote in his notes earlier in the season, "It's amazing how a mix of earth tones—cream, brown, black, gray, rufous, and tan—can produce a stunningly memorable bird." Since my favorite butterflies are the satyrs, fashioned of those same colors highlighted by eyespots, striations, and lichenlike mottling, I agree. But with his molt complete, this bird's colors had grown almost gaudy. Rich chestnut side stripes had thickened and spread up the shoulder and down the sandy back, where new feathers lay like elegant lapstrake. His choker band was positively burgundy, and the putty patterns on the head had become zebraic, clear white throat and eyebrow against the shiny black mask and puffed-up crest. It was as if our amazing guest was making one last valedictory visit, just to let us see his breeding plumes in fullest glory before northing.

Birder friends Ann and Alan dropped by for a last look, and the bunting showed as soon as they arrived in the kitchen with their spotting scope. I watched him all afternoon as a big American robin came to forage alongside the remaining Alaska robins, or varied thrushes, giving a field-guide side-by-side of these two rust-breasted relatives. A massive flicker dropped down, then the jays, and there was a lot of birdflesh noshing on those little seeds. On her jog that morning, spotting a scuffle in the hedge, Thea found a jay and a female robin in clutch. When the jay flew off, the robin remained, and Thea saw it was wounded. The jay had mortally stabbed her in the breast.

Who killed Robin Redbreast? Steller's Jay did! Alan has seen a jay take a winter wren and eat it, but a thrush its own size? Was she already hurt, or were they fighting over a fat worm? When the season's first Cooper's hawk sailed over today, we didn't judge it for its many murders, though both Cooper's and sharp-shinned hawks have been defamed for their predatory ways. But crows, magpies, and jays, which raid nests and take a grown bird now and then, have caught most of the bird lovers' ill-considered ire. How easy to fall into the moralism that humans have visited upon corvids as long as we have cohabited with them—the masters of getting along versus the virtuosos of the double standard. We create conditions favorable to jays, then blame the jays.

Leaving the kitchen window and heading outside, I found one big clump of five trilliums in the carpet of inside-out flower (*Vancouveria*) up behind the Broken Oak. A single small *Arion ater* slug was doing its best to turn the trillium petals into Irish lace. Meanwhile the big solitary trillium on the leafy floor of the grape-fern woods was unfurling after all. Right on schedule, our visitor came and picked it again. A little late, we made a resolution—should it survive this latest topping—to sign the spot the next year: PLEASE ENJOY THIS FLOWER AND LEAVE IT ALONE TO BLOSSOM. So we did, and for three Easters now the big lone lily has bloomed and faded to pink in its own time, unplucked.

Out beyond the giant tulip tree, the bleeding hearts splayed their frilly green fingers in our woods. The first of a cardiac unit's worth of the fleshy, rosy pink flowers were enlarging out of their buds. The blossom has one of the strangest floral shapes: the petals merge into the lobes of a little 3-D valentine, opening only at the bottom in a tiny ventricle for pollinators' entry. I wondered whether any insect could actually get in until I watched a Persius duskywing nectar at length from one fresh bleeding heart after another. Soon their scent will sting the sinuses with its sweet-spicy pungency. All day long the winter wren sang its million-noted song: a continual countertenor solo from Introit to Kyrie, Hallelujah through Sanctus, on to Voluntary and Magnificat, and right down to Exultemus. I spoke the Amen. Before long, frogsong took over and drowned out a lone coyote, as Jupiter, Saturn, and Orion sprang from the western sky.

One spring, out past the biggest stand of bleeding hearts and across the creek, on a little flat beneath a pair of big spruces that hold the ravine in place, trilliums abounded. They may still. But our neighbor's forest thinning—a good job, and he spared those spruces—left the floor inaccessible with slash, making me wish

I'd driven a harder border bargain with Ed Sorenson when I bought the place. Another April trilliums sprang up in unremembered numbers from Ed's long southern slope. Seeking to preserve his view of the valley, Ed cut many maples and alders on the hillside, then burned it. The fire got a little hot, scorching a big Douglas-fir, which fortunately survived, and revealing long-lost artifacts in the soil, discards and escapes such as a big cat's-eye shooter marble cracked by the heat. Among the other treasures that the fire released or revealed were masses of trilliums, whose seedlings or sprouts must have hidden beneath the heavy brush for decades. So out of the flames and an ugly, scarified slope came a temporary eruption of beauty in soft shades of green and white—a lava flow of lilies. Within a couple of seasons the trees and brambles reasserted themselves, and the lilies went into hiding once again.

Soon the rustic bunting was gone for good, the daffodils were almost finished, the hellebores heavy, and the trilliums well and truly out. When Thea drove to Astoria for a birthday oyster lunch with friends, I urged them to stop at the mouth of a little ravine by the Columbia that I had investigated days earlier. Trillium Canyon, as I'd christened it, was strewn with its eponymous lilies, billowing like waterfalls down its steep, mossy, ferny sides. They weren't disappointed.

In the early evening the sun, seen from the front porch, set over the curves of the river, and lights came on across the valley. But not many lights. I count only five from my vantage on the river bench, four sodium vapor orange and one mercury vapor blue. One of the orange ones lights the entrance to the covered bridge. Moving about the yard I make out a few more glimmers through the trees. In all, fewer than ten habitations can be seen from here, even in winter with the leaves off. I like it that way.

The nature of the neighbors can make or break a dwelling place. The fact that we have few, and fewer still in real propinquity, reduces the odds of intolerable conflicts. Guns, dogs, dirt bikes, and diesels all detract from the day's quiet, but they usually follow my father's frequent injunction to his sons to "keep it down to a dull rumble." It is comforting to have a certain amount of movement, activity, and general human life around, if only to prove that society still exists out there beyond the perimeter of your own private fog-preserve. Also, it is good to have neighbors who will keep an eye on your place when you are away, feed the cats, lend a hand when a tree comes down or a car crashes on the highway. Most folks here are open and friendly when you call on them or see them at Mike's store or the post office. The flip side is that you never know who is going to show up at your own door.

Our first caller appeared not long after we moved in. Marilyn Gudmundsen's visit was officially intended to invite us to Gray's River Methodist Church. She brought fresh rolls, homemade jam, and an armful of flowers—a one-woman Welcome Wagon. We asked her in to sit, and we soon discovered a common interest in England, where I had lived for several years and where she was probing her Forrester family history. This we discussed as we drank the first of many cups of tea that would be poured in each of our homes. A nurse, Marilyn had married Georg, a Norwegian seaman who was often away on United Fruit ships and supply vessels to Vietnam. When he retired, he took up a cattle farm among other Scandinavians in Gray's River, where Marilyn and he raised three sons. Years later, after a house fire, I lived with the Gudmundsens for a while and heard Georg's sea stories as we sipped his dry blackberry wine by the hearth. As for Marilyn's invitation to church, my mumbled demurral was far less articulate than the one Bobby Larson's brother Harry related to a local historian: "My mother wanted us to go to church, but my father wasn't really too rolled up in it." So while the church call failed, the friendship stuck; in years to come the Methodist Church, attended by many of our friends, including the Larsons after all, turned out to be a warmly supportive neighbor.

It is the gift of stories that most repays life among settled people. I often wish I had spent more time listening to the personal histories of old-timers who have passed away, such as Helen King and Harold Badger, and had asked Harold to show me his films of old Gray's River. I did, however, visit frequently with Ed Sorenson, and I learned much of what I know about Swede Park from his tobacco-raspy voice, which vacillated between appreciative and critical of the pretender to his family seat. Even though he sold the place to me, he never seemed quite reconciled to that fact, and of course I could never meet his hopes for how it should be kept up. Often he would drop in, tell me some chapter of the house's history and how the 1930s linoleum in the hall was excellent and could last forever (we've still got it), then suggest some yard work that needed doing. The grounds had had only basic maintenance since his mother, Ebba, had died, and we were making inroads against the brambles, but I think Ed remembered how the place had once looked and could look again. My leaning toward wildness conflicted with Ed's penchant for tidiness. On the other hand, my interest in the history of the home place and its trees, and my commitment to conserving them, gave him some comfort. When he and Lenore moved to a retirement village in Vancouver, it was hard for Ed to leave the valley, and he didn't live many years longer. We still see Lenore from time to time when she comes back to visit her Swanson family. But all the Sorensons, with businesses elsewhere, are gone from the valley now. I miss them, their connection to the land, and Ed's visits—even if he always thought I should mow the lawn.

Many's the time that folks have called in here to share tales, the time of day, the weather, or the way the river flows. Ernie Wirkkala, for one, will come by in his old green truck to return my sharpened saw chains. After arguing about taking any payment, he'll give me a story along with the chain. Ernie is a solid cedar stump of a man, with a broad Finn mouth and deep-set, expressive eyes that conspire in a quizzical smile when something strikes him as puzzling or funny. Part of a World War II ground crew for fighters in Europe, he treasures the memories of his few surviving buddies but hates war, of which he seldom speaks. Nor does he talk much of the logging he did all those years, though sometimes the corner of his mouth goes up when he recalls falling firs ten feet thick and asks me, "Was that wrong?" Ernie is not the only logger-vet of his generation who feels both pride in and compunction for what he did with his years, but he seems more thoughtful than most and has the gentleness to see trees as more than logs.

Still, getting out the logs is what men did here. Ernie loves to tell about growing up in the days of horse logging and steam donkeys. Like the time when, as a boy of five or so living in a logging camp, he hitched a ride into town on one of the log trains. On the way the brakes gave out before a long curve that ran down to a high trestle. The brakeman, thinking they were going to lose the locomotive to the canyon, grabbed Ernie and threw him off into the brush. The engineer saved the train after all, and a couple of hours later someone went back in a handcar to rescue the scratched and petrified kid. Ernie spent most of his working life in those woods but never forgot that one ride and sitting by the rails wondering, what was *that* about?

Steve Puddicombe, home from summer work in Alaska, might drop in to discuss local politics, move into broader politics, on to E. O. Wilson's *Consilience* versus Wendell Berry's *Life Is a Miracle,* and, via Berry, back to community, where we started. It's his favorite subject, and one he has acted on as school board member, volunteer fireman, conservation district chairman, and Master of Gray's River Grange. No one matches his fervor for progressive change and the protection of what's worth keeping. He also cooks a turkey for the fall feast, stokes a bonfire for summer solstice, and MCs the Christmas party at the Grange. In great demand as a paid handyman, he'll also accept a blackberry pie for a small job, as long as conversation goes with it.

Equally handy and loquacious is Bob LiaBraaten from Salmon Creek, who repaired our house after a serious fire. His talk, when he swings by to give us a jar of lemon curd or to fix something, tends more toward books, stories, and jokes than politics. Mary Steller, whose home is on the Deep River delta, stops in to trade tales of her donkeys for laurel cuttings. A home-school mom or a utility worker will bring a giant silkmoth for me to identify. As well as stories and news, neighbors arrive bearing goods. Diane Matthews brings her hens' fresh brown eggs; Bob Richards proffers his hoppy home-brewed ale and equally strong opinions on the decline of democracy; Carol Ervest shows up with a crab or some sturgeon, and in years when gillnetting is good on the Columbia, fisher friends might bestow a nice coho or chinook just when it is most welcome—and when is fresh, wild-caught salmon not welcome?

As often as not, visitors never get past the kitchen. Added in the fifties after the old kitchen burned in an earlier blaze, it is an unselfconscious period piece of blue and red Formica and cream-colored, handmade cupboards, slightly off square. It opens onto an airy yellow dining room, with a big table that once was Ebba's and chairs painted to match the classic red of a Swedish Dal horse. A print of Drottning Sophia of Sweden, found in the attic, presides between my great-grandmother's hand-tinted girlhood portrait with lilacs and a woodcut of Charles Darwin. Our annual Darwin's birthday dinners take place here in February.

The other half of the downstairs is given over to the living room, with ten-foot-high ceilings and tall sash windows. Here the old-growth-plank inner walls are exposed, and the outer walls are insulated by what some might suggest is a surfeit of books. The glory of this room is an old Universal wood-burning cookstove, in bright blue enamel, which Thea bought for thirty dollars on a radio swap show in Laramie in 1970. It was installed here fifteen years later, just in time for us to be married by District Judge Bill Faubion in this room. Bokis's favorite sleeping place, a round blue rug, lies beneath the stove. On cool evenings we burn small logs and splits of oak as we read in this old and lit-tle-changed room.

A handsome oak newel post and banister, restored by Bob LiaBraaten, are among the few concessions to structural orna-ment in Ahlberg's plain and sturdy house. The windowed land-ing supports an avocado tree raised by Thea from a seed saved from the compost—it's entirely out of hand. Now that the chil-dren have left home, their bedrooms have been commandeered for a sewing nook, a natural history lab, a correspondence corner, files, and more books, and enough space for squeezed-in guests. In our bedroom the two rectangular eyes, which frame the cov-ered bridge, are open to the valley airs every night except in heavy storm. The final room, once a nursery off our bedroom, is where I work. I am nearly as tightly contained within my tiny, jam-packed study as Firkin in her rushwork cat-igloo on the porch. To turn around and stretch, I make frequent forays down-stairs for tea. Which brings us back to the kitchen and the neigh-bors who call on us there.

THE YOUNGEST NEIGHBORS are a power unto themselves. I have only rarely yelled at them. I like that the school bus has children to stop for. Some of them take shortcut paths across our place to avoid the highway curve, and that helps us keep the footways open. And I loved the sunny Saturday mornings when Bill, building a house down on the floodplain, brought his daughter and her friend to race their horses—long dark hair, manes, and tails flowing behind—up and down the fields. Two young children, a brother and sister, used to come and ask to chase butterflies with me. Most years a few kids have been will-ing to brave our dark drive on Halloween to admire my jack-o'-lanterns and claim our candy, though the traffic has dropped off as small goblins have become giant basketballers.

For a while a passel of eight kids lived with their mother across the river. It was good to hear them enjoying the river on a hot day, swinging from a rope below the bridge and flying into the cold, clear water with whoops of pleasure. Less pleasant was the older ones' irksome habit of burning rubber in the covered bridge, leaving skid marks on the wooden floor as the sound ripped open the night. When a big bowl of blackberries laboriously picked by Thea and JoAnne mysteriously disappeared, word got around the valley that our household was not amused. There came a flurry of fleeing footfalls and T-shirted backs as the bowl reappeared, the berries a little smushed but mostly there. The boys' pellet guns gave us cause for concern, but Billy, a lad fascinated by blue herons, loved the valley and said he never wanted to leave it.

One summer several of these kids went at the pasture with dirt bikes and four-wheelers, circling and circling with maddening two-stroke shrieks and *bams*, turning the bucolic bridge-side scene into an ad hoc motocross track. Work became impossible. While the noises of tractors, chain saws, and loggers' cautionary air horns emanate from work being done and are more or less predictable and finite (logging operations, like haying, have their season, and trucks quit in the afternoon), the destruction of a summer's day by that random engine racket was a form of torture.

I tried to reason with the bikers' mother, but she said they'd moved to the country so they could be free to live and play as they liked. Our dialogue lost its neighborly tone. Later, at a public meeting over a different matter, she accused me of being against everything and of calling her early in the morning and using the f-word. I replied that this was patently ridiculous; everyone knows that I don't make calls early in the morning. But this too passed. The kids and their mom moved on, and the windows of the big house she'd built like a dormitory went dark. Once she had planned to set up a farm museum in her barn, and when I go there now, the beautiful scene of the valley and the covered bridge that she painted on a big barn window is broken, like whatever dreams she had for her lively brood-of-many-fathers here. I found that I missed the kids' whoops at the bridge, and I wondered whether Billy ended up somewhere with herons.

Unless you live in the true wild, you live daily with the sounds, smells, and sights of near neighbors: the *tap-tap* and hum of auto-mechanicking; the soft *clink* of tossed horseshoes up above the highway; the *clip-clop* of horse's hooves on the bridge deck and the *whoomp!* of a pheasant-rearing neighbor's shotgun down below; the distinctive sound of each truck as it comes and goes and each dog as it worries the night; the calls of husbands and wives and parents and children to one another; the separate timbres of weed-whacker and lawnmower. These are the ordinary, occasional background punctuations in the general quiet, familiar to any rural community. We make allowance for one another's chain saw and wood smoke. We don't apologize for living, and most do our best to live and let live. We try not to call the sheriff on each other too often, though endlessly howling hounds and all-night parties on the covered bridge have sometimes challenged that scruple.

DURING THE TIME I've lived in this place, it is the Larsons who have most defined it. Back when they still had a herd, the day always began with Bobby yelling at the cows and his sons and ended with the lights coming on in the barn as Ila Mae performed the evening milking. I came to believe that I almost understood the inflection and mood of the different *moooooo*s that issued from the fog, rain, or sun-shimmer, whether prompted by feeding time, milking time, the fullness of pregnancy, the loss of a calf, exasperation with cold rain and mud, or delight in a sunny day and fresh grass. The Larsons' tractor, too, had different resonances, depending on whether it was engaged in manure spreading in the spring, haying in midsummer, or baling after the hay had cured, cutting green-chop for straight-up feeding or harvesting veg to make silage through the magic of bacteria. The scent of that silage, a rich and sour reek that struck like a needle to the nose, reminded us where we live as much as anything. When the dairy herds left, I hated to see the old dames go, and now I actually miss the silage. More, I miss Bobby calling to his cows and Brian's horn going *da-da-da-dah-da* in the covered bridge every time he returned from milking for the Burkhalters downvalley. Doug still keeps a small herd of heifers and a milk cow or two, saving the fields from the sad cowless, mooless state that has befallen so much of this formerly dairy-famous county.

Still in bed with coffee, I picked up the ringing telephone. "Good morning!" Bobby said, "Now don't hang up on me. I'm thinking Captain Gray needs to come back here again."

Sometimes Bob recruits my help—to chair the park committee, say, or provide historic interpretation on the covered bridge or the Swede Park trees. Just as often he simply wants to try out his ideas on someone other than the cows. A little later Bobby may drop by, wearing a hooded sweatshirt and dungarees dyed with grass and tractor grease, to explain his plan. Any number of projects for the community have hatched under that hood while Bobby steered his tractor back and forth across the fields, spreading manure or cutting the hay it fertilized: our town water system, the covered-bridge picnics and festivals, a Grange park.

Bob's parents came down to the valley from their original place up in Fossil Creek early in the twentieth century. A third-generation immigrant Swede born in 1924, Bobby speaks directly, with a lexicon derived from the land as much as from the local schools he attended, spiked with good cheer, goodwill, and story. Officials who don't know him, hearing his "You bet" and "This here's the deal," may assume he is that imaginary creature "the simple farmer" and are taken aback to discover his formidable intelligence, imagination, wit, and perseverance. He often gets his way.

At the height of their dairy business, Bobby and Ila Mae built a modern ranch-style house near the milking barn. When they sold, they moved into a cabin on the site of the original house, which was long gone. To give themselves more room, Bob concocted a plan to drag an abandoned but sturdy house belonging to his family from its position by the highway upriver to the main home place. His plan had a precedent: Bobby's father, Victor, had built that original family home from two recycled logging-camp bunkhouses he had flat-carred down from K-M Mountain on the log train, then tugged into place on skids pulleyed from a deadman. No wonder Bobby thought he could pull off what others might have thought a daft scheme. For weeks he and his sons worked to shore the house up and build a huge sled beneath it in preparation for hauling it across field and dell with tractors or a Cat. But the state fisheries officials wouldn't even consider issuing a permit to pull a house through the river, and in the end the Larsons settled for salvaging good old clear-grained lumber from the house. For one such as I, for whom replacing a rotten plank is a major feat of engineering, it was invigorating to see Bobby take on such an ambitious plan in his seventies. He could have done it, too.

One of Bobby Larson's grander visions saw the county buying the tens of thousands of acres of the Cathlamet Managed Forest, which the Crown Zellerbach Corporation had owned for decades and which employed many local workers. Crown sold the holding to Sir James Goldsmith, an English junk bond speculator, and he later sold it to Willamette Industries. When the forest came up for sale again, Bobby saw the chance for the county to pounce, but the purchase would have required a huge bond debt, and the idea cut no mustard in the county seat. Now that the modest state trust forests that fund the county have been overcut and the commissioners are coveting timber reserved for marbled murrelets, Bobby's brainstorm shows for the bold notion it was. If Wahkiakum County owned that huge forest estate, it would have plenty of saw logs to fund its operations while plenty of trees continued to grow. There would be good local jobs in the woods and no need to cut the older trees the murrelets need. Sustainability might actually be possible.

Lately Farmer Larson has lobbied the county to consider annexing parts of neighboring Pacific County that would make more sense being in Wahkiakum and to investigate a deep-water port on the Columbia. These notions aren't likely to win many adherents, especially in Pacific County. But they too show remarkable imagination. Some shake their heads, but I just enjoy how Bobby reads the world around him. One recent evening when he and Doug were taking hay to some cows at the old Norman Durrah place, now theirs, down the valley, Bobby leaned against his pickup, pushed his hat back, spread his fingers, smiled, and said, "If a person watches the moon, listens to the weatherman, and is ready to go, why then it can be done." He was talking about the hay harvest, but his words could apply to everything he does.

That mornings' call was about a bicentennial reenactment of Captain Robert Gray's historic arrival in 1792. Gray was a merchant seaman sailing out of Boston to barter for sea otter pelts along the West Coast for the China trade. It was his crossing of the Columbia River bar in the ship *Columbia Rediviva* several weeks prior to Captain George Vancouver's arrival that gave the river its name and eventually led to the Canadian border's placement north, rather than south, of Washington and Oregon. We know that Gray rowed inland on the river that bears his name. On little evidence, village tradition has it that he came upstream to the head of tidewater, our town site. So Bobby cooked up a plan to replicate Gray's landing on its two hundredth anniversary.

Sure enough, on May 23, two period ships' boats (loaned with remarkable generosity and trust by the Oregon Historical Society, then towed here and recaulked by George Gregg and me) rounded the river bend below the Valley Tavern. They were rowed by the entire high school basketball team, commanded by Steve Puddicombe as Captain Gray, with mates Hoskins and Boit, all in period dress or some approximation thereof. Scores of schoolchildren enjoyed lunch provided by the Grange and watched as Gray & Co. were received by a party of Chinook Indians (arrayed in Plains Indian garb and headdresses, but never mind). Gifts were exchanged, including a small cask of who-knows-what. It all worked out well, even the actual landing, thanks to another of Bobby's ideas—a plan for a boat ramp in the village tidal basin.

When the Deep River bridge was replaced by the state, the old bridge's still-sound concrete slabs were available for the taking. With apologies to Archimedes, if you give a farmer a tractor, he can move anything in the world. When the Zimmermans saw those heavy slabs, they envisioned a floodwater dike along their farm road, and indeed they erected it. Bobby saw a community boat ramp. He asked me to write the permit applications, since messing with the river these days is a complicated and highly regulated business. The permit was granted, and the ramp stands today. I use it for my canoe, steelheaders and smelters put in and take out there, and it may still be there ready for Captain Gray's next coming in 2092. As Bobby and I were standing by the riverside talking after a recent Grange meeting, he brought up the reenactment. "That was about the best thing we done," he said.

In the classic statement of diminished expectations, Thoreau wrote in *Walden*: "The youth gets together his materials to build a bridge to the moon, or, perchance, a palace or temple on the earth, and, at length, the middle-aged man concludes to build a woodshed with them." For Bobby Larson, I think it is the other way around.

AT ONE COVERED Bridge Festival, we were dancing to a hot rock 'n' roll band with two other couples, naturalists like us. I'd been bartending in the beer tent all afternoon, sorry that we didn't have Pyramid Pale Ale as we had the first year and beginning to wonder if a few folks hadn't had more than sufficient Blitz by now. A stocky, middle-aged logger I recognized but didn't know staggered onto the dance floor and shouted, "Everything was fine around here until you goddamn environmentalists showed up." I tried to talk him back to his table, where a buddy was egging him on.

The logger went on about government regulators (one in our group worked for the Department of Fisheries) and government grants (I'd had a book grant, but not from the government). "Ed's place was nice and clean before," he said, "and you've let it go all to hell. Now it's just a brushy mess." He was about to throw a punch when some other folks convinced him that this wasn't an appropriate occasion for brawling, and he backed off. Later another logger, a good friend, told me not to sweat it. "He was a thug in high school," he said, "and he still is." But a neighbor for all that.

A few springs before that, a pair of loggers showed up at our back door one day wearing the standard stagged-off jeans, calk (pronounced "cork") boots, red suspenders, and tin hats. "Are you that guy Powell?" one asked.

"Yes, Pyle," I said, "Bob Pyle," and held out my hand.

"Did you write that book Evergreen?" asked the other one. My book *Wintergreen* had been critical of some local logging practices.

"That's me," I said.

"Well, we want to buy a couple of copies," said the first man, shaking my hand, "and have you sign 'em." Unlike the belligerent at the bridge fest, they understood that I wasn't antilogging, that my argument was not with the logger but with Big Timber, companies whose short-term profit decisions had hurt the people of our timber town as well as the woods themselves. More of the reaction to the book in this timber-dependent district has been closer to the back-door sentiment than to the one on the dance floor—or at the least tolerant.

Only one neighbor has caused us real grief, and not just us. This person was a welcome buyer when one of the retiring farmers was selling his property. The buyer went on to purchase much of the valley, assuring the residents that all he had in mind was farming. And indeed he raised cattle and cut hay for a while. Then he announced plans for a dense subdivision of secondhand doublewide mobile homes, right on the floodplain beyond the bridge. In preparation, he logged and 'dozed the best trillium stand in the valley. The county permit coordinator, the planning commission, and the county commission all fell over themselves to approve Covered Bridge Estates. We wondered if this would be the end of the valley as we knew it.

ANOTHER NEIGHBOR, George King, created beauty without even intending to. George, a retired military man with a millimeter of crewcut under his army cap, a voice as soft as moss, and a permanent smile, lived in a white brick house up on the next river bench with his war bride, Serena. A devoted fisherman who liked small engines, he always tuned and repaired our mower. While tending his own garden and woodlot, George used his riding mower to shear not only the grass but also the vegetation in the open woods behind his house. On one April visit, we walked out there to find acres of heart-leaved yellow stream violets and lush *Maianthemum dilatatum,* or false lily-of-the-valley, in extravagant bloom—and among them, thousands of pink fawn lilies, *Erythronium revolutum.* The color of pink Popsicles, with drooping, recurved petals and broad spotted leaves, the usually uncommon lilies mixed with all the other wildflowers in a glorious carpet of green, cream, yellow, and pink. George's fortuitous once-a-year mowing made the perfect management regime for this faerie sward, and we came back to enjoy the stunning show year after year.

Trillium time arrives with the overpowering green of April: the leafing dogwoods and ninebark along the sloughs east of Skamokawa, the elderberry and Indian plum and unfurling vine maple, the willows past pussy-bloom and the alders past red catkin time, the tulip tree leafing out above the canopy in peeper-green two-lobed wagglers, tremulous on the breeze against high sky the blue of Steller's jays' eyebrows.

Unlike the babylons of big-leaf maple blossoms, the flowers of sugar maples never caught my notice until this spring, when two of our three trees burst forth in chartreuse showers. Each tree can bear male or female flowers or both, and each flower may also express either gender or both. Yet despite their robust ambisexuality, *Acer saccharinum* flowers are so delicate that I had overlooked them until one morning when the sun caught them from behind. Then, watch out—lemon-lime sparklers! I'll never miss them again.

Edna St. Vincent Millay, in her poem "Spring," protests that it is not enough when

> April
> Comes like an idiot, babbling and strewing flowers.

On the contrary.

5 ⋆ Arrivals

O honey-bees,
Come build in the empty house of the stare.

— W. B. YEATS, "Meditations in Time of Civil War"

Every day and every night of the shoulder season, winter
into spring, the Swede Park census grows. The parade of
newcomers swells, peaking in May when the great incoming becomes almost frantic. Each day new names appear on the yellow
pad in the kitchen on which we record each first bird and every
butterfly sighting of the year. Of course the migration begins
much earlier. Killdeer cry all winter but thicken overhead for a
few weeks each fall and spring. Common mergansers never
completely leave, but their numbers subtly increase about now,
as the real winter absentees check back in. The first turkey vulture yaws its V back into the valley, and a languid darkness on
the grass reflects its shadow on the sky. Way back in February, an
unzipping sound, echoed by a russet blur around the side of the
unleafed snowball, gave away a precocious rufous hummingbird
days before there was any nectar. Having made it this far, he'll be
okay.

Through March and into April, the immigration picks up
speed and mass. Even as the wintering ruby-crowned kinglets
move out, their stand-ins appear in the form of slightly huskier

Hutton's vireos. The "bird alert" trill of western tanagers and the clipped robin-song of black-headed grosbeaks turn on, then off, as these birds stop by, then split, seldom sticking around for long but nesting elsewhere in the valley. Actual robins, on the other hand, plop down for six months of omnipresence; a pair of rust-breasted dumplings canvass the mossy lawn, the male black-headed, the female paler overall. Warblers signify migration to many of us: the separate songs of Townsend's, black-throated grays, orange-crowns, and yellow-rumps all pipe through the burgeoning foliage. Then one warm day we hear the lazy *wee-dee-dee* of yellowthroats issuing from the willows by the river (their famous *witchity* call seems one speed slower here). And finally the brilliant brassy burst of the Wilson's warbler, a gathering coloratura trill tumbling over itself at the uphill end. Four or more males will try out territories in Swede Park, and at least two will succeed in attracting mates. For many weeks the Wilson's regale every outing, both with song and with glimpses of their lemon yellow, black-skullcapped selves.

Bats come back too, appearing in the evening air as if materializing from the newly warming vapors. One mid-May dusk I reviewed the changing of the shift from my chair on the front porch as a swallow and a bat flittered about together before the bird took to its roost and the mammal took possession of the space before the house. The swallows had already been around for a while. Right about the Ides of March, someone will see barn or tree swallows scything the cool air over Deep River. One afternoon of on-and-off sun I sat writing at the porch table, wearing wool. At that time tree swallows nested regularly in a clay pot hung from the eave for the purpose. I hadn't yet seen a swallow of any species. All of a sudden a light-and-dark swoosh scored the air beside me. There, in the budding wisteria below the nest pot, clung the gunmetal-blue and silver-white vision of a tree swallow. I swear it was panting; I swear it had immense relief written all over its little hirundine face. I know for a fact that it had just completed its two- or three-thousand-mile migration, and I was there to see it arrive. What luck!

Our own violet-green swallows, awaited with exquisite anxiety ("What if they don't come back this year?"), seldom miss April Fool's Day by much on either side, though certain cold springs have detained them up to a fortnight, scaring us silly. When they do arrive, they shimmer around the housetop, round and round, tittering. I throw open the sash, then run out and titter and squeak back at them in sheer stupid gratitude, imagining reciprocity. It doesn't matter if they actually pay me no mind; there is no doubt that they recognize the *place* and come back here on purpose. For days or weeks they will visit the nest hole on the porch between long sorties over the valley; then they will settle in, clean out, trading old feathers and moss and straw for new, and start nesting. For months we will revel in their comings and goings, those magical swoops, every time we hang out the wash, sit alone or with friends or cats on the porch, or go for the mail. No other migrants, save maybe the later Swainson's thrushes, are more welcome.

Some arrivistes, however, are less so. There used to be a round hole in the clapboard gable above the kitchen, probably cut by a flicker. One of my first springs here, I noticed stains on the wall below the hole. Bits of straw began sticking out, then piling up in the garden underneath. I stationed myself to see all comings and goings, and what I saw were starlings. All naturalists aspire to furnish lodging for various species of wildlife on their own grounds, but we can be as prejudiced as anyone, and starlings—introduced aliens that compete for cavities with native hole-nesters—were not what I had in mind.

I climbed into the small attic over the kitchen planning to remove the starlings, but I was not prepared for what I found. First there was a great untidy flutter and squawk as the building bird lit out of the hole, bright against the black wall when seen from within. I focused my flashlight on the spot from which it had erupted, and my eyes nearly popped in the fiberglass-and-shingle gloom. The nest—or, rather, its foundation—was built up three feet to match the height of the hole and was four feet across at the base. Perched on the very summit, like a tiny crown on Jabba the Hut, was the nest itself, as elegant as any songbird's. I don't know why starlings need such a big nesting mound, but at least it was now clear why they needed so much straw.

No eggs had been laid. I removed the entire structure into a big trash bag, filled it to bursting, and carried it out to the compost heap. There I carefully went through the whole mess, tabulating the following recognizable objects: straw (from hay), leaves of oak, maple, black walnut, tulip tree, beech, bramble, holly, and montbretia. Also moss, club moss, lichen (*Usnea* and other species), bracken, cedar foliage and bark, cardboard wire wrapper, thimbleberry twigs with galls, fiberglass insulation (some big pieces), synthetic rope fiber, plantain seed heads, wood slivers, sticks, alder cones, charcoal, several species of dead grass, lawn grass clippings, sheet plastic, bark strips, chicken feathers and down (but, remarkably, no other feathers), red yarn, beetle elytra, cardboard strips, budded wisteria tendrils, cotton string, an orange-painted splinter, alder and cottonwood catkins, cellophane, strapping-tape fiber, two five-foot pieces of black plastic baling twine, metal foil, marah vines, roots, cigarette filter tips, clods of earth, thistledown, beech mast, dandelions and various other flowers, and red plastic twist ties.

Then I climbed back up and nailed a piece of wood firmly over the hole. The starlings moved down to the covered bridge, returning now and then to feast helpfully on European crane-fly larvae, or leatherbacks, in our mossy lawn. I've seen nothing like their edifice since—at least not until the bushy-tailed wood rats came. When people around here speak of rats, they usually mean wood rats, also known as pack rats. Near the old wharves and waterside communities around here, Norway rats (*Rattus norvegicus*) have become established, and the county may also have black rats (*Rattus rattus*)—*real* rats. We've only ever seen

two Norway rats around here, both young, one nabbed by a weasel and another that Bokis subdued by sitting on it. But many an
attic or outbuilding in these parts hosts *Neotoma cinerea*, the
bushy-tailed wood rat. These large, intelligent rodents establish
stick-'n'-stuff domiciles of such permanence that anthropolo-
gists have cored their multigenerational urine crusts as a means
of dating ancient human habitations in the desert. Around here
they usually get the boot or hot lead, or they move on when their
chosen habitation finally rots into the ground. I suspect that the
attic of our outbuilding has been haunted by wood rats off and
on for decades. When we began hearing the loud stamping of
broad feet overhead, a rhythmic drumming characteristic of the
species, we knew we had one.

You can also tell when wood rats are in residence by their
strong ammoniac odor. You might begin noticing that small items
have gone missing and biggish scat pellets have appeared in their
place. Except when mating or rearing young, they tend to live on
their own. We found it fairly easy to live-trap our wood rats using
dried prunes for bait. We transported them, one at a time, several miles up into the forest and released them on huge old
stumps whose many crumbling cavities seemed a reasonable approximation of their "natural," prehuman habitat. Pack rats have
handsome faces, with large, shiny eyes and rounded snouts that
are more squirrel-like than rattish, richly variegated pelage, and
long, fully furred tails. I'd love to have them around if they were
tidier in their habits and less kleptomaniacal. Apparently they'd
love to be here, too. I didn't tag our releases, so I can't be sure
that any individuals actually returned, but somebody sure moved
in soon, and more than once.

After putting off the dusty, awkward job for years, I finally
clambered up over the garage rafters to excavate the wood-rat
nest. The platform it was built on spanned three rafters and
looked as if it had been placed there especially for the animals'
pleasure. This rat-nest receptacle turned out to be a stacked pair
of deep window frames, six feet long and three feet wide, which

were completely covered with debris that rose three feet in the middle and overflowed on each side for another two or three feet. The superstructure was composed mostly of kindling that we had stacked in the old smithy below—cut branches an inch or two in diameter and from one to three feet in length—and old cedar shingles pulled down when the house was reroofed. The architecture, if a random jumble, was impressive for its magnitude and ambition. Once I'd removed the bulk of it box by box, handing the cartons down to my brother-in-law Ted, I measured and weighed the surprising mass. According to the late Northwest naturalist Earl Larrison, *Neotoma* edifices sometimes exceed fifty bushels' worth of material. Our nest wasn't *that* big, but it did fill Thea's old bushel basket twenty-five times. A bushel of dried corn weighs seventy pounds, but this matter was much less dense, ranging from two pounds for a bushel of foam to fourteen pounds for one of cut limbs. The total came to ninety pounds plus. Nearly a hundredweight of stuff, shifted by one or two rodents the size of large squirrels!

The job turned out to be much more arduous than I expected, causing me to lie across rafters in hot still air, scooping and whisking the debris amid clouds of powder from decaying fiber and rat shit. I wore a dust mask but had to remove my glasses, which immediately fogged up, and my eyes stung with the fine dust of decades. I only hoped that this species of rodent had nothing to do with hantavirus. But the ordeal had its compensations. As I burrowed through the ruins and removed the overburden, I discovered two actual nests. The larger, filling a bushel by itself, was a more or less discrete ball of foam rubber chunks tightly interwoven with scraps of many kinds of fabric, thread, moss, leaves, hair, wool, paper, and one fishing leader with a big silver hook. My guess that this was the birthing chamber was confirmed by the find of two bodies, mostly mummified: one, a baby, was mouse-sized; the other was much older, two-thirds as big as an adult. I was amazed to find that several years after the last occupation, the little one still had living maggots feeding on it, and the larger bore a cluster of eggs. But there is, after all, a long succession of decomposing insects.

The smaller nest-within-a-nest, which filled a shoebox, consisted mostly of long grass blades cured into straw along with some lichen and shredded rubber foam, fabric, and other soft materials. I wondered if this were not my rat's cozy sleeping bag. Most of the smell had long since dissipated, and while there was a plenitude of half- to one-inch-long charcoal-pellet rat poop, most of it was deposited away from the nest. A long wooden gutter lying nearby was filled with rat scat, like a latrine. Lying there on my belly, sifting through this private chamber, I felt like a looter of the lost ark. I was even more struck by the wood rat's providential and fastidious habits than by the dimensions of its accomplishment.

Those dimensions were, nevertheless, prodigious. The sheer diversity and abundance of the rats' gatherings were astonishing. Here is what their violated nest contained. On the botanical side, Thea and I identified sticks, bark, leaves, needles, vines, or catkins of alder, maple, red and English oaks, hornbeam, laburnum, blackberry, ivy, tritonia, birch, beech, pine, and Port Orford cedar; sword, deer, and bracken ferns; ornamental horsetail stalks; and several species of mosses and lichens. Strips of veneer, up to three and four feet long, came from old paneling. Of fruits and such, there were dozens of butternuts, both whole and gnawed, big white oak and tiny red oak acorns, black walnut husks and shells, English walnuts, a peach pit, wisteria pods, maple samaras, marah seeds, onion skin, orange peel, and a mummified Asian pear. From the kitchen garden came the fruiting stem of a tomato, dried garlic leaves, and an ancient Chas. Lilly radish-seed packet. The animal kingdom was represented by tiny red ants, a false black widow, a European house spider, cocoons and eggs sacs of moths and spiders, noctuid moth and termite wings, elytra of emerald bupestrid beetles, old mud dauber wasp foundations, millipedes, larger and smaller fly pupae and maggots, three bones of large mammals, and one perfect little *Haplotrema* green snail, vacant.

Besides about ten million sticks, the milled wood included scraps of modern cedar shingles and old ones stamped with the names of two long-gone local shake-and-shingle mills: "Knappton Brand No. 2" and "Johnson and Swanson"; hunks of pine and fir one-by-fours, one-by-ones, one-by-twos, and a cedar one-by-three; a routed banister rail, finish molding, painted window trim, and wall laths. The wood rats, more advanced than we are philosophically, made no distinction between "manmade" and "natural"; to them, we're just another aspect of natural history. So the great heap included many human artifacts: strips of wire insulation, rubber, and woven asbestos; copper wire, both bare and insulated; sisal twine and cotton rope, cord, and twine; nylon strap and ropes of various gauges. A ragbag of fabrics included scraps of blue cotton kite tail, pink plaid blanket, orange life-jacket fabric and filling, T-shirt, shoelace, flannel sheet, canvas, muslin from an old insect net, red thread, gold velvet trim, a nylon zipper, and a blue sock the washing machine missed. There were flakes of composition shingle from two roofs, green and speckled; plaster and wallboard, cheap paneling, Celotex, acoustic tile, aluminum strip, and a Styrofoam peanut. Masses of plastic featured a strip of rainbow-zigzag shower curtain, clear and yellow tarp, and voluminous, rotting white, yellow, gray, and blue foam. And plenty of paper! Kraft grocery sack and handle, one fragment labeled "Port Townsend Paper #8"; labels from cans of True Value latex paint, green paint thinner, and Western gypsum; gray and brown cardboard, cellophane, masking and electrical tape, toilet paper, paper towel, tarpaper, waxed paper, and one Phillies cigar band. And several paper items bearing hand marks: A tag—"Sold to Dr. Robt. Pyle"—from what? A shingle label marked "sold." A scrap from a yellow pad bearing Thea's handwritten list of fishing gear, and a piece of white notebook paper with the beginnings of a story typed on it: "The Gold is in the Generla Store. The Sherff . . ."

What one hopes to find in a pack-rat nest is the recognizable object that has been missing for how long? In this I was not disappointed. A partial inventory of items borrowed by our resident rat revealed one orange plastic Squibb toothbrush, used for cleaning oil off engines; a full tube of Bentley-Harris stovegasket cement; leather straps, clasps, and clips from a purse; a four-inch length of rusted chain with rings at each end, reinforced with friction tape, possibly a piece of horse tack; a short, wooden-handled screwdriver; and the handle of an orchard saw left out in the woods. Aluminum and plastic film canisters still carried labels for moth and beetle specimens, and two plastic prescription pill bottles told what Thea's parents were taking in 1972 and 1984. I hooted with glee at the most bizarre find: two well-gnawed bass drumsticks, one of cork, leather, and wood from my days in the Seattle Irish-Gaelic Pipe Band, and one of red-striped felt and aluminum from the University of Washington Husky Marching Band.

I found no coins, keys, or jewelry, as are often reported by wood-rat excavators. But I found something even better. As I picked among the sticks and shingles out in the sun, a glint caught my eye. Lodged there was a little cardboard box in a plastic sheath and, within, a cluster of fishing lures: several shiny Mepps spinners of silver and brass, a little Red Devil spinner (my favorite as a boy), and two beautiful wooden lures of my father's: F6 Rio Grande Kings, painted yellow and green and orange and black. How I remembered these, and the brookies and rainbows and browns he caught with them!

Later I came across reels of monofilament, a dried bottle of Pfluger Speedy Reel Oil, and a folded packet of shiny Wright & McGill Eagle Claw snelled hooks—"They Hook and Hold"— gold-plated Aberdeen size 3, circa 1938. All these things had lain for years in my father's creel out in the studio. Noticing one day that the creel had been gnawed on, I took it to a rented office to protect it from the "mice." When that office was burgled, Dad's damaged creel was left, but his old reels were stolen—along with everything else in the creel, I assumed. Finding his beautiful lures in the bushy-tail's lair meant recovering something loved and long lost. The wood rats had saved these treasures for me.

I TAKE PLEASURE in the fact that our abode lodges many other animals besides ourselves. They are not always convenient—the mouse turds in the linen drawers, the moth holes in my grandmother's blue silk carpet—and we do resist those species with lethal means. But overall I would rather live in a home with some troublesome tenants of other species than in one with nothing but agreeable humans. So what if the hibernating lady-bird beetles become tedious in spring when they grow hungry before dispersing and flop into every beverage and bite us on our nipples and eyelids as we sleep? They also eat the clothes moth larvae. And if the impossibly long-legged *Pholcus phalangioides* leave their polka-dot spider frass on books and doodads beneath them, they also entertain us, jiggling on their webs in the corners. There are so many more tenants. I enjoy the golden-green jewels of bupestrid beetles that sometimes appear on the floorboards, and the big, brown inchworm moths called *Triphosa haesitata,* with their soft striations and elegantly pinked margins, that sneak into our house to hibernate in drapes or the cool cellar, then flutter from room to room like chimerical butterflies bringing dreams of spring. We try to let them out when spring really comes, before they die struggling against a sunny window.

We are hospitable to most of the wildlife that finds its way inside, but recently our welcome was tried and found wanting. Returning home on a warm spring afternoon, I noticed a disconformity on the wall outside the bathroom window. Hanging there above the oil tank was a throbbing mass of brown: a swarm of honeybees. The workers were agitating around a small hole in the siding, and the queen was not in evidence. Honeybees have been scarce because of the plague of *Varoa* and tracheal mites, and wild hives have virtually vanished from the countryside, so I was delighted to see these bees alive at all. Some were making wax on the wall, but more and more were coming and going from the hole. A hive was a-building, all right—within our own walls. Would it be smart, I wondered, just to leave them be?

I had always heard that when you have an unwanted swarm, you should call the local beekeeper, who will gladly come and get it and leave some honey in exchange for the free hive. But in fact, Sue Hubbell writes in her *Book of Bees,* the tired queens and kicked-out swarms they obtain this way aren't really good for much, and apiarists take the swarm chiefly to maintain good relations with their neighbors. Our nearest beekeeper, Paul Zimmerman, was past going out for hives, his wife said, and the next nearest had died, but another man had taken over his hives. Mr. Busse came and tried to sweep the cluster into a super, but they wouldn't stay without the queen, and she was already firmly ensconced in the structure of our house, making it her home. He left beeless and less than amused with the effort, so we bought the quart of honey he'd brought for the traditional swap.

And so the bees came to live in our house. I would have liked nothing more than to extend our hospitality to the honeybees. But everyone we talked to said the same thing: "You can't have bees in your walls!" For one thing, other "vermin," such as mice, would be attracted by the honey. For another, if the colony grew big enough and then died, the combs, without the thousands of fanning wings, would overheat, allowing the honey to leak through the walls or pour out along the floor. I pictured myself standing by the sweet cascade, scooping it up with an open jug or just licking the walls.

Various people offered the same two remedies: spray the bees or tear out the wall. Since the colony was lodged in the wall behind the oil tank, the second option would be a massive project. As for the first, the likelihood of my spraying toxic chemicals into our walls is roughly equal to the odds of that golden throng metamorphosing into the golden fleece overnight. I asked a beekeeper at a farmers' market for advice. "What you want to do," he said, "is go down to the hardware and get some bee and hornet killer. Spray a double dose into the wall, making sure you seal up all the holes. But don't breathe that stuff! It's *really* bad." I bought some honey and thanked him.

As much as I liked the idea of providing a place for the peaceful manufacture of one of my favorite foods, I concluded that the only sensible recourse was to get the bulk of the bees out before they could make much comb and start filling it with honey and bee brood. I installed an escape, a little device that allowed the workers out but not back in, and by the end of the third day, most of the swarm was hanging outside again, unable to reach their queen. I couldn't find anyone with an empty hive and a spare queen, which might have lured them in and conserved the swarm. But it didn't matter: when I looked again at dusk, the bees were all gone.

It was too much to hope that they had just left. In the morning it became obvious that they had found another way into the space between the studs and reunited with their queen before dark. We found the second hole and plugged it with a cork. The next day was one of our December days in July, and only a few bees managed to squeeze out the escape. Rain continued, with temps in the low fifties. The bees hung moribund on the clapboards.

This state continued for the next few days. Some bees died and lay on their backs on the oil tank like sacrifices to the season. Then at last came a day when the summer reasserted itself. The last raindrops spangled the glaucous stems and leaves of broccoli stalks as tall as a child. Nasturtiums spilled out of a metal tub, offering spicy sips of nectar at the ends of their tubes. Marah vines sprawled across the ruins of a sometime rock garden, their American-flag-star flowers studding the green mass among coiled tendrils and big palmate leaves. Up in the roadside oaks, a small flock's worth of fledging chestnut-backed chickadees stripped the aphids that spattered everything underneath with their sweet shellac.

All this time bees were issuing from the escape in earnest. Watching from the bathroom with binoculars, I could see their fuzzy forms pressing against the gate of thin copper tangs, which parted to let them out but not back in. Each escapee took to the air in what passed for bee expectation, going forth for nectar and pollen, then returned to find general chaos around the blockage. Bees circled back and tried to get in, but most, realizing that they could not get back to the hive by that route, crowded instead around the pheromone-leaking cracks. By the middle of the warm afternoon, the air was filled with winged golden pellets flinging every which way, their confusion palpable. And as the day began to wane, the swarm bubbled against the wall much as it had just over a week before. I shared their frustration. I assumed they would hang and stew there for days until they all died, their only option without their queen. I hated being the source of their bafflement.

That evening the friendly cat, Firkin, brought in an innocent shrew, and the ghostly cat, Virga, slipped onto the porch to suck down a dish of salmon eyes and cheeks, then disappear. And when I next looked at the bees, all but half a dozen were gone. Had they swarmed away after all? On the next sunny morning, they were back at the aperture. It seems they had found yet another way into the hive where the wooden wall meets the semiporous stone foundation. Now what?

That day I happened to speak with Mace Vaughn, the pollination biologist for the Xerces Society in Portland. "You have bees in your wall?" he said. "Honeybees? How cool!" He went on to tell me that all the hoo-hah about the perils of bees in a wall was just that—hoo-hah. Their colony would be well sealed with wax and unlikely to run with honey. And if we already had mice (we did), the hive would hardly cause them to increase. All in all, he said, the bees were a blessing, guests to be honored and enjoyed. That was exactly what I wanted to hear. I went home, yanked the excluder and the cork with deep relief, and settled back to enjoy our bees.

I know that some survived the next winter, because I could hear their humming. But in the early spring, shortly after the first bees emerged, I was chatting with the oil delivery man and distracted him. A pink geyser of diesel fuel overflowed the tank valve and soaked the soil all around. That night five inches of rain fell, saturating the earth with oil. The spill was bad enough, but I was horrified that the persistent fumes might have poisoned the hive. For days and days I rued that event, as much for the bees as for the butt-busting effort of digging out yards of polluted dirt from a very cramped space. And when the first bee reappeared, I couldn't have been more pleased.

The bees not only recovered, they positively thrived. By late summer, their numbers had built to such a point and the heat had increased to such a degree that the bees thrummed in the walls to circulate the air and stay cool. I had never heard the singing of bees before as we heard it now. Day and night the buzzes were audible in the living room, bathroom, and outdoors. First one loud, high-pitched buzz, like that of a fly trapped in a spider web. Then a series of broken beeps, like a nuthatch's call. Plus other beeps from around the original source, a kind of entomological call and response. The buzz lasted some twenty seconds, the beeps about ten, the sequence recurring every few minutes. It sounded like an emergency: bees in extremis.

Just as the workers had discovered one entry point after another when I'd tried to block their ingress, now they found a new means of egress: into the house. We hustled about with a small net and other implements to help them—maybe thirty or fifty bees a day—toward open windows. I learned not to do this in bare feet after treading on downed bees and receiving the first stings since they had set up residence. By the time the cool weather returned and the songs and invasions had tailed off, I realized that another hot summer would necessitate some adaptation on my part: removal of a high wall's worth of bookcases and the sealing of whatever cracks the bees were coming in by. Well, the library needs serious pruning and dusting anyway.

But the following winter the bees perished. There was some activity at the hive on unseasonably warm days in December and January, but no sign of the bees on snowdrops in February, nor in March, when the heather and crocuses were at their best for bee food. Those flowers had bees, but they weren't issuing from or returning to our walls. The mites must have found them and depleted their vigor during the dormant season. Or perhaps the wall-mice, which I hear nightly, gnawed their way through to the queen and brood chambers during their defenseless time of torpor. This time we'd done nothing to displace or dispossess our guests, but I felt forsaken just the same.

One day in early spring a few bees appeared at the hole, and I reckoned they must be gleaners visiting from another hive, attracted by the smell of the propolis or by pheromones. But these explorers increased in number, and one day in early April a great beard of bees appeared on the wall beside the hole. A swarm had arrived — just like the first time! The bees settled in, and a scent wafted from the hole like a breath blown across a meadow. When the styrax bloomed, with its great waterfall of white flowers full of pollen and scent, the bees returned to the wall with pollen sacks bulging like comic-book moneybags. And by the time the thistledown flew, they had already swarmed and kicked off another colony elsewhere.

Hundreds of species of native pollinators frequent Swede Park. Today the comfrey was thronged by small bumblebees. Wasps, bees, hover flies, and many others spangled the blossoms of the Asian pear at its peak this spring. Some people might say I should be much more excited by these than by the introduced semidomestic honeybees, which have displaced native pollinators in some places. But they have also furnished pollination services where natives have been depleted by other causes. Surely the coevolutionary dance called apiculture is one of the gentlest partnerships between humans and other animals. And that they should come back to Swede Park, where H. P. Ahlberg kept honeybees in a handsome pagoda-like bee house and was the first in the area to use hives with removable frames, is entirely suitable. Ahlberg knew, no doubt, what his contemporary Maurice Maeterlinck meant when he wrote, in *The Life of the Bee,* "The closer our acquaintance becomes, the nearer is our ignorance brought to us of the depths of their real existence."

WHILE THE ANNUAL immigrants return again and again, and the bees seem to stay on, some of the creatures that we see make only cameo appearances. A gray homing pigeon showed up on the porch roof one day with a blue band on its left leg, green capsule on the right. A ferret appeared at the cellar window, ran under the oil tank, then down the slope of the butterfly garden. And a yearling doe walked into the front yard sporting an orange ear tag and a ribbon of orange tags around her neck. She followed us onto the porch and wanted to be scratched and petted.

When Ed and Lenore Sorenson, from whom we bought Swede Park, left Gray's River for a retirement village in Vancouver, they gave their chickens to neighbors across Fairview Road. At least one of the chickens ran away. We began noticing bird lime on the road at the base of the mail path and finally spotted a fowl roosting fifteen feet up in an overhanging birch. The chicken, a barred mongrel of indeterminate sex, began foraging deeper and deeper into our precincts. As the fall weather closed in, it chose a neglected fuchsia basket hanging on the back porch as its new evening roost and remained all winter. The chicken paced all over the place, feeding on bits of broccoli, bright yellow mushrooms in the lawn that were no species we'd eat, snowberries, old sprout seeds, and homegrown sunflower seeds from last year's nodding amber giants.

Each darkening afternoon, after pecking about the yard and avoiding Bokis's desultory stalks, the bird returned to the porch for the night. As country folk who don't keep chickens, who rely on friends who do keep them for good orange-yolked eggs from free-range chickens, we'd never had the pleasure of a softly clucking hen about the place. But in spring the Colonel, as we had perversely but presciently named the bird, took on definite roosterish attributes. His comb and wattle became more prominent. I put out popcorn for him, as he was my kind of chicken— no eggs to gather, and he didn't crow until eleven A.M.: a very civilized fowl. Smart, too, for a chicken: every time a Steller's jay mocked a red-tailed hawk's scream, the Colonel dashed into the garage for half an hour. Or was he dumb to be so fooled?

One day when the leafing-out oaks were still red, as sun struck the eastern edge of Swede Park, then moved into the yard, I looked out and saw the Colonel's coxcomb ablaze as he basked in the shine beneath equally ignited leaves of an unfurling scarlet oak. As spring accelerated, his outings became cockier, his garden scratchings fiercer, and his raids on Bokis's kibbles more blatant. At planting season we assisted him in relocating to George and Carol's well-tended flock on Puget Island, where his malehood flourished. I missed his stolid, indented presence in the sphagnum of the hanging basket on the back porch, missed the eye to eye every time I went outside for firewood, for air, to fetch or recycle an ale.

On the front porch the hanging nest pot made for us by our late friend Elaine Myers has been claimed by tree swallows and both black-capped and chestnut-backed chickadees. How they sort it out I do not know, and some years the vacancy sign stays out all summer. One year the tree swallows brought up five young, with one egg unhatched. They had adorned the pot with grass, straw, leaves of beech, oak, and willow, feathers and down of ducks and chickens, and a small river snail's shell. A few yards away the violet-green swallows perennially nest in one of several vent holes in the soffit directly over the front porch stairs. The robins usually build in a thick pink camellia out back, or sometimes in the adjacent snowball bush, in one of the old, tangled clumps of *Rhododendron ponticum,* or in the buddleia. Flickers, sapsuckers, and hairy, downy, and pileated woodpeckers all hang out and sound their different drummings, making cavities for others even if they do not stay to nest themselves. One summer, when returning goldfinches decided to construct their elegant teacup in the styrax right outside the kitchen window, Thea and I vied for dishwashing rights so we could watch them. Towhees, thrushes, and wrens, white-crowned sparrows and song sparrows, flycatchers and warblers and crows all nest on this patch where we too nest. Even the Vaux's swifts, whose urgent high cries tinkle off the evening sky of May, have found local lodging. Fresh out of large hollow snags in the forest, they have adapted to the chimney of the Fittses' farmhouse, following the lead of their eastern relatives, the chimney swifts.

By mid-May the male hummingbirds that arrived with the blooming of the salmonberry in early spring have concluded their aerial arcs and zitting screams, their crimson-and-cinnamon display meant to attract the female's eye. She, somehow impregnated while all that blazing vertical sex show was going on, will keep the nest. The male, having done the deed, will set off on the next stage of his figure-eight migration, high into the Cascades or Rockies in pursuit of the alpine nectar bloom. We don't always find the hummers' nests, there is so little to them. One spring, walking down the path to the pond, Thea spied, on a horizontal twig of a maple sapling, a tiny oval pillock given away only by the black-needle bill sticking out. The mother's sleek back lidded the cup, making a green-leaf operculum invisible to the sharp-shinned hawk cruising the wood. Wee as a bonbon, the nest's inner lining was fashioned of spider web; the main structure, smaller than a Reese's cup, was made of lichens and down. Another nest, on an apple bough, used cattail fluff, and one found on the ground incorporated feathers and my silver beard trimmings put out for the purpose. When the female took a nectar break, we spied on her four eggs, each about half the size of an Altoid. Later the young zipped and flitted around the garden like popcorn popping. They are impossible to count, but they must represent the final fruit of three or four hummingbird nests each summer.

Some nest holes swap occupants from year to year. One contested tenancy has been that of a hole about fifteen feet up in the Lincoln Oak, facing the river. It is the rotted-out base of a long-ago lost limb, making a hollow just big enough for several species to see it as hospitable. Chipmunks and chickarees pop in and out. And though we've never yet seen them alive here, northern flying squirrels must have called the hole home, for a great-horned owl left a broad silver tail on the lawn beneath the oak each morning for a week or more.

After cleaning out the gray gliders, the owl moved on, and tree-nesting ducks came around. For several springs we watched excitedly as wood ducks—both the glorious males and the soft-hued females—flew laps from the river to the tree, over and over again. They landed on the branch nearest the hole many times but never settled in. Common mergansers also checked out the premises, making similar circuits from the valley to Swede Park and back. They seemed to need several passes to get their coordinates right before alighting to examine the potential nest site. I thought the fish ducks would be too large for the modest hollow, but they did finally nest there in successive springs. We watched the rust-crested gray female merganser returning to the nest dozens of times, though I never saw the green-headed white male in the tree.

On May 16, 1993, we watched the merganser family quit the nest for the river. First the female leaves and calls to the ducklings, which one by one climb the wall to the bright hole and leap into the unknown. We didn't actually see the ducklings tumble out in their free fall—a tense moment I remember well from the wood ducks in Disney's *Beaver Valley*—or bounce on the mossy turf, but we arrived soon after. Passing beneath the tree on Loop Road on her way to Rosburg, Thea noticed the mother duck and young ones crossing the pavement. She dashed back to call me, and I ran down. From the road we could see them waddling down the slope and into the tall grass of the unmown field. We counted eleven plump and downy ducklings scrambling behind the mother, two or three of them riding on her back at any given time, or trying to.

Already the entourage had crossed our slope of salmonberry, maple, vinca, and bracken, then negotiated the dropoff to the road through roses and oaks and broom, the open road itself, and the bramble and thistle border. Then they disappeared into the deep meadow. We drove to the north vestibule of the covered bridge, but even from that elevated vantage, we couldn't make out their progress through the tangle. I proceeded to the south end of the bridge, from which I could see both ends of the thirty-yard blackberry thicket lining the shore, and saw them emerge from the field at the east end of the brier patch, bounce onto the narrow shingle, and plop into the water like rubber duckies. In they went for the first time, close behind their mother, without hesitation. We watched them paddle out into midstream, where two aunties seemed to be awaiting them, doubtless having heard their constant peeps. Immediately the other females began to fawn, but the mother would have none of it and chased them away. Quickly she herded her brood over to the shaded far bank, overhung by vegetation, where they remained until we left. Less than fifteen minutes had elapsed since the baby mergs had left the cozy womb of the oak and entered the big broad world. Their journey from the lip of the nest to the safety of the river spanned a hundred yards.

IN THE TEMPERATE north, neighborhoods are transient. A large part of the populace is always coming or going. It is not just the north–south migration of birds that creates the annual exodus and influx. Certain insects come and go too. Neighbors often tell me when they see "monarchs" arrive in the spring. But lacking milkweed, we lack monarchs as well, except for the occasional overreacher; like many Americans, my neighbors sometimes take resident yellow swallowtails for migratory orange monarchs. But big darner dragonflies and certain butterflies, including painted ladies, red admirables, and orange sulphurs, arrive from points south and east each spring or summer. And there are altitudinal as well as latitudinal migrations. Steller's jays and varied thrushes nest up in the hills but descend to our level for off-season feeding; the difference may be only a few hundred feet of elevation. Gray jays live higher in the Willapas, and even the worst winter has never brought one down to us. Fritillaries too come down from the hills, small bright western meadow fritillaries in spring and large pale hydaspes in high summer.

While animals make their movements over both the miles and the months, our plants pursue their comings and goings chiefly in the dimension of time. Ever since the first Indian plum broke bud just weeks after the winter solstice, leaves have unfurled by the billions. And ever since the hazel catkins and crocuses burst forth, garden flowers of many kinds have doubled and redoubled almost daily. While there will be new bloomers to come for months yet, the efflorescence is now at its best. What a litany their colors and names make! Orange Oriental poppies, blue bachelor's buttons, sweet William, snowball, iris, thyme, red and purple rhododendrons, waves of daisies, comfrey, violets, roses of white, pink, red, and yellow, kerria, laburnum, sweet woodruff, forget-me-nots, tulips, mock orange, billions of bluebells, and columbines, columbines, columbines—the hummingbirds' delight.

Now the birds have all arrived, and the hover flies, and the bats. We will never have more denizens in residence than we do right now. The compensation for living in a land of many leavings is that everyone comes home, if only you wait.

6 · Swallowtails and Swainson's

Butterflies . . . glancing against the bright, delighted leaves
—ANTHONY BUKOWSKI, "Time Between Trains"

The whistles of Swainson's thrushes announce the summer. A May eve it is, with rain returning gently after days of sunshine, with swifts and swallows chittering overhead. A succulent salad of false lily-of-the-valley, candled with its own snowy bloom, spreads out beneath the unfolding pink hands of the Lincoln Oak. All of a sudden, out of the deepening shadows, comes a light, delicately piped query: *Sweeeet?* Soon there are more calls, some drawn out, some terse: *Whit?*

After some days of this, we begin to hear the song itself—two, three, five introductory notes followed by an ascending series of silver hoops: *Dee dee dee deeoo da deeoo da DEEOO!* And finally the aggressive, abrasive rattles that are difficult to reconcile with the tenderness of the first call and the sweetness of the song: *Chuck-baREEEE!* Songs of Wilson's warblers and juncoes have been dominating the day, but now in the damp evening the thrushes take over. Standing in the kitchen dooryard, I detect three incipient territories by their song, whistle, and chatter. Half a dozen thrushes query the dusk, and summer is here, all over western Washington.

I've always thought our dawn chorus was pretty modest, compared to that in the East. But waking unusually early one June dawn, I heard the Swainson's chorus continually from four-thirty to five o'clock. The robins followed, reversing the evening crescendo of thrush-song after the robin wheedle shuts down. By eight, when I usually arise, the swifts and swallows are tearing through the sky, zipping, unzipping, zipping it up again with their sickle wings, high sweet chittering, and staccato screams.

Birds at Gray's River, May 31, 2002

Loop walk, six–nine A.M. 42–60 degrees F, sun rising to light cloud and haze and blue sky. Cool, fragrant, quiet.

double-crested cormorant: four flying over SE, then NE
great blue heron: four flying upstream, one down, one alighting atop
    oak by river
mallard: possible quack from downriver
common merganser: female and six young paddle under bridge; three
    males upstream
red-tailed hawk: several cries (real ones, not jays!)
bald eagle: one adult flying upstream overhead
osprey: ditto, right after the eagle
northern harrier: brief sighting (gray male, white rump) heading
    downstream
turkey vulture: two over E Swede Park
killdeer: protective parents at Larson's meadow, Torppa's beach
spotted sandpiper: mating pair on pebble strand, others along river
band-tailed pigeon: several overhead
rufous hummingbird: many; two females vying for holly nectar,
    ignoring cherry
belted kingfisher: several rattles
northern flicker: calls from several sectors
willow flycatcher: many calling, none seen
warbling vireo: at least three males singing, E and W of mailbox
common crow: many

raven: calls
violet-green swallow: over river at covered bridge
tree swallow: ditto
barn swallow: ditto, and nesting in Torppa's barn
rough-winged swallow: over river, warm thrush-brown
cliff swallow: over river, nesting under blue-roofed house eaves
black-capped chickadee: one, below Makis' slope
winter wren: one singing in Swede Park woods
Swainson's thrush: several along Loop Road woods
American robin: many
starling: in and around covered bridge
cedar waxwing: pecking at lichen in apple and cherry trees
Wilson's warbler: ditto, lower Swede Park
orange-crowned warbler: two males, one female, maples S of
    covered bridge
yellow warbler: one male alarm-call, seen in elder, N end covered
    bridge
yellowthroat: one male, one female, in elders and grasses N of
    covered bridge
western tanager: a single "bird-alert" call
song sparrow: many, mostly among the brambles
savannah sparrow: Covered Bridge Road
red-winged blackbird: males on perch, female with two young in
    road, at Larsons'
brown-headed cowbird: one male near covered bridge
English sparrow: Larsons' farmyard, covered bridge
purple finch: pair alights in road, S end of covered bridge
goldfinch: many, male and female, singing above Loop Road

Over Memorial Day weekend, our friend Fayette, who birds here each spring on visits from the city, spotted these additional species around the Loop: Canada goose, Vaux's swift, scrub jay, Pacific slope flycatcher, Bewick's wren, black-throated gray warbler, MacGillivray's warbler, spotted towhee, white crowned sparrow, and lazuli bunting. So between us we tallied fifty-two birds of May on the midvalley loop. And each season sees passers-through or lingerers that are less likely to be noted at other

times. Over the twenty-five years that I've been following seasonal changes in Wahkiakum, I've tallied a grand total of 137 species of birds in the county, 127 in Gray's River Valley, and 94 at
Swede Park proper. At this time of year, when everyone who is
going to nest here is likely to be in place, the diversity of birds is
at its highest.

That's true for mammals, too. On our walks Faye and I both
saw weasels carrying prey. I was watching a female redwing
working the west road verge opposite Larson's Pond with two
peeping, fledged young, looking very much like sparrows with
enormous heads. They could fly a little way. The mother was
feeding them bits, perhaps urging them to forage for themselves.
A male redwing appeared overhead, loudly squawking, then a
couple of others arrived. The female flew up at the first male as
if to drive it away. Then an animal ran right past the chicks on
the road toward my feet. I thought it was a chipmunk until it
darted into the snowberry hedgerow, dropping another animal
on the edge of the road. The carrier was a short-tailed weasel,
Mustela erminea; the package, a young Norway rat. Maybe the
male redwings were going after the weasel all along, rather than
harassing the female and young redwings.

LIFE IN THE country is spent in the constant company of
predators and prey. Popularists commonly characterize evolution
as "eat or be eaten," but it is really a matter of eat *and* be eaten.
Everyday acts of predation subsume one life so that another may
go on a little longer. I think, for example, of the day of the merlin
and the snipe. One March, when some lepidopterist friends
were meeting at Swede Park, we took a break from discussing
checklists and field notes by stretching our legs with a walk to
the covered bridge. From the far side, looking back, the house
stood out among its leafless oaks and the slope below, spattered
with daffodils. Then the air parted before two brown blurs, one
just a heartbeat ahead of the other. The streak in the lead resolved into a snipe, which tore into the tussocks at the edge of

the river. The other shape swooped upward, swung around, rose, stalled, and settled into the crown of a cottonwood. Its slaty, hooded form announced it as a merlin, a falcon bigger than a kestrel but smaller then a peregrine.

We all stepped onto the apron of the bridge and watched the two birds, both stock-still in their respective positions. Minute after minute the striped snipe hunkered in the tall grass—visible to us, but only because we had seen it fly in. Minute by minute the merlin stared down at the snipe, knowing exactly where it was and willing to wait. Had the snipe been just as patient, and waited in place until nightfall, maybe the pigeon hawk would have blinked and gone away. Or maybe it would have roosted there too and resumed its unsettling scrutiny at the dawning.

But the snipe didn't outwait the falcon. It burst from the tussock in standard snipe fashion, emitting the hoarse cricking call without which it seems almost unable to fly, as if its wings were attached to its voice box by a ratchet. Barely a wing stroke later, the falcon launched too and closed on the slower shorebird in seconds. This time the snipe flew over instead of under the covered bridge, a fatal error. The merlin triangulated and met its prey above the bridge. The snipe zigged, the falcon zigged; snipe zagged, hawk zagged. On the next zig the two streaks merged, and striped brown feathers fell toward the river. Barely bigger than its prey, the lead pellet of a hawk carried the long-billed fowl upriver to an alder stub, alighted, and commenced tearing it apart. In a joint reflex, we all closed our mouths.

My friend Neil Johannsen once commented, "Merlins are so cool: they hunt small birds by simply outracing them. Unlike many falcons, they don't stoop to conquer. Instead, it's a flat-out drag race in the air." That was it exactly. And because the obscuring curtain of leaves was still drawn back at that time of year, we saw it all. In May the drama might have gone unseen, the spectacle a secret. Timing, too, is crucial. One time when Thea was coming around the back of the house, she paused to watch a nestful of fledging violet-green swallows in the cranny under the eave. Just then a movement in the corner of her vision resolved into a sharp-shinned hawk. In a stopwatch second the sharpie took a swallow on the wing and disappeared with it toward the Broken Oak.

Among other seizures: A Cooper's hawk bulling through the flock of band-tailed pigeons feeding on autumn oak mast and taking one with it. White-faced hornets relieving the parsley of fat anise swallowtail larvae. A little downy woodpecker pick-pick-picking at the winter wands of thimbleberry, mining their swollen nodes for gall-making wasps. The great-horned owl, uncommon in these parts, that moved into the Lincoln Oak until its supply of flying squirrels was exhausted. Even our snails have predators: harvestmen (opilionid spiders) and ground beetles with long, narrow snouts, mouthparts of both modified through parallel evolution for probing deep into snails' whorls. We see these predators on the back porch or creeping into the kitchen.

A single tiny feather on the stoop, warm browns banded with black, is a bad sign. When Thea opens the laundry-room door, with its round cat door, and a storm of similar feathers and fluff flies up, her suspicion comes true: Firkin has nabbed a wren. Winter wrens, the most abbreviated birds in the wood, with the most attenuated songs in the world, like to hang around our back porch. Along with kinglets, they gather spiders, which without such predation would soon enclose both porches in web-works. And the wrens whick around the stems of the salal and huckleberries that frame the native-plants garden and screen the porch from the road and the yard. Occasionally they nip into the kitchen or the studio, curious mites that they are. This time the wren popped right through the cat door and into Firkin's happy grasp.

Cats are routinely condemned as major predators on American songbirds, and so they are. But Firkin's antecedent, the great Bilak Bokis, numbered among his trophies barely a feather. He collected the tails of eight species of mammals: deer mouse, western jumping mouse, Townsend's vole, Townsend's mole,

Townsend's shrew, shrew-mole, Townsend's chipmunk, and northern flying squirrel. His mammal life list also included baby brush rabbit, baby rat, bushy-tailed wood rat, and a bat or two. We've been sorry for all of these, but we can hardly condemn his bag. Our refrigerator, among the welter of magnets and messages, bears Thea's checklist of deer mice trapped on the cellar landing. Her "mouse year" begins in September, when the mice come indoors, and last year had fifty-nine checks by Thanksgiving. Live trapping would be preferable to killing them, but we would have to drive for miles several times a week to transplant the captives, unless we wanted them back inside directly. Coexistence is out, too, when you consider the drawers full of chewed and pissy sweaters and linens, the mouse-turd troves in the folding sofa, and the specter of hantavirus. Happily for them, these prolific mammals are not likely to be extirpated by traps. Nor by cats.

If our pets have mostly been mammalogists, that's not to say that they have never caught a bird. Once, when a female rufous hummingbird visited a pink columbine by his stoop, Bokis simply reached up and snagged it. I'm sure it was irresistible. I blame myself for allowing the columbines to grow so near his usual sunny-afternoon post. And there was the odd towhee or junco. But sometimes the tables were almost turned. When Bokis was a kitten, I watched a barn owl stoop at his small black form, then pull up just in time. And once, when a bald eagle alighted in the butterfly garden, Bokis stalked it and went on point. That might have gone badly. The line between predator and prey can be slender.

As with the hummingbird, such takings are never the cats' fault but ours, for introducing semidomesticated predators into the ecological mix. I always regret losses of native creatures to our kept felines, but my heart was truly taken when the beautiful but wild little silver tabby Virga caught the Swainson's. I told it in a poem:

The Grief of Thrushes

When I saw the brown lump still between the gray cat's
      paws
I took it for a Townsend's vole—one of those great cat
      sausages,
their tunnels so hard on the garden. Take the voles, we say,
      and be content; leave their gall bladders big as marbles
      for us, and leave
the flying squirrels, the jumping mice, and all the birds
      alone.
But this was no vole. It lay compliant, but alive, struggling
just a little. Cupped in my hands, it seemed a song sparrow,
      but the bill
said *thrush*. Oh, kitty! Not the Swainson's, who come in May
and make of June evenings a madrigal of whistle, chitter,
and trembling call—not one of theirs!
But it was. And here's the bad part: the mother. The whole
      time I held
her young, she flew around and around the wood, calling,
calling. That whistled plaint carried on into the dark, round
      and round,
long after I placed the thrushlet on a pile of leaves. Its bill
      opened
in silent answer, one leg dangling, one wing stretching, then
      it died,
as the cat looked around in disgrace. Never mind her partial
      exculpation: the discovery of downy feathers where the
      chick had hit the window
before the pounce. In the morning, eyes gone, snail's silver
      streak shimmering over wing, still the mother circled,
      and called.
Just as I wonder, in an old graveyard serried with the stones
of one-, two-, five-, six-year olds, how the parents stood it,
so too with birds: just a momentary itch of absence
would be the merciful thing, most of their young taken
by car or crow or coon. But who knows? If you'd flown
ten thousand miles, found a mate, fashioned a nest, hunted
      down

ten thousand caterpillars, only to lose it all to a cat at
    fledging, maybe you
too would circle and keen, circle and keen. I don't know
how it is with birds. But when their time comes to move on,
I hope they wear their losses lightly.

I spend the early evening with the cat and a glass of wine on the porch, listening to the Swainson's tentative beginnings, which wax into a scintillating rondo, a whole section of disembodied flutes each more beautiful than Papageno's calling to Papagena in Mozart's magical opera. The swallows bring in a billful of insects every few minutes, making their last trip before rest at nine o'clock. A heron flaps easterly, an eagle toward the west, their forms just visible in the dusk. Thrush song finally fades, and I know once again why I never want to leave this place.

SO WHO WAS this Swainson, whose name is sung so sweetly every evensong all over the forested West? And for that matter, who was the Townsend whose name seems affixed to half the small ground-dwelling mammals around this place, not to mention Townsend's warbler, solitaire, and big-eared bat? Townsend's mole, like his vole, is the biggest species of its genus in North America, so John Kirk Townsend presumably had no difficulty spotting it in 1835, one hundred miles up the Columbia from here in Vancouver. Born in 1809 in Philadelphia to a Quaker family, he became acquainted with John James Audubon as a youth. At twenty-five he was tapped by Nathaniel Wyeth to join his overland expedition to the West, where he traveled and collected plants with the botanist Thomas Nuttall, he of *Cornus nuttallii,* the Pacific dogwood. Unlike his fellow collector David Douglas, of fir fame, Townsend returned safely from Hawaii; he held the post of surgeon at Fort Vancouver for several months before voyaging east via Cape Horn. He was not to live much longer. A splendid preparator of vertebrate specimens, he concocted a preservative formula and used it liberally; he died of arsenic poisoning at the age of forty-two. But in the peculiar kind of immortality that only taxonomists and their friends attain, his mole, vole, bat, and solitaire live on, along with a genus of large-petaled western daisies named *Townsendia* by Nuttall's friend Thomas Hooker. Perhaps Nuttall suggested that honor in expiation for cooking and eating an owl of a new species that Townsend had collected for purposes of description.

William Swainson, born in England in 1789, became chiefly a biological illustrator, publishing three books of *Zoological Illustrations* in the 1820s. Leaving tame England, he traveled and collected natural history material in Sicily, then extensively in Brazil. Failing in a bid to become Keeper at the British Museum of Natural History, he freelanced and wrote the bird section of John Richardson's *Fauna Boreali Americana* without ever actually traveling to North America. He too made friends with Audubon and traveled with him to Paris. But perhaps inevitably, as rival describers of America's avifauna, they fell out. Swainson went off to New Zealand, where he died in 1855. By all accounts he was full of himself to an irritating degree. Surely his description of such beautiful birds as Barrow's goldeneye and Bullock's oriole was something to be proud of. But if he had ever heard the glorious voluntary of the thrush that bears his name, at four-thirty in the morning or nine at night, he might have been humbled—or else made absolutely insufferable.

ON THE WALL of the Royal Entomological Society of London, alongside Swainson and Townsend's contemporaries Darwin and Wallace, hangs a portrait of Moses Harris, described on a brass plaque as "The Aurelian"—an early title for a lepidopterist, derived from the golden flecks on the chrysalides of many butterflies. In 1775 Harris published a little book called *The English Lepidoptera: Or, the Aurelian's Pocket Companion: Containing a Catalogue of Upward of Four Hundred Moths and Butterflies, the*

Food of Their Respective Caterpillars, The Time of Changing into Chrysalis, and Appearance in the Winged State: Also, the Places Where They Frequent and Are Usually Found; with a Concise Description of Each, and Their Dimensions.

One of the most charming aspects of this early field guide is its butterfly and moth calendar. By glancing down the charts of the pages, with their old *s*'s that look like *f*'s, you get a sense of the Georgian English seasons passing in a parade of colorful flying insects. You know that when Harris went out along hedgerows in June he would find the large gatekeeper and, in briery swamps in August, the pearl skipper.

I know of no better way to get to the heart of a place than through its phenology—the progression of the seasons as told by its animal and plant appearances. Everyone does this, if only by noticing when the street trees leaf out and shed. Gardeners are keen phenologists, as are hunters, loggers, and farmers. I keep track of the comings, goings, bloomings, and burstings of all sorts of living things—migratory and resident birds, native and alien plants, amphibians silent and noisy—whose patterns bear a sharp concordance from year to year. But I attend especially to butterflies and moths. We record every species of butterfly (and some notable moths) seen each day, their relative abundance, and other memorable details. The annual panorama of lepidopterans "in the Winged State" limns the year precisely. As with birds, the diversity of butterflies usually peaks in May or June, though their abundance rises through August. "Butterfly season," however, is bracketed on both sides by a long increase and decline, with particular punctuations throughout.

You might think butterflying was solely a summertime game, yet I can begin some years on Groundhog Day. In a mild winter not all of the cabbage-white caterpillars, being a hardy species and becoming more so, pupate, their usual off-season habit. I can go into the winter crucifer garden and find lively green velvet caterpillars hunkered in the purple Brussels sprouts, still doing slow damage. But because they are the only wakeful butterflies (or larvae, at least) in midwinter, I tolerate them. And the butterfly calendar proceeds from that point on.

In late February the honeybees have just about finished up the pollen from the yellow danglers of hazel, now curling and going reddish. The soft green tongues of Indian plum are nearly two inches out of their leaf buds. The lacy foliage of bleeding heart pokes up through the elderberry duff. Then one bright morning around Leap Day, the first flicker of willowware blue will ricochet through the air. The spring azures have emerged. As always, we see the first ones out on the Altoona Road, where Gray's River runs into Gray's Bay of the Columbia River and the southwest-facing hillsides catch the northing sun. This is where spring first shows in Willapa. At Pigeon Bluffs on a sunny afternoon, the pioneer azure appears on the mineral mud, just the way Frost's blues cling "where wheels have freshly sliced the April mire." Soon we will have them at home, sucking minerals from the wood-ash heap or the first nectar of cherry laurels.

Even earlier, two species of geometrid moths ("earth measurer," named for their inchworms) precede the azures. They are about azure-size, an inch or less in wingspan. One, *Enchoria lacteata,* is soft cocoa brown; the other, *Mesoleuca gratulata,* is (as the name says) half white, half black, blue, and chestnut. Both species are common, adaptable, and diurnal, flittering all through western Washington and Oregon and inspiring any number of inquiries about the early "butterflies" that "aren't in the book." I call them honorary butterflies, but their dun colors and whiffy flight let you know these are no azures as soon as you get a good look. The sight of their delicate wings all over the heather and spirea herald the spring as loud and clear as butterflies. Never mind that we (and they) may still face weeks of gelid rain.

The blues, like the first royal purple crocus sticking up through the brown mat of old oak leaves, bring drama. The

males are clear lilac-tinted blue, like sky seen through a polariz-
ing lens—in a word, azure. Females are a darker, deeper blue,
with broad black margins on the triangular wings. Once thought
to belong to the Old World species *Celastrina argiolus,* known in
England as the holly blue because its larvae feed on the developing flowers of holly and ivy, our version favors ninebark and red
osier dogwood, which is one of the most widespread plants in
the Northern Hemisphere. The azures likely followed the dogwood across Beringia during interglacials. A number of different
species have evolved since, specialized to feed on cherry galls or
hop flowers. So the identity of the basic "spring azure" is a matter of debate. Lepidopterists now think that our Pacific Coastal
azure may be a full species: *Celastrina echo,* the echo blue, but
loath to give up the lovely old name "azure," I refer to it as the
echo azure. By whatever name, a cluster of these brilliants pud-
dling on a Columbia shoreline thrills the winter-chilled heart
every bit as much as Frost's sky-flakes fallen onto the muddy ruts
of Vermont. And when one spring (never before and not since),
they chose the bluebells as their chief source of nectar, crawling
up the sides and probing between the petals to reach the nectaries, blue on blue was a gift no one could really expect, much
less deserve.

Even as the azures emerge, the overwintering nymphs come
out of hibernation. Any day in mid-March we are likely to see
the russet flashes of tortoiseshells and anglewings. Satyr, faun,
and oreas anglewings and Milbert's and California tortoiseshells
all pop out of the woodpecker holes, birdhouses, and abandoned shacks where they have overwintered. They look for
sap or the earliest flowers, then mate and seek nettles, currants, willows, or rhododendrons, depending on their species, on
which to lay their eggs. Rhododendrons also attract the early-
emerging rust-and-lilac brown elfins, which dress up the sparse
Easter garden along with the little gray two-banded checkered
skippers that buzz around the big-leaved avens, and the cit-

rus flashes of West Coast ladies nectaring on vinca's purple disks.

By the Ides of March the pale linen specters of margined whites roam the forest roadsides, nectaring on the candy flower in the verge. Not long afterward their European counterparts, the cabbage whites, bust out of their sliverlike winter pupae lodged in windowsills or on garden stakes. After twenty years of looking for Persius duskywings in the county, I stepped outside on a hot day-before-Easter to see one sipping from just-opened bleeding hearts by the studio steps. The larvae of *Clodius parnassians* feed upon those same bleeding hearts, and the adults emerge in late May on isinglass wings with coal and cherry spots. A big female, almost too heavy with eggs to fly, settles on blackberry blossoms for hours. If the stars are right, the lilacs will bloom late enough to receive the grateful hungers of the first anise and pale tiger swallowtails to emerge. Western tigers eclose as the horse chestnuts candle and remain with us all through the summer. As the days approach their longest, it is truly the time of swallowtails and Swainson's, the former owning the midday, the latter, dawn and dusk. Tigers, both yellow and white, worry the purple rhododendron by the mail path all day long. Just as large, but an unmistakable cinnamon orange, a rare monarch shows up on the solstice.

Early summer arrives with the fiery flickers of western meadow fritillaries down from breeding on high forest violets, and mylitta crescents, up from meadow thistles. One male crescent quarters a patch of lawn that is claimed by his kind every summer (why? no thistles grow anywhere near) beside raspberries that have swelled to dropping. Strawberries and lettuce go on and on in the garden as broccoli heads unfold and cabbage whites cruise arugula in clear preference to kale. The day ends late; both Larsons and Fittses are still cutting hay at 10:30 in the evening. The sky fades from golden-dull, with a paler margin over the hills, to dark. The progression reminds me of the imaginary "evening" sky in the Denver Museum of Natural History's planetarium show as its lights dimmed to bring out the pinpoint stars. That was long ago. In the real sky here and now, Scorpio crawls across the low southern ceiling.

One morning soon the first of the big white-banded, cinnamon-tipped Lorquin's admirals will appear along the willowy streams and in the gardens, where thousands of flowers of dozens of kinds are blooming. Small brown wedges resolve into dun skippers, tawny ones into sonora skippers, where the sedges and grasses grow long. At night we watch for two giant silkmoths of the northwest woods, the honey brown polyphemus and chestnut red ceanothus, bedazzled by lights in the later and later evenings. By day the cinnabar moth shows up. Imported to battle tansy ragwort, it has orange-and-black-banded caterpillars, called tansy tigers by the local children. The brilliant scarlet and gunmetal blue wings outshine all the native butterflies and moths.

High summer sees eye-spotted chocolate wood nymphs dancing across the lawn in their flip-flop fashion. Two of them do-si-do on the wing, then part, one swerving past a worming robin so as not to tempt it into flycatching. Bright vagrants from the south, such as California sisters and Virginia ladies, show up on the butterfly bushes that have finally deigned to bloom. A stunning second-flight anise swallowtail, the color of undyed Tillamook cheese, arises from the parsley bed and flirts between mauve and pink buddleia, where an old, faded male tiger can't leave her alone. She circles and swerves back to the bar, legs dangling like some complicated undercarriage.

Summer runs down. Orange multiplies as sulphurs materialize in the valleys and hydaspe fritillaries drop in from the clearcuts. Purplish coppers, second-brood crescents, and wafty pine whites seem to await the fresh nectar of native Douglas asters, which suddenly break bud. By this time the happiest of Swede Park butterflies, judging from its numbers, has positively burgeoned. Woodland skippers flit through nearly every habitat *except* deep woodlands, and they skip about Swede Park by the hundreds. Thyme and mint along the garden walk fairly drip with skippers; aster heads and wands of butterfly bush bend beneath their dozens. As afternoons cool, scores of skippers bask toward the sun on the Asian pear's broad leaves. They last, almost every year, right up to the first of October.

In the fall tortoiseshells seek their hibernacula, and late-brood whites and azures glean the waning nectar of leggy broccoli and hawkbit. The only butterflies to be seen by Halloween are robust ash-and-cinder red admirables breasting the cold nights. One unseasonably warm Thanksgiving a pale orange sulphur floated across the front lawn, and mourning cloaks may come out at a mild winter solstice. But on the whole, the butterfly calendar wraps up as the last anise larvae pupate or freeze on the shriveling cow parsnip in November. Then we shall dream of mellower days, when swallowtails dally among sweet Williams, and Swainson's call from the shadowed banks.

FOR NOW, at summer solstice, everything is gluttony. Caterpillars convert leaves with haste and immoderation. Brown slugs ingest the marigolds as if there were no tomorrow, which, if Thea has her way, there won't be for them. Our doe walks through the back yard, making herself welcome by munching the thimble-berry beneath the buddleia. But she can't stay good: she paces over to the currants, blueberries, and Asian pear and takes a bite of each before Thea chases her away. Minutes later I spot her just off the front porch, nibbling the *Maianthemum,* and her crunching tells me that those lush, heart-shaped leaves really *are* salad.

The porch swallows swoop up into their nest hole with greater facility and frequency, and I can hear the reasons peeping through the battens. Brown flutterings outside my window are the Swainson's, jumping the bushes for red huckleberries.

We cover the blueberries and red currants with netting to try to save a few for ourselves. As for our own takings, currants are already appearing on the oatmeal, and our own good lettuce and snap peas grace every meal. All this harvest seems early, with spring such a recent memory—but not as precocious as the oldest leaves of Indian plum, already going yellow. Though the official first day of summer is just past, the first signs of the season's fullness and consequent mortality have already appeared.

7 · Days of Mist and Thistles

These afternoons I stare a lot, imbecilic with pleasure
— DONALD HALL, *Seasons at Eagle Pond*

Hundreds of goldfinches line the fencerows and wires, whistling and wheezing, then drop like gold nuggets into the thistle fields. The air is compounded of their yellow arcs and a gauzy film of thistledown. It is a morning of mist, as if last night's milky way had fallen to earth with the dawn. The mist obliterates the bridge and then brings it back, like Brigadoon.

For two days now a thistle seed has struggled in a web in the corner of the open window. Golden skippers, brown wood nymphs, black flies, brown vultures, pied swallows, and russet hummers sizzle, flicker, glide, sickle, and dash across that frame, and all the while the thistledown flutters in place, stuck in silk, gossamer on gossamer, each downy filament reaching for the freedom of the air.

Insect song is more understated in this land of conifers than in the eastern deciduous forest. But today, as the mist dissipates, I hear a high-pitched ringing from the taller trees in two or three different quarters. It's warm, and we had rain last night after a near-full moon ducked under clouds. The singers must be the leaf-green, fork-tailed bush katydids, which we rarely see. They lend the day a high-strung, fragile, silky feel.

A day like this in early July is almost too perfect to be legal. The slant of eastern sun turns the long pale panel of the covered bridge into a silver ship looming out of the lapping sea of mist that fills the valley floor. The lifting fog melts into a soft morning of brooklime skies and lambswool clouds. Forenoon, high noon, and afternoon run together, spinning on the bezel of the day in one slack refutation of time passing. Three o'clock, seventy degrees, the air so still you can't even feel it. It cools almost imperceptibly into dinnertime, and the least breezes rise with the gnats that whine at the edge of hearing but don't bite.

Thea takes a barrowful of fresh shredded limbs and leaves to the far compost, returns with a load of leaves and shreddings that a year has worked to a sweet, rich, deep brown, bound for gardens and pots. The cat stands sphinxlike in the last of the sun on the newly cleared slope she had forgotten was there. Cedar waxwings move through with a vocal shimmer and whisper, dogs and crows and ravens bark, a little late traffic whishes. On KMUN out of Astoria, *Evening Jazz* gives way to *Bedtime Stories*. Last night's breeze carried the ocean's salt, the Columbia's sweetness. Tonight the cool breath of Gray's River smells earthy.

This sort of day makes indoor work seem shameful. So working outside, whether in the garden or the woods or on the front porch at the writing table rescued twenty-five years ago from a tumbledown farmhouse that is now mostly soil, is a sacrament. Almost all the birds are silent now, save for an anonymous chipper; but the river's plash, as if making up for the quiet birds, is as loud as it gets. When the mist rises again, the river will be muted by its woolly muffler.

IN SOME NORTHERN places, spring strikes hard and fast before a long hot summer. Here spring trails off gradually into an abbreviated summer. You know you've turned the corner toward stretched-out fall when the swallows fledge and shift from nest to valley, when the Swain-song falls away; and when many mornings start misty and the day mimics the season by taking half its hours to rise from cool to warm before quickly cooling again. Estivating slugs are moved by mist to roam; on the Fourth of July an eight-inch banana slug perambulates the compost, looking right at home among the other pieces of overripe produce.

Now, too, is when thistle goes to seed. While "thistledown" is a pretty word, and the sight of a million silky paragliders filling the summer sky is undeniably beautiful, the plant itself has more detractors than lovers. I should say "plants," as there are about 464 species of thistles (genus *Cirsium*) in the world, 109 in North America, and 4 in the Willapa Hills. Only the Scots, who made the thistle their emblem, seem to revere it outright.

Thistles are composites (members of the aster family) whose heads have only the narrowest of disk flowers, bunched together like a badger-hair shaving brush. The flowers of most species are mauve, red-purple, or lavender, though some are pink or scarlet or, like the big, edible-stalked elk thistle of the high western mountains, white. Thistle scent is usually sweet, like honey and overripe plums. But if you stick your nose into a thistle head you're likely to get pricked, as the flower, sepals, stem, and leaves are abundantly armed with sharp points. Walking through thistled ground in shorts leaves my legs scratched and itchy. Artichokes are big thistles. What we eat is the flesh at the base of the armed bracts and the "heart," the head of the stem and the flower receptacle. The choke, the part we cut away, is the bunch of fibers that would become giant thistledown if allowed to grow.

The classic Scots thistle is reckoned to be the same as the common bull thistle (*Cirsium vulgare* or *lanceolatum*). According to tradition, it became the Caledonian national symbol by puncturing the bare feet of Danish invaders, whose howls of pain gave them away. The Scottish motto it inspired, *Nemo me impune lacessit* ("No one provokes me with impunity," or "Wha duar meddle wi' me"), equally describes the plant and the incited Highlanders. But I'll bet lowland Scottish farmers hold no more love for thistles than English farmers across the border. The sad fact is that thistles tend to invade hayfields and ruin the quality of the hay. Not only are they poor forage, but the spines can cause injury and infection in a cow's mouth—imagine those prickles lodging in the soft gums of a Holstein.

Our native thistle species are important parts of local plant communities, but they tend to occur in less disturbed areas, such as mountain meadows or coastal headlands. Alien thistles dominate the much-altered lowlands, especially bull thistle and Canada thistle (*Cirsium arvense*), a European import despite its common name. These "weeds" aggressively displace more "desirable" plants, so farmers and nature reserve managers often spray them with herbicides. But agriculture in this area is not as intensive as it used to be, even in the years I've been here. Ed Sorenson couldn't abide a single stalk of thistle in his velvet pastures, a feeling shared by many other dairymen. Self-respect was involved, and shame, if one were to fail in the effort to eradicate the thistles; the righteous ire of neighbors is an effective motivator. And landowners who fail to control weeds listed as noxious may be subject to penalties. Yet as the dairies shut down and the county's agriculture petered out, management of the fields relaxed. In spite of the imprecations of the longtime weed-control agent, Carl Blaine, cost-share programs for herbicides, and the threat of mandatory control, more and more landowners let their thistles be. Each year at the Grange Christmas party, I read "The Night Before Christmas" to the children. When we get to the part about the reindeer flying off "like the down of a thistle," and I whisper "Gray's River's best crop," a volley of half-guilty chuckles always arises around the room.

Yet not everyone hates thistles. Swallowtails, fritillaries, monarchs, and many other butterflies find their nectar almost as compelling as that of *Buddleia davidii* (butterfly bush), another Eurasian invasive. And two butterfly species hereabouts, the little orange mylitta crescent and the painted lady, use thistle foliage as their caterpillars' preferred host plant. When the native thistles were displaced, the crescents and ladies adjusted to the European kinds. Mylitta's range and abundance no doubt increased greatly on that account, and in a really good painted-lady year, the needs of both butterflies and farmers are met.

The painted lady—*Vanessa (Cynthia) cardui*—occurs so widely as a native species that one of its alternative names is the cosmopolitan butterfly; another is Cynthia of the Thistles. Though it cannot overwinter in freezing zones, it annually invades Europe from North Africa and the United States from Mexico. From year to year the numbers of painted ladies range from few to quite a few. Robert Vandenbosch at the University of Washington has recently shown that El Niño events and sea surface temperature are significantly connected with mass movements of painted ladies. But certain years all systems are go: low parasitic load, abundant spring nectar in the desert, weather conducive to northing. Then, it's blastoff time for painted ladies.

The summer of 1992 was such a year in the West. We first spotted the ladies in April, flitting among the goldfields of dandelions down by the bridge, and their company grew from that point on. Vanessas flooded northward in such multitudes as to force the closing of Interstate 5 in southern California. The newspapers ran over with ink devoted to the vast "invasions" of orange-and-black butterflies, which many mistook for monarchs. I wrote letters to editors, explaining what was going on and urging farmers not to spray their thistles that summer. Indeed many did not, and the ladies devastated the thistles for them. It became hard to find a thistle without *Vanessa* eggs, clusters of the black, spiny larvae, or the frass-filled webbing of launched larvae. Our neighbor Steve Puddicombe had never sprayed the fields of his spread, known as Wintergreen Farm, before. That summer he allowed an insistent field tenant to do so. But *V. cardui* will shift its diet when the need arises. So as soon as Steve's field was sprayed, legions of painted lady larvae moved on to his garden, where they obliterated his potatoes, Russell hybrid lupines, and almost everything else.

As the summer progressed, successive generations of bright painted ladies populated the gardens and roadsides. It was a great butterfly year altogether, with wood nymphs appearing in the valley for the first time from the drier east end of the county. The thistle fields below us brimmed with bright leps, even rare monarchs that had overshot their milkweed and appeared here, perhaps caught up in the ladies' train. By fall there was scarcely a thistle stalk to be seen. Not until 2005 did we see another painted-lady year like that one, with Cynthia of the Thistles haunting April dandelions by the covered bridge, looking for *Cirsium,* readying for a full onslaught. Most summers lack such a lady invasion. Instead, we see thistle fluff aloft, power lines full of goldfinches coveting the gift of seed, and above the covered bridge, mist and thistledown melding into a single substance.

I FIRST LAID eyes on the bridge in 1975. Denny Gillespie, a friend from graduate school, was working to conserve historic buildings in southwest Washington. Through a pelting July rain, Denny and Sally and I drove out from Longview to see the handsome but rotting Redmen Hall in Skamokawa (now beautifully restored); the old Eden Valley School (now sunk thirty years deeper into the sod); and the Gray's River covered bridge.

I've always been a sucker for historic structures, the funkier the better, and as covered bridges go, this is one of the funkiest. No twee, red-painted, white-trimmed Madison County confection, nor even the gabled and pertly whitewashed type that graces many an Oregon stream, the Gray's River covered bridge is functional and plain. Like the houses built by the Scandinavian settlers, it lacks the ornamentation of bridges built by German and English pioneers. Its roof of corrugated metal is bowed in a shallow arch rather than peaked, and the cedar siding is unpainted gray. In fact, the whole affair is a composition in grays, perfect for the river it happens to span.

Washington never had as many covered bridges as Oregon, and most were of the hoop-roof type like ours and carried rails, not roads. One or two little covered truss bridges survive on logging roads in Willapa (we've seen one up by Pe Ell, above the Chehalis River), and another has been covered in recent years beside a historic grist mill in Clark County. Near Colfax in eastern Washington stands a marvelous big red covered bridge of the open, or "sandwich," type, roofless but with double siding covering the truss beams. It was built for the railroad but now serves as a farm driveway over the Palouse River and as a haunt for owls and swallows. But ours is the last historic covered bridge on a public roadway in the entire state. When I first saw it, it called to me, and in answering, I assumed a shared responsibility for it that I could never have imagined. I did not anticipate the floods that almost took it; the hundred Harleys, fifty-one red-and-white Ford pickups, and endless pilgrims who would come to call on the bridge; the festivals and picnics and weddings and film crews for advertisements; the long months when the bridge was not there during its restoration; nor the bagpiper at the gates of dawn who piped us awake one midsummer day, then disappeared into the rising mist.

The earliest settlers in this part of the Gray's River Valley included Charles E. Schoebe; Henry O. Lamb; Nis N. Nymand; John, Anton, and Hjalmar Klint; and Hans P. Ahlberg. They knew that a bridge would be necessary to connect farms on the south side of the valley with markets and neighbors. The firm of Ferguson and Houston in Astoria was engaged to design a Howe truss span of 156 feet. The bridge was erected in 1905, replacing a suspension foot bridge that (according to Ed Sorenson) was then moved to the middle of Gray's River village and later to Chris Sorenson's farm. The farmers who lobbied for the bridge did the construction, notably Ahlberg, on whose property it was built. Over the next several decades, the Klint, Hull, Sorenson, Badger, Durrah, Cook, King, and Larson families all benefited from the new river crossing.

BOBBY LARSON MAINTAINS that the chief function of the siding and roof was to make the bridge suitably dark for sweethearts to share a smooch, and so it does. The practical reason for covering wooden bridges, though, was to protect their beams from the elements. The original tarpaper roof, added in 1908, frequently blew off, so a tin roof replaced it. Cables, guy lines, and a central pier followed in later decades.

In 1971 the covered bridge was designated a National Historic Site. The handsome brass plaque announcing this fact was mounted on a two-legged concrete plinth off the north apron of the bridge approach. Not once but twice this pedestal was taken out by teen drivers speeding through the bridge and losing control, ending up unhurt in the field beside the sign's busted base. Remarkably, the two misdirected drivers—their adventures a year apart—were brother and sister. Even plaqueless, the bridge became famous to the point that it was one of the most visited tourist sites in southwest Washington. Hanging from a string just inside the bridge, an informal register of visitors was kept first by Lenore Sorenson and then by Barbara Chamberlain. Its ruled pages carry pen and pencil signatures and comments by covered-bridge buffs and other visitors from all over the country and the world, amounting to some forty thousand pilgrims per year. Of the likely fakes, "Edmund Hillary" was the best.

The setting remained pastoral, and the only available souvenirs were covered-bridge postcards sometimes carried at Rosburg Store and Redmen Hall. When I moved to Gray's River, the bridge had seen better days, and I worried whether it would last. More than once, as county crews grew weary of making repairs and commissioners tired of paying for them, replacing it with a concrete slab looked easier and cheaper—a dull end that has befallen many a covered bridge in Oregon, and all but this one in

Washington. One such casualty was the *other* Gray's River covered bridge, which few people know about. I didn't, until I heard rumors of its former existence at a Grange meeting. Glenrose Hedlund recently gave me an old photograph of the bridge, which crossed the river just upstream from the head of tidewater at the village. It was boxy and unpainted, with a nearly flat roof and cantilevered sides. According to Merlin Durrah, it was the long, steep, curved approach that led to its demise. When heavy trucks became common in the valley, he told me, the county road department just let them rattle and batter the bridge to bits until it was replaced with a colorless modern span.

In 1982 the same late-winter storm that toppled half of the Broken Oak at our place peeled off the top of the covered bridge like the lid of a sardine can. Then, in the great flood of 1986, the raging river tore out the central pier. Fortunately the bridge did not go with it. The pier, built of rough, stony concrete, shaped like a ship's prow, took the brunt of the river's force. A door in the side of the bridge gave access to the top of the pier. I spent some of the most serene moments of my life sitting there cross-legged on summer mornings as the mergansers awakened out of the mist. But the old pier was not set deeply into the bedrock, and the irrepressible floodwater finally took it.

The county replaced the roof and, in 1987, the pier. The new pier, basically a reinforced concrete staple with brackets for the bridge, is not as handsome as the old one. But it is set into steel pilings driven deep into the riverbed, and the upriver side is fronted with a sturdy wedge to deflect the floating battering rams of logs driven before the deluge. Nothing will budge this pier, short of orogeny. But now the support was stronger than the bridge itself, which was showing signs of rot and disrepair here and there. Serious questions arose about its future.

The Grange asked Ralph Munro, the popular secretary of state and a friend of the bridge, for the state's assistance. After careful examination, the state Department of Transportation gave the county four options: do nothing and the bridge would eventually fail; continue to make stopgap repairs, which will be expensive and may not be enough to save it; remove and replace it with a modern structure; or conduct a major restoration and reconstruction. The radical fourth step was the only option acceptable to the bridge's supporters, but how could it be funded? We trotted out the visitor registry to prove the bridge's great appeal. County engineer Wayne Rickert corralled state centennial and federal grants to cover most of the $295,980 price tag (the original building cost $2,615). The Dulin Company of Centralia worked with the original blueprints, found in an Astoria attic, to reconstruct a bridge such as no one had built for decades.

Removal of the sides of the bridge in the fall of 1988 revealed the Howe truss in all its clever complexity of clear-grain fir and iron fittings. But it also showed that the dry rot had progressed further than anyone had guessed. After the last old plank came off, you could see cows right through the bridge. The ancient cedar siding was stacked in Larson's meadow, its chartreuse staghorn lichens facing up to the sun and rain, in hopes it could be reused.

Some of the old-timers began to grumble as the bridge remained down for weeks and then months. But we were spared a major flood, and in the spring, as the workers' shirts came off, the new laminated and pressure-treated truss beams went up. The original steel hanger rods and compression fittings were used again, and any salvageable old planks were rehung on the downstream side, with new siding on the upstream. One day in late summer, the work was finished. On a brilliant morning with that fresh cedar wall shining in the sun like salmon steaks hung to dry, I walked down to the bridge and hailed the men. "Thanks, you guys," I called. "You've brought off a miracle." Just before they packed up to leave, I handed a bottle of good Washington wine to each of the builders: Jerry Niemczick, Vaughn Aust, Curtis Piper, and Mark Jessen.

The Grange set September 30, 1989, for the rededication ceremony. When the day came, the rain held off. Bobby and Doug had mowed Lenore's field for parking, and folding chairs were lined up under the bridge's porch, ready for VIPs and seniors. All the officials made speeches, charitably short. The honor guard of World War II vets—Norman Anderson, Jim Fauver, John McIlwain, Bob Torppa, Ernie Wirkkala—marched stiffly up to the portal in their blue-peaked, gold-piped caps and shot their old rifles to the raising of the colors. Helen King, the oldest living valley pioneer, whose family farm the bridge had connected with the world beyond, cut the ribbon. Then Raymond Badger drove Helen and other pioneers through the bridge in his Model A. The doubting Thomases, several of whom died over the next couple of years, were all there to applaud the bridge's resurrection.

So we got our bridge back. To be sure, some things were lost: the funky old pier; the old-growth fir beams that had been grown, logged, and milled in these hills; and a sweet-natured tortoiseshell cat, christened Bridgette by Brian Larson. She had haunted the bridge for years, visiting the fishermen for handouts of bait and warming herself on the hoods of their rigs. We suspect the coyotes came for her before her bridge was taken down. Yet some things are better: the metal and asphalt deck from 1952 was restored to handsome wood, as in the original, and the weight limit was raised from three tons to fifteen, allowing the milk truck and the school bus to cross the bridge.

Some covered bridge purists quibble that it's not the same, with steel box-beams inserted (and masked) at each end and in the middle. One such grumbler wrote the editor of the *Chinook Observer,* objecting to the use of the word "historic" to describe the bridge. I replied that the structure should now last another hundred years and that this makes us happy, especially considering how easily we might have ended up with a bland concrete span. "So while the official covered bridge registry may not list our bridge as 'historic,'" I wrote, "we beg to disagree. It is a mix of the old and the new. Besides, the Gray's River Bridge is one of the only large covered bridges built to an original design in modern times anywhere—surely a historic event!"

Fifteen years on, the reincarnated bridge looks much the same as the old one did, now that the bright orange cedar on the new side has gone to gray, as all things here eventually do. Salvaged pieces of the old truss can now be found in various farms and homes, such as the new ceiling beams in Steve Puddicombe's Wintergreen farmhouse. And the Federal Registry plaque was put up again in time for the one hundredth birthday party the locals threw for the bridge in the summer of 2005. This time it is mounted with original bridge bolts onto two massive chunks of old-growth bridge beam that I had taken home, and it is placed well out of the path of speeding teens.

AGAIN LAST NIGHT I awoke from a dream into the certain awareness that something was with us in the bedroom and that it was softly flapping around and around. When this happens, I rise, fetch a butterfly net, help the bat back into the black night, maybe pull the window sash down an inch or two, and go back to sleep. For no reason that I know of, other than the abundance of bats and swallows, mosquitoes are scarce here, and most of the old houses lack screens. I like having bats around, but not everyone does. Once I was reading in a piny library off the lobby of a rustic Colorado lodge when another guest burst through the front door, so frantic that we expected to hear of fire or worse. "It's bad," said the man in a quavery voice. "We've got a *bat!*"

The proprietor was about to send the man back with a can of Raid, but I offered to extract the bat from the cabin. It was a tiny *Myotis* to cause such a fuss, happy as a gnat to be back in the alpine air. At breakfast my host proudly told the other guests, "The professor saved us from the bat!" Actually, I'd saved the bat from them. On several occasions before and since, I have used my butterfly net to catch and release bats trapped indoors—once to the *Batman* theme *nah-nah-nah*ed by a throng of watching teens.

After a bat was found in the nursery of our former governor's infant child, the mansion was debatted and the state health department issued warnings that any persons seeing a bat near their sleeping quarters should have a vaccination against rabies—at about a thousand dollars a shot. But bats come into our bedroom on many a summer's night. We'll wake to that soft flutter, or maybe we won't, as a little brown circles the room a few times before it finds the open window again or I rise to show it the way out. Or those soft brown wings will brush our faces, like the ministering visitors in Pattiann Rogers's poem "When at Night." We know the rarer big brown bats by the louder, deeper pitch of their flitting. Once, when a big brown flew into our son Tom's room, he awoke to its draculoid bulk and freaked out. But our bats want bugs, not blood, and the incidence of rabies in bats is very low; we far prefer their company to stale air. That's how I happened, one day, to feed a bat.

Home from a summer trip, I went upstairs to air out our bedroom. One window had been left open a crack, and on the windowsill lay what looked like a very dead bat. But it moved its head and looked at me. Judging it dehydrated, I tried to give it water on a bit of soaked paper towel. At first it just raised its head, but as I moistened that tiny muzzle, the petal-tongue began to lap the wetness. Like a parched plant given water, the bat came around. But it was still weak, so I carried it outside (wearing gloves—I'm not *that* cavalier about rabies). I set it down on the mossy top of a big shelf fungus conk on the side of the Lincoln Oak and left it there with the damp towel. When I looked an hour later, there it was, hanging up beneath the conk in the manner of its kind, sleeping it off.

But along toward dusk, seeing the bat was still there, I began to worry that it was too weak to hunt. It had managed to crawl a little way, but could it fly? So I took matters—and the bat—in hand again. With my free paw I grabbed an insect net. Together that bat and I prowled the garden, sweeping the vegetation for small prey. The first item I tried to feed it was a grass moth, which I held with forceps in front of the bat's face. It made feeble nips, but couldn't handle the moth. I tried again with a gnat, and the bat managed to get the insect between its minute sharp teeth and swallow. Next a midge, which went down a little easier, then a small crane fly. By then, the bat was looking around for more. Here, let's try a grass moth again—ah, got it this time!

And so it went, as we collected together, the bat growing stronger and more interested with each insect, its face powdered with pale moth scales. Soon it was lunging at each proffered dainty with zeal. And when I tried a bigger moth, the bat's natural prey, after all, the miller vanished faster than a Vienna sausage tossed into a kennel at kibble time. Six or eight more times we did this. The light was fading. The little brown bat lay across my gloved palm, belly down, foxy little ears straight up, nose twitching. Then it drew its wings in toward its body. And in the blink of a bat's eye, it lifted off from my hand and became one more dark form against the night sky.

TWO THINGS TEND to happen on hot July nights: big tree limbs, heavy with risen sap and leaves, fall, and cats, out hunting, end up going home with coyotes to feed their pups. Milkweed, Brownie McGee, Virga, and Bridgette the bridge cat were all likely taken by coyotes. I was always afraid the same fate would befall Bokis, but it never did. We joked that the coyotes must have metal detectors and left Bilak Bokis alone because of the heavy metal plate in his gimpy leg. But for a few days we had cause to fear the worst. The coyotes had been close and vocal. Scat appeared on the mail path. And Bokis failed to show, morning after morning. Since his monthlong disappearance as a kitten, he'd never been away for more than a night, except after the house fire, when he took shelter from the mayhem somewhere for a week, then reappeared and submitted to a month's boarding during the house repairs.

But this time there was no apparent cause, and no clues. As the days ticked by, the coyotes seemed guilty by default, and we prepared to mourn our remarkable cat. I was heartbroken yet still hopeful. David and Elaine Myers had come over from Eden Valley for a visit. When we went into the studio, Elaine heard a sound. "I think it's coming from under there," she said, pointing to a floorboard—one I had recently replaced. We all listened, and there it was, a faint but unmistakable mewling. I grabbed a hammer and ripped up the board . . . and out popped Bokis! He was weak and dehydrated but okay. Maybe the mice that had lured him down there to begin with had also sustained him.

That night, when we sat together, Bokis clung especially close to me. My brother Tom and I had moved some pieces of furniture, left to me by our great-aunt Helen Phelps, from Denver. Among them was an armchair I had coveted most of my life, an old family piece whose arms end in beautifully carved heads of retrievers. It had always been the Dog Chair and, once installed at Swede Park, it quickly became the favored perch of Bokis, with or without me. When he sat on the cushion by himself, he looked as if the dogs were his personal guardians. And for days after his lucky rescue from his own personal House of Usher, he scarcely left the Dog Chair's protective embrace.

AS JULY WANES, young birds leave their nests. One silly young robin gets trapped in the studio, another under the red currant nets put up especially against hungry thrushes. I release them both, but they seem far more indignant than grateful. On the dippy tops of birches, infant cedar waxwings importune the parents they already resemble. Dull-toned baby hummers throng the early butterfly-bush bloom. Thea finds a quartet of kingfishers lined up where the small power line crosses the river and comes back to get me. I spot their nest in the washed-out bank created when the winter floods took a big bite out of the field by the bridge (it's an ill wind . . .). And the swallows. From dawn to dusk the violet-greens fly in from the valley to plunge and swoop up into their nest in the soffit hole above the porch. They don't quit until darkness deprives even their acute eyesight of any more catches or safe landings.

Then one morning we hear a racket outside, much like the sound the swallows make when they first arrive, but even louder. For hours six swallows—parents and young—loop in and out of the porch, shrieking, piping, and yelling. They drift out over the valley, come back, and do it again. The fledglings try to get back into the nest, and occasionally one succeeds; the parents try to drive them away from it, sometimes riding them right down to the ground. I don't know where freshly fledged swallows sleep after their first flight, but eventually they lose interest in the nest and join the great mixed company of violet-greens, trees, rough-wings, and barns hawking over the river and the valley, now and then returning for a valedictory swoop through Swede Park. It seems so recently that they arrived; I'll see them on and off for the rest of the summer, but they've been out for a day, and already I miss their gentle cohabitation.

In the languorous late-July afternoons, the airspace over the garden is like O'Hare at midday: gliding swallowtails, dashing painted ladies, and zipping baby hummingbirds fill every flight path and come close to collision. If it gets hot enough, we might walk down the river path to a grand old big-leaf maple hung with licorice ferns, club mosses, and a rope swing. A deep pool opposite Larson's Island is a fine place for a swim. A good place too for fat crayfish, which proliferate on the cobble bottom and don't pinch if you grab them right. We'll contribute a few of them for a crawdad feed at Kent and Irene Martin's in Skamokawa, insufficient exchange for the salmon he brings back from his summer's commercial fishing in Alaska. I'll pluck a basket of plums to take along.

When Bokis and I walk down to the plum grove, where the

first plums and blackberries come into ripeness, the air smells sweet and tangy. Thistledown floats and seems to stick on the scent-laden air. Goldfinches loose clouds of their silky seeds, and barn swallows play with the floss over the river, catching, rising, dropping, catching, rising, dropping. Black walnut leaflets, among the first to yellow and drop, float while spinning on the breeze, but even their little mass must eventually fall. As for the down, I'm not at all sure that thistles, like mist, haven't completely reneged on their contract with gravity.

8 · The Time of Hay and Berries

the thorny arms of berry vines
give up their fragrant flesh and drop
musty fruits, one by one

—THEA LINNAEA PYLE, "Reincarnation"

The first wood nymph comes dancing around the corner of the porch, announcing the arrival of summer's long last stand. Doug Larson is cutting hay. Around and around Lenore Sorenson's field the old Farmall, baling-wired together for yet another season, spins in a narrowing ellipse. Spud, the brown dog, runs alongside but gives the machine plenty of room, his brother having gone under the flail last year. Occasionally he pounces like a coyote on a turned-up vole. Crows flop down on the windrows for the same reason, giving a raven hell when it has a look-in. The northeast bridge field is entirely ringed with brambles, many still in blossom, their scent (along with honeysuckle, mock orange, and white roses) filling my window's breeze. I remember when the first blackberry bush sprang up on the riverside, and now look at it. That field, which once looked like a golf green, thanks to the dairy cows, wants to go to broom and bramble and will do so the first year it isn't cut. Doug, his strong arms as brown as Spud, steers the tractor around in ovals, just as he and his father, Bobby, have for

decades. The cut grass sprays out of the flail like a green foun-
tain.

WHILE THE FARM folk are getting in their hay, other animals
are busy hauling nectar and pollen and meat. Of the dozens of
species of pollinators we see at work in our garden, several carry
on their lives in communal hives. The hives are seldom obvious,
and if made so, as in the case of ground-nesting yellow jackets,
it is often to our distinct disadvantage. One day last summer
Darrell Sorenson, one of Ed's sons and a great-grandson of H. P.
Ahlberg, brought his daughter and granddaughter to see the old
home place. Thea walked them out to the pond, where the
Sorenson boys once kept a little rowboat. I stayed behind. A few
minutes later I heard shrill cries, as Thea and the little girl came
running back to the house, waving their arms. They had stepped
on a ground-nesting yellow-jacket hive and were immediately
engulfed by the pheromone-driven guards. They ended up slap-
ping baking-soda paste on frightening stings near their eyes.

The greatest of the beehives around here is the paper palace
of the white-faced hornet, *Vespula maculata*. These hives are
usually about the shape and size of a small watermelon. But
they take many other forms depending upon their location, often
conforming their lines to the substrate. One that Thea found
pressed against columnar basalt in eastern Oregon looked like
an outgrowth of the putty-colored, lichen-blotched stone flutes.
A nearby nest occupying the corner of a doorjamb on a pictur-
esque old barn curved into the angle almost up to a horseshoe
nailed overhead, as if it were part of a set designer's plan. Still
another was woven into the wire diamonds of a chainlink fence
in a Bellingham alley, shielded by shiny pear leaves. Each of
these hornet hives was an object of exceptional beauty, completely distinctive. Each was also an advertisement of major pain
for anyone dumb enough to disturb it.

Such as the local lads who tried to steal our apples a few

years back. I would happily have given them all the apples they wanted, but no doubt it was more fun to swipe them. And still more fun to lob yellow apples at that funny gray globe hanging from one of the branches—until they hit it. Never had those boys dismounted a tree so quickly, or run home so fast! These hornets are *big*: black-and-white and bald-headed, they carry one of the most painful stings in North America.

Now we have a new hornet nest, fresh this season; I let one maker out the kitchen window this morning. This hive is not a branch-balloon, but a curvaceous vessel built into a crease in the Tall Oak's trunk, some thirty feet up. And *built* is the word: paper-making wasps, including these hornets, masticate and regurgitate wood pulp, extruding sheets of paper every bit as sound as those from the mill across the Columbia in Wauna, every bit as ornamental in their earth-tone striations as any handmade Japanese art paper. It was Thea who discovered one source of the fiber for this particular edifice. One day she happened to spot a hornet visiting the clothesline, about seventy-five feet from the hive. Inspecting the wooden clothespins bought new that season, she saw that every one had been scraped by the logging jaws of the hornets. Their surfaces were not only weathered gray but also rasped into a soft nap and so scored with strips and stripes that they looked much like the reverse image of the paper they made. Later Thea watched the hornets harvest clothespin pulp.

In the early spring, when honeybees began to visit the first crocuses, overwintering queen bumblebees also appeared. I believe they commonly breed in vole holes in the earth. We see them less often later in the season, but smaller yellow-and-black bumbles are abundant in summer. Recently I discovered a hive of small, kitten-gray bees. Preparing to move some large oak logs downslope to where they might be split, I had to pry the great rounds out of the articulated roll in which they'd lain since Phillip Wirkkala had bucked the latest great limb fallen from the Lincoln Oak. When it came time to shift the last vast oak loaf, already parted from the butt log, which I intended to leave in place for the cat, I saw that it had several little hollows. I positioned my peavey, a stout pike with a swivel hook opposite the point. A few compact, hoary bees first hummed around, then issued from the taper-sized holes. They seemed unaggressive and did not sting me, but I wasn't sure how they might behave if the hydraulic splitter rent their cozy quarters. So I let that log lie and contrived a shingle roof to protect the formerly guarded cavities from the rain.

Now, peaveying the heavy oak rounds down the slope as Thea cuts bramble canes, I look up as she shouts. A sharp-shinned hawk has just flown between us, two feet from my face, a peripheral blur. Later a long-waisted hunting wasp skims through the vegetation, clutching a fat yellow crab spider. Crab spiders often occupy perches against which they are already cryptic or change color to match their background. This helps protect them from color-sighted birds but not from UV-sensitive wasps. A big white-and-pink crab has sprawled across a deep purple spike of butterfly bush for days, asking for it. As we regard the newly cleared slope, our once and future butterfly garden, a bird drops past the buddleia onto the exposed ground. Attracted by the many invertebrate refugees unhoused by my rude dislodging of the oak logs, it flashes the pied pattern of a black-throated gray warbler: sometimes heard, almost never sighted in summer's thick curtain. The crab spider escapes for now.

Writing on the porch as the day fades, I barely see a form move across the lawn, left to right, in front of the steps. It passes just a few feet from Firkin, who watches with evident concern. It seems bulkier than she is. I hurry to the west end of the porch and behold a doglike form mincing to the log boneyard, sniffing, then loping off to the compost and beyond: a juvenile coyote. As it pauses by the woodpile, I see that its fur is short, mottled, and matty, its ears enormous, and its legs long and stiltlike. I suppose it will move on up the path toward the creek. We haven't heard their songs lately, but the coyotes are always around. Firkin might well be concerned. Virga, the other cat who arrived when she did, disappeared last winter, probably recycled as coyote.

Our own primary items of prey in the fecund wreckage of summer are the berries. Blackberries say high summer here and connote languorous afternoons, scratched-up hands and wrists, purple-stained fingers, and the promise of pie. Three species of blackberries proliferate in western Washington. The only indigenous one, and the only one worth picking, according to many locals, is *Rubus ursinus,* known as dewberry, native blackberry, or just "the little ones." Dewberry trails through the clear-cuts and over the road cuts in endless wiry vines with short, ankle-raking stickers and triplets of leaves that carry good color all winter long. The little-fingernail–sized berries aren't very seedy, are the most flavorful of all, and ripen around mid-July.

The second, much more prominent species has long been called *Rubus discolor,* or Himalayan blackberry. Botanists have recently revised its proper identity to Armenian blackberry, *R. armenicus.* By either name it is one of the most aggressive alien weeds anywhere. Himalayans seize the land, gobbling acres, blanketing banks, consuming abandoned farmhouses and their Studebakers and anything left alone in the rain for five minutes or longer. True enough, their tangles furnish cover and food for songbirds, the endangered Columbia white-tailed deer, and many other creatures, but the thick barbed-wire ropes grow inches per minute, or so it seems, as they hang thirty feet from the trees by midsummer. They are generally seen as a plague upon the land—until berry season, when they transform into worshipped manna for a month or two before the herbicides and brush hogs are brought out again. Himalayan blackberries can be as big and black as Bing cherries. When Dory comes for a weekend in berry season, she and Thea fill their buckets in a couple of hours. The drupelets are fat, extremely juicy, and, when truly ripe, delicious, though devotees of dewberries find the Himalayans' flavor watery and the fruits coarse. They are far preferable, however, to the third species of bramble, the European or evergreen blackberry (*Rubinus laciniata*). Its leaflets are deeply dissected compared to the Armenians' ovals, its thorns wickedly recurved into hooks that won't let go, and its fruit stony with seeds, more bitter than sweet unless nearly overripe.

I am a berry slut and won't turn down any of these. Bearlike, I gladly rake the strawberry-red thimbleberries, orange-to-blood salmonberries, deep blue blackcaps, evergreen huckleberries, crisp red huckleberries, even the almost-ignored purple salal. Thea too likes all these at their best and will gladly gather and cook with the profligate Himalayans. But her special love is for the native dewberry. When she finds a female patch (it is a sexually separated species, unlike the others), she watches it and guards its whereabouts as jealously as her best chanterelle grounds, and she is not alone in this.

In berry season Gray's River gets together. The custom began in 1905 with the county fair, held at a Grange park on the riverbank below Swede Park until 1911, when the Wahkiakum Fair moved to Skamokawa. Annual Grange picnics began in 1926 and continued for decades. Then in 1988 we held a covered bridge picnic, with old-timers and newcomers gathered in the shade of the Larsons' maples beside the bridge. Old photographs covered easels and card tables, and picnic tables sagged beneath a generous potluck. Larsons and Badgers, Durrahs and Fauvers, swapped stories and argued over whose double-cousin married which aunt. Carlton Appelo commented that it was a good thing the K-M road was finally put through, or there's no telling what folks around here would look like. Refreshments included hamburgers, potato and Jell-O salads, and abundant blackberry pies. It being the time of low water, a cross-river tug of war broke out. The north-shore team, including a couple of hardened young loggers, finally yanked the dregs of the southern side into the gentle but chilly current.

That picnic spawned a full-fledged festival in 1991, complete with dance floor and beer garden. John Twiss flew his biplane over from Astoria to perform aerobatics. He didn't quite fly under the covered bridge, but close enough that a lot of breaths were collectively held. The next year Dave Henderson brought his ultralight, and you could take a flight over the valley or ride through the bridge in a wagon pulled by Joel Fitts's heavy horses. At night people of all ages danced their socks off to local bands such as Sunrise and Jessica or the K-O Peak band. The festival ran for seven years until it wore us all out. In another form it resumed again last summer (with a fresh committee) for the covered bridge centennial jubilee, and it looks to continue. The blackberries certainly will.

LIKE MUCH OF what is worth being here for, most of our summertime events owe their existence to the Grange. Once a radical farmers' league, which arose in 1867 to resist the all-powerful shippers and railroads, the Patrons of Husbandry has since shrunk along with the family farm. National and state Grange policies often conflict with my own feelings on issues such as pesticides and endangered species. But at the village level the Grange can still be the best thing, if not the only thing, going. Here we would have no covered bridge, let alone a water system or computer center, without our local Grange.

I joined the Grange soon after I moved here, at Bobby Larson's invitation. My hope was that it would be a good place to get to know local people and to hear the stories of the old-timers before they were all gone. In this I have not been disappointed. But there is a price: meetings can run long and are not always exactly gripping. One slow evening at Grange I noticed that the owl was missing from the Gatekeeper's staff. Someone had stolen it—as well as an auxiliary owl that came from Naselle Grange when it closed—during some repairs to the Grange Hall. That night we draped the Grange charter in memory of our Worthy Sister Opal

Kraft, who had been the last gatekeeper to wield the owl. Born to a local family in 1915, Opal left the valley to teach special ed for many years, then returned. In her sixty years of membership, starting in early childhood, she had held every Grange office, from Flora to Master, except Gatekeeper. A peculiarity of Patrons of Husbandry elections is that no one is supposed to campaign for office or even let his interest be known, so I had not been aware of Opal's desire to be Gatekeeper. I'd had a lock on that office for years, having subtly campaigned after all. Following the election one year, Opal told me she wished she could have been Gatekeeper, but it was too late to change the result. I felt bad. Then I was absent at the next election, and Opal was chosen instead. I was delighted to learn that she finally got to be Gatekeeper for a few weeks before she passed away.

"Now we'd better get it right," Chuck Parker said to Norman Anderson as the Steward and Assistant Stewards prepared for their slow march around the hall. "You know what a stickler Opal was for ritual." She also loved a laugh. But we were grave as Chaplain Ila Mae Larson placed the black crepe over the ninety-eight-year-old framed charter of Gray's River Grange #124 and the proper words of heavy hearts were spoken. Then kind thoughts and funny stories went around about the sturdy Opal, whom no one could quite believe was gone. Her mortal remains had been laid beneath the turf of the Grange cemetery, under hemlocks, beside her forebears, and where, according to the minutes, "the moles continue to work, unabated." Thus was another pioneer of this valley sent to grace. I glanced over at the Gatekeeper's station and at the pole's bare neck. The missing owl had been a beautiful bird, hand-carved nearly a century ago with scallops and hachures for plumage, fierce orange eyes and bill, flecks of gold indicating that this was once a gilded fowl, and, yes, it was spotted. It was likely as old as Ahlberg, founder of Gray's River Grange, builder of Swede Park, neighbor of Opal's ancestors. After the draping of the charter, I again became Gatekeeper. But the hall seemed naked with both Opal and the owl in absentia.

At the normal installation of officers the next January, Steward Chuck Parker, magnificent in a special pink sash and a freshly trimmed van Dyke, invested the new officers with the graceful intonations of the nineteenth century. The Lady Assistant Steward was enjoined to come to the aid of any women who might be fainting, while the Worthy Gatekeeper was instructed to keep a sharp eye on all those entering and passing out—two charges that always elicit a few smiles in the semisolemn proceedings. Chuck draped each officer in a blue-and-gold sash, which always reminds me of Cub Scout colors. Then he bestowed the officers' implements—a straw horn of plastic fruit for Pomona, a basket of ripe barley for Ceres, a bunch of artificial flowers for Flora—along with staffs topped with a spud (a weeding blade), a pruning hook forged from a sword, a shepherd's crook, and, for the Gatekeeper, the owl (Master Esther Gregg had affixed a fluffy finger puppet to the staff as a stand-in), with suitably metaphorical job descriptions. The Overseer was instructed to encourage reading, "so that none of our number shall remain ignorant of nature's laws." Flora was enjoined to look to the gardens of the district, and the Steward to watch for weeds and tares. Then each officer was escorted by the Master to his or her post.

For some years I served as Lecturer. This officer is supposed to provide a "literary program," and he really did in olden (pre-TV and highway) days. I took that charge seriously and read a bit of poetry and good rural writing. But the Lecturer has lots of paperwork to do, which I neglected. Once elected Gatekeeper, I preferred that post because a favorite British butterfly goes by the name and because I got to hold the staff with the owl on top. Also, the Gatekeeper's office was undemanding, with no paperwork. I sat in the very rear of the hall, opposite Doug Larson, the laconic and eternal Steward. My role was limited to standing at the opening the meeting, closing the front door, and reciting "I hereby close this outer gate with faith, hope, and charity, and will guard it with fidelity." For some reason the Gatekeeper has an old beauty-parlor chair instead of the theater seats all the others occupy, and though any movement on its plastic cover is likely to sound like a fart, this throne is by far the most comfortable seat in the house for a long sit. So, as much as I missed Opal and the owl, I was glad when I was elected Gatekeeper once again.

PLENTY OF FOOD is served after the meetings; diets do not marry well with Grange. Oyster Stew Night and Pies for Polio are my two favorite meetings of the Grange year. I rejoice if I am in town for the late-winter meeting that features Norman and Myrtle's rich and peppery oyster stew, and Pie Night speaks for itself. Last year's began with Ila Mae Larson speaking the prayer, asking that we be good and faithful servants, protecting the widows and the orphans, and keeping ourselves unstained from the world. Everyone was eager for pie, so the order of business proceeded fairly promptly. The minutes of the last meeting were old history, the Christmas party and high water in the hall having intervened. In the Cemetery Report, Norman Anderson advised that "the moles are back again, and quite a large hole has developed up there." Bobby Larson took the floor to speak on the possible revival of the Covered Bridge Festival, visits to Alzheimer's patients, the Fourth of July, the county fair food booth, and "the whole deal." We voted to let the Water Conservation Board use the Grange Hall without paying the usual fee, as a gesture of thanks for saving our park's jerrybuilt but sound boat ramp from the gargantuan root wads that washed down the flooded Gray's. The meeting threatened to veer into the Army Corps' plan to deepen the Columbia River shipping channel, but fortunately the siren pies called. We formed the traditional circle, held hands, sang "Blessed Be the Ties That Bind," put away the vestments and implements, and climbed the stairs to the dining room.

Pies for Polio began in aid of the March of Dimes; nowadays members bring and buy pies to benefit local charities. Apple, cherry, pumpkin, rhubarb, various creams, berries, and combinations, some from Costco in Astoria, some from home, waited on the raised stage by the kitchen. Ones and fives were offered, the proceeds going to a flooded-out family that year. The floods, the river's desire to have its way, the proper responses, and the bullheaded agencies that are supposed to prevent floods were the hot topics of conversation as the coffee was poured and the pies diminished. Over my fourth slender slice, Merlin Durrah, a cousin of Opal's and a retired log-truck driver, described the splash dams in the hills where, long ago, logs were stored until the time came to blow the dam and send them all downstream. "You talk about tearing up the stream banks!" he said. "And now the Fisheries is worried about a little work to keep the river in its bed instead of making a new course and running right through Marie's place?" The river, which had run a foot deep in the Grange Hall a few weeks before, will not easily be kept. But as the pies vanished, so did the valley's problems, in the warmth of the Grange Hall if not outside in the changing world.

One August evening at Grange as the summer's light faded, the Larsons and I lingered over coffee, discussing the good haying season. Bobby Larson, for many years the Master of the Grange, was telling me how he decided when to mow. "When you watch the moon," said Bobby, "you know. In fact, it's the same phase of the moon right now, but that was two moon deals ago. We had that long, hot, late summer, and the grass was this high. But you only have until the sun goes down, and then the dew's on it. I knew I was pushing the baler, the windrows were so wide with a lot of it canary grass. I only had a couple more passes, then the baler went haywire. We went down to Fittses'. Joel said he had something on Friday, but he'd come get it Saturday, and he did. When we finished getting it into the barn, there was room for only two bales left."

"So you can use the reed canary grass?" I asked. I'd thought this coarse, invasive grass was useless for forage.

"You bet," Bobby and Doug said as one. "After timothy, canary grass is the favorite hay for horses, and the heifers like it fine too." They used the chopper for baling, which cut the head-high canary grass into palatable lengths, and sold two truckloads to Doug's brother Mark's ex–in-laws.

But the season hadn't all been happy. Another local farmer, who raises beef, had lent his bull to a neighbor to breed his few remaining cows. The borrower hadn't bothered to electrify his fence, so the bull walked right out. He wandered over to Larsons' and forced Doug's best cow—a recent mother to a tiny calf—up against the barn, and gored and killed her. The bull's owner intended to make it right, but the cow was gone nonetheless. Doug's face was sad as he told the tale; he loves his cows. "She had such a good bag," added Ila Mae. "Sometimes you'd see four calves suckling on her." Fortunately Doug had another fresh cow willing to take the calf. They trucked the dead Holstein over to their far field for the coyotes and vultures.

With the heavy rainfall and the distance from markets, farming was never easy here. H. P. Ahlberg took cucumbers and other vegetables to market in Astoria by sailboat or rowed a skiff upriver to sell his produce to workers at Knappton Mill. Marie Fauver showed me an old photograph of her place, the turned fields brimming with fine potatoes. Her uncle John Klint had worked at the logging camp at Brookfield on the Columbia, but he walked the ten miles back across the hills to cultivate potatoes to pay off his land. In 1912 he sold eighty-five sacks of his spuds to the Portland Lumber company for thirty dollars, and fifteen hogs for seventy dollars. Many families have tried various crops since, usually coming around to dairy. Few farm anymore. In the face of bad bulls, floods, and economics, the Larsons, Tom Zimmerman with his fresh winter kale and snow peas coming on, the Fittses' horses and heifers prancing in the meadows, the Burkhalters' dairy cows, Derek's beef cattle, and those who make hay keep farming alive here still.

After one coffee refill too many, I stepped out of the hall, down the stairs, and into the same dark riverside mud that H. P. Ahlberg had trod—almost dry for a change. A bright moonglade lit the river. Looking into the shimmering water, I thought of the long string of stories that Grange had brought me: Merlin Durrah's byzantine, interlocking family histories; Carlton Appelo's account of how his mother, Agnes—whose silver braids I recall as she served her last years behind the counter of Appelo's Store in Gray's River—took the payroll up to the camps on the logging railroads or how she carried two rolls of barbed wire out to Jim Oatfield's car, while Jim could barely lift one. Bobby Larson telling how some of the lads turned up in drag at a dance in the forties. When the stories of the founders and the travails of particular cows, horses, or black sheep forebears went around with the coffee and cookies, I felt more and more woven into this history that I have chosen as my own.

And I worried about the stories to come. Like the lowered ceiling in the hall and the furling of the stage curtain, with its romantic landscape surrounded by painted ads for defunct businesses, the theft of the Gatekeeper's owl was a reversal. When I joined Grange, the membership was robust enough to conduct the fancy floorwork for the full fourth-degree ceremony. Since then, attrition and the relaxing of protocol nationwide have cut back on formalities. At the last installation, the watered-down ritual for new members seemed pallid compared to my own elaborate induction twenty-five years before. The Puget Island and Skamokawa Granges had closed, leaving only Elochoman and Gray's River in the county. I couldn't help but wonder if Grange itself was going the way of agriculture in Wahkiakum.

But at the next election, Krist Novoselic was elected Gatekeeper. The former bassist and cofounder of the band Nirvana, Krist, now deeply interested in political reform, settled one valley over and joined Grange in hopes of building on its progressive past. He used his influence in Olympia to obtain from the state Grange a new-old owl, handsomely nickel-plated, rescued from some Grange Hall that had gone down. To put off such a fate here, he and Steve, Karl, Jim, Rick, Delvin, Krist, and other members have devoted themselves to restoring our hall. Dedicated in 1905 and repaired in fits and starts since, the building has been showing its hundred years. Already we have a new (all-important) kitchen and a furnace that actually heats the hall without drowning out the reading of the minutes, and the building has been raised above flood level.

So we still meet, brothers and sisters with very different opinions who converse civilly for the most part and wash down too many homemade cookies with hot coffee. Stories are still told, which may be more important than the fading ritual and shrinking herds. Krist has now been elected Master, and he has instituted progressive election changes that reduce the endless and cumbersome old process to a brisk half-hour while allowing members to actually run for offices of their choice.

Our members from across K-M Mountain in Skamokawa, stimulated by new energy in the community, are taking steps to restore their own beautiful but badly flooded hall and begin anew. Even as the veterans dwindle, the Granges they made—like their villages—carry on.

At least for now.

ANOTHER INSTITUTION THAT has been touch-and-go around here is the rural post. The national Grange was the primary engine behind both rural free delivery and rural electrification. But country post offices have been flickering out almost as fast as family farms in recent decades, as the U.S. Postal Service deems it uneconomic to keep them open. Unlike Oregon, across the Columbia, where many towns have lost their postal identity (Jewell subsumed to Astoria, Elsie to Seaside, miles and miles away), until recently Wahkiakum County had kept its four postal facilities. Cathlamet and Skamokawa persist, but it finally came to some inspector's attention that Gray's River and Rosburg were pretty darn close together and too sparsely populated to have two P.O.s.

For many years Jean Calhoun was our postmaster. The many-boxed lobby of her post office occupied the enclosed porch of her own home. In slacks and print blouse, she stepped out onto the nylon-grassed wheelchair ramp to collect the mail from the outside post box, accompanied by her handsome and beseeching black-backed, white-bellied pussycat, Pooser. Jean's P.O. was the depot not only for mail but for news, bird spottings, connection with neighbors, emergency notifications, and payment of utility bills. It was the place where we all checked in to make sure the world was running aright. All country post offices have the potential to function in that way, but a diffident or taciturn postmaster can easily keep things all business. Jean was economical with her speech but never close-tongued. One day she telephoned to tell me that she had a redpoll at her feeder. This northern finch is a favorite of mine that I have rarely seen. But country bird names don't necessarily correspond to Roger Tory Peterson's; I knew, for example, that Jean called goldfinches "yellowhammers," the accepted name for a European finch. I headed down to the P.O. pronto, half expecting to find a house or purple finch. But a redpoll it was—the first ever recorded for Wahkiakum County. Jean stood behind the grate and issued her standard all-purpose summary: "So."

After Jean finally retired, she wanted her house for herself. About the same time Mike Swanson at the Rosburg Store, our other pocket-handkerchief post office down the road, hoped to reclaim the space the P.O. displaced. The postal powers in Portland had already announced that one or the other would go. Of course the Rosburgers wanted it in Rosburg, the Gray's Riparians in Gray's River. For a time it looked as if we would get our way and at the same time reclaim the oldest building in town, the Walker House—a shingled cabin built by our first settler, Samuel Walker, in the 1860s; the postal service was interested in adapting the house for the two-village facility. That would have been especially suitable, because Julia Walker was the town's first postmaster. The Walkers sorted mail in their bedroom and passed it out to patrons in the parlor.

But the owner of the Walker House was unable to agree on the terms of lease with the postal authorities, so the deal fell through. Jean passed away before getting her front room back. At her estate sale the minor artifacts of a long life in the valley were laid out for all to rummage through and buy for pennies. I would have loved to get the brass mailboxes, both to remember Jean's daily labors sorting letters into them and to sort my unanswered correspondence, but they quickly went for a tidy price. I selected some old accordion file folders and Jean's venerable black-and-blue unbrella, and Jean's son Roger gave me a fine photograph of Jean and Pooser, backdropped by the olive-green split box, the community bulletin board, and the tacked-on letters that read P O S T   O F F I C E   G R A Y S   R I V E R   W A   9 8 6 2 1.

The new Gray's River–Rosburg Post Office was built up a steep drive off the highway in Rosburg, three miles oceanward from here and no longer the short, safe bicycle ride away that the old P.O. was. Both Zip Codes still function for now. But 98621 no longer shows in the national Zip Code directory, and someday some manager may rub it out altogether. Then this historic place, whose post office dates to 1872, just eighty years after Captain Gray first entered the Columbia River in the *Columbia Rediviva,* would join Deep River, Altoona, and Brookfield on the Columbia as a postal ghost town.

Jean's partner in keeping the appointed rounds was Hermina Carroll, the mail lady. She collected the sorted, rubber-banded letters from the P.O. in an ancient and much-duct-taped cardboard box, then drove the route and delivered the mail in her venerable rococo station wagon with a stuffed leopard bungeed on top. As she approached our mailbox, Hermina smiled out through a haze of smoke over a dashboard crammed with medals, ribbons, statuettes, and doodads, extracted our packet from

the box, and leaned across to place it in the mailbox. Whe_
retired, that cardboard carton was about to be given the toss.
Thea's distress, I rescued the relic.

Life here would be impoverished, maybe impossible, without the mail. It brings not only bills and checks, both the
Wahkiakum County Eagle and the *Washington Post Weekly*, and a
few letters truly worth getting, it also provides a reason for a good
short walk almost every day. When I walk for the mail, I monitor
the population of thrips in the old galvanized mailbox, which is
just beginning to rust on top, or the state of bloom or fruit of the
salmonberries along the stream, or the courtship of Bewick's
wrens in the hems of the Douglas-fir by the black walnut, or the
response of our one vine maple to my pruning of the oaks, maples, and beeches around it. We read the mail on the porch if the
day is warm or on the couch just inside if cool, then recycle it or
set it aside to enjoy again and eventually answer. I've always felt
there is something sacred in a piece of paper that travels the
earth from hand to hand, head to head, heart to heart.

The volume of real mail has dramatically diminished since
the advent of e-mail, and many transactions that formerly would
have been carried by Hermina's cheery successor, Sharyl Hjaltalin,
now flow through the wires. But as the dreaded electron stream
has flooded more and more of life, I've found it incompatible
with my writing and daily life, and we've banished it from the
house. I now dip into e-mail only once or twice a week at the
Gray's River Computer Center. Yet another successful project of
the Grange, the center took advantage of a Gates Foundation
grant to provide high-speed Internet access in rural communities. Set up in the old Rosburg School and run by volunteers, ca-
pably led by Norm Bolton and Judy Durrah, the center is a wonder. It allows us access to e-mail and the Web when necessary,
close to home and for free, with no worries about maintenance.
And I can use my antediluvian computer at home as a simple
and pure writing device, free of all online blandishments, devil-

ment, and clutter. At the center I am as likely to listen to Merlin expounding on how to set up a North Bend logging system across a canyon or to Judy and Marie debating the best way to make oatmeal or sharing genealogy software tips as to attend the tawdry substitute for correspondence called e-mail. I may go back to letters altogether, thus doing my bit to bolster business for 98621.

The other leg of country communications, of course, is the telephone. We are extraordinarily fortunate in this bit of the American outback to have a small, independent telephone company. C. A. Appelo founded the Western Wahkiakum Telephone Company in Deep River in 1927, and his son, Carlton, is still the company's president. The Gray's River exchange used to be located in Appelo's general store in the village, which only recently burned to the ground, but since the seventies it has occupied a modern building at Swenson's Corner. Competitive long-distance service, as well as our local calls, repairs, and billing, still go through this small, friendly office where we know everyone, rather than via some faceless telecommunications behemoth in a distant city. It hasn't been that many years since we connected with an operator when we dialed 0; you would know Mary Kandoll by her Scottish lilt, and you could call the operator to find out a sports score or the state of the tide on Deep River, or to ask (or pass) the time of day.

Carlton, a recipient of the State Heritage Award, published detailed historical accounts and photographs of local settlements in his telephone books for many years, and his own capacious archive of local history has been curated and is now available for research. He has always been extremely active in regional and national telecom organizations, which may be how he wangled one of the first licenses in the country for Direct TV, a great boon to a small company. Indeed, Wahkiakum West, with only 4.8 customers per mile, furnishes high-speed DSL Internet service to every household that wants it — something the adjacent Bell system cannot yet provide. I still use the rotary telephone that was installed when I came here, and every time I dial I hope (as with so many aspects of life in this thinly peopled district) that Carlton's phone company will last and last.

NIGHTFALL, the last week of August. Mars, swinging close by, dominates the southern sky. Below it Spica glitters red and blue like a deputy's cherrytop a few miles away. Earlier a bat flicked through the airspace of the front yard, and a Swainson's thrush, silent for weeks but enlivened by a light rain, struck up a little protest of feeble *whit*s as I made a dusk run to the compost. The blackberries will last for a while longer. Between the last hay, almost in, and the berries' fullness, a scent like honey glazes the night air as it begins to cool.

Given such signs, it must be time for the Wahkiakum County Fair. With its produce and animals, 4-H displays, hobbies and quilts, elephant ears and Tilt-A-Whirls, musical acts and ribbons, the fair still attracts almost everyone in the county in late August. Last summer I went to Skamokawa on Saturday in time for the annual salmon feed. County commissioner Dan Cothren served me up a massive slab of alder-baked chinook, and I walked it off by visiting the guinea pigs and the funny feather-footed chickens. Then I took my turn manning the Democrats' booth, handing out buttons and bumper stickers and fliers for our slate of candidates. Right next door sat Chuck Parker, my Grange brother, doing the same for the Republicans. I told him I'd take his handouts if he'd take mine, but we both knew exactly where we'd put them if we did.

I had exercised my main role at the fair earlier in the week, as judge for the beer and wine competition. Someone has to do it. Marilyn Gudmundsen's late husband, Georg, a Norwegian seaman turned farmer, used to make a splendid dry blackberry wine. I always hope to taste its match at the fair, but only Sunrise Fletcher's vintage has come close. That was the year his blackberry won Best of Show and his hop wine the Judge's Award. This year Sunrise was a judge with Steve McClain and me, and didn't enter. Bob Richards's good bitter ales were also absent from the competition. This left us with little but cloying liqueurs to sample and reluctantly adorn with our store of ribbons. Thank goodness for George Exum's fine fruit wines, but even his best dry kiwi was overwhelmed by the alcoholic raspberry syrup and crankcase Kahlúa. Afterward Steve, Sunrise, and I were forced to adjourn to the Oasis to rinse our palates liberally with Bridgeport India Pale Ale.

At the fair Grangers staff the public food booth, working long greasy hours and earning much of their operating budget for the year. For several years the county's Granges have sponsored a popular spelling bee, and they furnish much of the direction for the vigorous 4-H and other youth activities. But the most conspicuous signs of the Patrons of Husbandry during fair time are the elaborate booths dressed by the local Granges—formerly four, now only two. These displays, shaped roughly like a big pinball game, usually involve lots of prize produce, designs painted in dried beans and grains, a Bible, a flag, and perhaps a nod to the year's theme. I learned early on that the booths are judged less on originality than on fidelity to tradition.

In our first year as Grangers, Sally and I served on the booth committee with Brian and Connie Larson. A talented artist, Sally designed a handsome and imaginative response to the assigned theme of "renewable energy," depicting a 3-D farmyard using solar, wind, small hydro, and even methane power, the latter from a mound of manure. Brian tossed on a Bible at the last minute. Up against three rival booths consisting mostly of grain pictures, canned goods, and such, we were pretty sure we'd bring home Gray's River Grange's first blue ribbon in years. When Sally saw the results of the judging and our pink ribbon, fourth out of four, she spat out a terse and damning assessment of the judges that pretty much summed up her English appraisal of an American country fair: "Those *clothheads!*"

The pigs, sheep, impossibly soft rex rabbits, and dressage horses are all still there, and this year Krist will be the superintendent of the goat barn. But the cattle are more often heifers and steers than milkers. The sweet picture of a dairy daughter snugged against the soft, brushed side of a warm tan Jersey at the end of a long fair day is fading, and candidates for dairy princess are seldom from milking families anymore. All three of Joel and Noreen Fitts's daughters—Suzie, Amy, and Genevra—served in that honored role, and they had plenty of competition, one girl sponsored by each Grange. But at that time there were some forty working dairies in the county; now there are just three. Not long ago young Kyle Burkhalter, from one of the surviving dairies, spoke to Grange about how his great-grandfather John introduced Swiss Brown cattle to Washington and assured us that they do *not* give chocolate milk. Now Swiss Browns, Jerseys, and Holsteins are as endangered here as marbled murrelets.

Gray's River Valley grows the best grass in the land, but as cattle feed it can't compete with subsidized alfalfa from eastern Washington irrigated with cheap federal water from the Columbia Basin Project. That fact, along with shifting milk supports and economies of scale at the big dairy co-ops like Darigold, knocked the milking stool out from under a creamery industry that once won ribbons in Olympia and medals in Chicago. Alta Meserve's article in the *Gray's River Builder* of September 5, 1936, told how Ed Rice won the gold watch, gold medal, and gold diploma for his butter at the Pacific International Stock Show. "Milk to the local creamery is delivered daily in the early hours of the forenoon, fresh and sweet," she wrote. When the dairy farms go, so goes a century of connection with the grass. Even the frogs were more numerous when the damp fields were pastured: as Brian Larson pointed out to me, the cows created pondlets with every step and kept the blackberry brambles and reed canary grass down.

We're out of step here, an eddy in the economic mainstream. So far we've avoided jumping onto the global juggernaut. Yet if this is a pastoral vision, it's getting dimmer. What remains is the pasture, and the hay. But who knows? Maybe enough of us like it this way that we'll just hang in there. Maybe we'll endure, even thrive, in this backwater where cell phones don't work very well and where computer games go cold in haying season, when there is always summer work for young, strong kids willing to heave bales into the back of a pickup, their tanned arms scratched by hay and berry vines.

9 ✦ Departures

As the season advances, and those birds
which make us but a passing visit depart,
the woods become silent again, and but
few feathers ruffle the drowsy air.

—HENRY DAVID THOREAU,
"The Natural History of Massachusetts"

As the birds thin out, the spiders come into their own. European cross spiders sling their webs between any two available supports. Eastern garden spiders have shown up beside the covered bridge. Arachnids also proliferate indoors before the cold comes. When you live in an old house that is anything but airtight, especially in the country, you have no choice but to share your home with many boarders. Some of them originated in the Old World, having stowed away with the pioneers. On a Saturday night–Sunday morning at my typewriter, as I watch moths fly in the window, a big apricot *Pyrrharctia isabella* tumbles in, with a European crane fly in its wake. I hate to think of the Isabella moth, after crossing the road over and over as a woolly bear last autumn, getting stuck in here to dry and die, so I catch it and put it out; but the gangly crane fly bumbles into the corner web of *Pholcus phalangioides*.

Both of these ancient European adversaries are called daddy longlegs by children, though that moniker properly belongs to harvestmen, or opilionid arachnids. *Pholcus*, of which there are hundreds in our cellar and usually one or two in the shower, is called hanger spider in England; its Latinate name means "jointed squint-eyed creature." They look fragile, but one that washed down into the shower drain completely recovered after I fished it out. When bothered, these innocuous but impressively leggy arachnids shimmy like crazy on their messy webs. I doubt that the delicate woof will trouble the robust crane fly, but one long leg gets stuck, and *pow,* the big female *Pholcus* is on it, quickly putting out silk. What a lot of leg! Fourteen long ones between them, maybe twenty-five or thirty inches' worth if laid end to end. The spider and the fly have similar dimensions in leg length and span, but the crane fly's body is much bigger and will nourish the spider for weeks if she can hold on.

For a while the battle of the daddy long legs looks like a draw, as several legs stick out, kicking. Then just two, then one, flexing pointlessly. After five minutes the mummified crane fly can struggle only by flexing its waist, which keeps the spider from getting in to pierce it. Meanwhile a little male *Pholcus* runs up and perches nearby. Ten minutes in, the female is still wrapping and dancing, the fly is still twisting, its hind legs sticking out behind and bound at the toes. *Pholcus* works at binding up the whole unwieldy package so she can suck unhindered by the wiggle. But the poor straitjacketed fly (all its legs at awkward, broken angles) still resists, giving the spinner fits. When she tries to settle in for the suck, the waggling resumes, throwing off her bite. She gives up and resumes her embroidery. Then the little male moves in and swings one of his forelegs around in a circle, almost touching her; she lunges and he scampers ten inches away. He has his own tiny gnat in a web far down the wall. Finally, with four of her legs in an X above and below her would-be victim, the other four embracing the body, the female *Pholcus* applies her head to the crane fly's. He kicks. She clings. He writhes. She hangs. The male *Pholcus* starts up again. She's hungry. He's horny. Ah, the hunt!

The spider has her beak into the side of the fly's head now, and though it still wiggles unhelpfully, she seems locked on. Her male, rejected, retreats on his own to the shelter of the philodendron. The big fly shudders infrequently but violently. After half an hour it is still not yet fully dispatched, but the spider is no longer deterred by the weaker wiggles. Eight legs and sticky silk, exquisitely coordinated, trump six and wings. When I vacuum these corners after the frost, I'll find the dusty husks of the struggle. For now the crane fly is nearly still. To live through the long sodden months as a leatherjacket in the lawn, then to emerge on a tender evening into maiden flight just for *this!* But for the *Pholcus* it's a fine night; she looks fat and glistening.

I MOVED THE heavy split oak up from the mail path to the driveway in the green wheelbarrow on a mid-September day when the rain gently reasserted itself after sixty days without. The smell of cider fueled the uphill heave past the apple tree, the scent of overripe blackberries powered the roll back down to the woodpile. I was uncomfortably aware of unhousing snails, slugs, wood lice, spiders, ants, beetles, particolored fungi, and much else as I worked. But our own comfort takes precedence, and I had to get the wood in before the big rain came. In the evening Greg Parke came over from Skamokawa, where he was the fire chief as well as a cabinetmaker and musician. He said that the oak we'd had milled for lumber when another big branch came down, which has been stacked and stickered these fifteen years, is still sound. Something fine could be made from it for our house.

The next morning another woodworker showed up, announced by plangent, urgent hoots. The huge, scarlet-mitered pileated woodpeckers used to haunt the rotting forks of a great European beech across from our entrance. Since the county took that tree down, the stumpfuckers (loggers' vernacular, a name shared with big longhorn beetles and wasps with long ovipositors for parasitizing the larvae of woodboring beetles) have been irregular at Swede Park. Any day they show up is a red-letter, red-crested day. For half an hour the big Woody dipped from tree to tree, whooping as if a raccoon were at its nest. Then, with a long staccato, it flew away west, and silence resumed.

Most of the bird song is over by now. But I awoke to jay song—the strident, petulant, rising screech of the scrub jay. A paler jay than Steller's, this species moved north into Washington not many years ago. One morning in bed I heard the call, familiar in Oregon, and leaped to the window for a look. There, atop a rhododendron, was the first scrub jay recorded in western Wahkiakum. Since then they have taken up residence at the Fittses' farm a mile downvalley. Now and then, as if taking an outing, they come over to the covered bridge or visit our porch to steal the cat's kibbles. Unlike Steller's jays, which just eat the cat-food kernels, the scrub jays bury them in the lawn. This morning several scrub jays squawked from a bent and broken King apple tree, overtopped by brambles, down in the meadow. Thea and Dory harvested buckets of blackberries from that leafy tump last week. Now a couple of bridge visitors were doing the same, along with the scrub jays, the blue of September's birthstone.

The day before the equinox, a big red-legged frog sat content on an ivy leaf below the hose spigot. Just a few feet away, a tree frog chuckled, a slow, deep hint of the shrill, valley-filling obbligato just six months past and hence. When I went for the mail, a little group of swallows swooped over me, round and round. I fancied they were our resident family come to say goodbye, even as I fancy that they greet me upon arriving each spring. I squeaked back. I could see a few white flickers of swallow wing out over the valley, but most of the flashes came from starlings back-and-forthing over Larsons' place, their rough cuts nothing like the obsidian slicing of the swallows. And then came distinctive *cri-i-ick*s from the sky, as bunch after cluster of sandhill cranes poured over, shimmered over, sixty in all—one for every elk grazing in the valley below.

The long, hot summer—for us, hot is anything over seventy degrees for any length of time, although eighty happens, ninety comes for a day or two, and one hundred has been known—had brought a bumper crop of wild cherries. Cedar waxwings came to get the little fruits, shining rubylike in after-shower sun. The waxwings' excited, electrical lisping made the cherries sound delicious. They left a good many lying on the ground among long grass and long-blown farmyard roses. So on the way back I couldn't resist sampling what looked like a refreshing pie cherry. A bitterer substance I have seldom tasted.

I wrote letters at the porch table all afternoon and into the dusk, until I could no longer see my own scratches. Then I sat on the steps and watched the bats and the stars come out. Firkin sat near me and purred, so happy when anyone shares her porch. A pair of bats circled the yard, taking termites and crane flies. Then an unexpected thrush—a Swainson's—whistled. From the tentative sound, it might have been just arriving, but no, this was benediction. Tomorrow it would be gone.

After moonrise, a killdeer whine-piped along the cobble and a great blue heron opened its bill and let out a sound like a hoarse, bass burp. So the after-summer nights and days are not completely devoid of bird sound. But the chorus of the spring has long finished, and soon even the silent ones won't be here. A great exodus is under way. Much of it is invisible, the migrants leaving in the night like motel guests skipping out on their bills. But one year I witnessed a decampment so flagrant that it left me breathless.

It was the autumn equinox, six months to the week since the swallows had arrived. I was on the porch drinking my morning coffee and reading the mail, basking with Bokis. At eleven I noticed that the sunny sky beyond Swede Park was *full* of swallows, milling and hunting by the hundreds prior to checking out. Most of them were violet-greens, but trees and barns were also visible. Half an hour later, they had all shifted to the south side of the valley, acting out Keats's line "And gathering swallows twitter in the skies."

By one o'clock, numbers of swallows were hawking above Elk

Mountain. One thinks of swallows and bats as locking onto their targets like Top Gun, and it's curtains for the prey, but that is not necessarily so. Many moths employ a battery of evasive tools, including ears that can hear the bats' squeaks and clickers to jam their sonar. Bats miss moths as often as they strike, as you can see by watching them interact around big lights. It is harder to gauge swallows' success in sifting the aerial plankton, but I know they're not infallible. Twice I watched swallows desultorily go for a painted lady on high and miss. As they soared over Elk Mountain, more and more of the swallows kept on going. And by three, they all were gone. I'd had their company for six months; now I would miss them for just as long, while they lived another life I could never know.

As the swallows departed, I saw the first Asian ladybirds arriving from the south.

WHEN THE PHOLCUS finally subdues the crane fly, I sit back and suck the frozen strawberry I placed in my tea two hours ago. During the coming months, I'll be just as likely to suck up a ladybug in my tea. Asian ladybird beetles (*Harmonia axyridis*) are everywhere. Some are a clear, pale orange; others are russet, citrus, or chestnut, and a few are black. The orange ones have anywhere from zero to nineteen black spots; the black ones, two big, bright, fire-engine-red spots. Yet they are all the same species, and our house has thousands of them, clustered in the corners and creeping up and down along the moldings, the walls, the fogged window glass, on the ceiling. They circle my eyeglasses and my computer screen. One hikes the edge of a sheet of paper and then, like a train switching tracks, passes on to the keyboard before me. Coming to a corner, it flicks its six brown legs, like eyelashes with joints, seeking further purchase. Finding none, it opens its orange elytra, unfurls its wings like folded panels of isinglass, and lifts off. Then it crashes into the monitor with a small *thunk* and falls onto its back. The black, shieldlike thorax, white-spotted behind the eyes, articulates like a neck. The little legs probe the air, the wing cases open again, and the wings hammer against the tabletop until the half-globe rights itself and takes off on another tangent.

Introduction of the Asian ladybird beetle has not, on the whole, been a good thing. Of course original intentions were admirable. The March 1905 issue of a children's magazine, *The School World,* was devoted to injurious insects and promising controls. "The San Jose scale that is doing so much damage to fruit and shade trees in some localities," it said, "will soon be met by another lady-bird beetle that feeds upon it in Japan, the country from which the pest was introduced." Though still sold and released widely for organic garden pest control, the beetles are having other, unexpected consequences. These effective new predators take the eggs of spring azures and other butterflies and attack other beetles, including native coccinellids (ladybirds). Whether through predation or competition, indigenous species have declined to the point where some kinds are disappearing almost completely where *Harmonia* has taken hold. So when I see *Pholcus* catching Asian ladybugs, I have to silently applaud.

The number of ladybirds in our house varies from winter to winter, from a few hundred to thousands. In a big year the beetles may turn up anywhere—in my hair, in my food, in my mouth, poking into every corner, as eager to get out as they were to get in. I open a sash, and they tumble by the dozens out of the rope wells. By March the hungry, thirsty ladybugs bite exposed flesh and become intensely tedious. I watched two of them, one orange, one black, working out on the curved horn of a partially sucked candy cane, head to head and butting until one stepped aside. Experimenting with flavors of jellybeans, I found they lined up at the coconut ones like cattle at a trough, but rejected the licorice, as most folks do. On the first warm, sunny days of spring, just as on the hot days of fall, the air is full of bright sparks with motors and flight plans. Then all of a sudden the ladybugs are gone, and I almost miss them.

Some very good books have been written about nonhuman

householders, including George Ordish's *The Living House* and Vincent Dethier's *The Ecology of a Summer House*. They speak of dozens of species of animals with which the authors shared their abodes, some of which occur at Swede Park. I'd guess that this hundred-year-old human habitation sustains at least one species for every year it has stood. I've never heard of another house where you can find cave crickets with three-inch antennae, several native slugs and snails, and four species of salamanders (Pacific Northwest, red-backed, long-toed, and ensatina) without even going outdoors.

The indoor wildlife of Swede Park occupy particular habitat niches, just as the outdoor dwellers do. Clothes moths, by far the least welcome lepidopterans on the premises, frequent Bokhara carpets and my grandmother's blue silk Chinese rugs. Honeybees and deer mice inhabit the walls. Minute gray beetles dwell in the dust on my desk. Various woodboring beetles and their hymenopteran parasitoids and their hemiparasites emerge now and then from floorboards and windowsills. Starlings take up residence in the stovepipe as briefly as bats do in the bedroom. The center of diversity of this zoo of opportunity is the permeable stone-walled cellar. This is where the cave crickets lurk among the rocks dislodged by plumbers, where salamanders show up in the sump-pump well, and where Bokis stalked an array of rodents that would have been much better off outside.

I used to keep a grotty little pub called the Slug & Leek for myself and friends down in the cellar. The pub sign depicted a banana slug rampant on the stalk of a great leek. The three grades of house ale I aspired to brew were Very Ordinary Bitter, Best Specimen, and Old Slugbait; the house motto was "Have a slug, take a leak." Fayette and I played darts in the dim light and watched the rough pointing between the stones ooze and spurt when the river was in flood, creating a solid stream across the concrete floor to the sump pump with its periodic background hum. The walls of the Slug & Leek were lined with English public-house memorabilia, including species lists of beers and birds from our forays in the U.K., but over the years the resident banana slugs stripped the labels off all the bottles as they laid their opalescent sheen and shiny, loopy shit over every artifact.

CANOEING GRAY'S RIVER at the end of summer. I load *Ms. Wahkiakum* atop Powdermilk, my Honda, after noon, as the grandkids of neighbors troop across the corner of the woods and down the driveway, headed for the covered bridge. At eighteen feet, the wood-and-fiberglass Old Town is longer than the car and hangs over at either end. But they are the same shade of ivory and fit together well as an amphibious combo. I have had the canoe since 1979 and the car since 1982. In amplexus like this, they anticipate the Honda hybrids, conspiring for efficiency through the mere sipping of gasoline and the use of paddle power instead of by the alternation of gas and electricity.

I wend through the valley, avoiding the Harleys and the weekend beach traffic on the highway. The blackberries at the boat ramp are so good, cooking in the sun like hot berry pie, that my launch is a little delayed. Lianas of marah and English ivy hang from the alders over the ramp. The tide is up pretty high; a couple of fishers stand on the shore above, and a boat is docked below Duffy's Irish Pub. Ravens gravitate to the baroque outcrops of the tavern, which has been creatively cobbled together by a non-Irishman named Salazar on the crumbling shell of the old Valley Tavern. "You look real purty out there," calls a friendly voice from Duffy's deck. "The water's fine," I toss back. "So's the beer," says the logger; work in the woods shut down early today because of fire danger.

Japanese knotweed leaves float by like chalky palms on the tidal current. I glide below the blacksmith shop, its rusty roof and sagging saltbox soon to settle into the fundament, and the Grange Hall, walls and name newly painted, ready for many more winters.

Flat, broad, still water carries thin late-summer scum at the slack of the tide. I detour to save a bumblebee from drowning. It

accipiter, the sharp-shinned hawk, commonly skims all the bird feeders and gardens around here. The Cooper's, about the size of a red-tailed hawk, is much more common than the larger gos but rarer than the smaller sharpie. Sometimes we suspect the hawk's presence, as on this morning's mail walk, when we heard dozens of crows and jays screaming, obviously mobbing something in the tulip tree. Checking it out, we put up the Cooper's. And whenever the band-tails congregate in the boughs of Ahlberg's oaks, we're not surprised to see that big gray shadow appear, as pigeon feathers fly.

One mid-autumn morning I was working in my study when I heard a double thump outside. Running out to have a look, I saw what looked like the UNICEF dove spread-eagled on the mossy mat of the front lawn—a band-tailed pigeon, dead. My first thought was for dinner, my second for what killed it, so I acted on both. Lifting the hefty bird, I carried it to the compost heap and commenced to pluck it. The rich, truly dove-gray morning suit came off in puffs and struggles, covering the kitchen slops with a pearly alluvium. When I got to the bluish flesh, I cut shallowly into the skin of the breast, as I remembered from preparing bird skins in ornithology class. Then I carefully slit the peritoneum and exposed the digestive tract.

I found seven big English oak acorns in the crop, two in the gizzard (one broken up, one whole), and acorn mash in the stomach. No wonder the bird couldn't get enough lift when the Cooper's came along! Apparently the pigeon, trying to fly off, struck the front of the house, then dropped onto the porch roof and onto the ground, its neck broken. The accipiter split, so I got the bird. Hunters have since told me that a dove doesn't need to be gutted; they cook it whole, so that the stomach contents add to the flavor, then just pluck out and eat the breast meat. But I scoured the gut nonetheless. When I had a naked pigeon, I marinated it in wine and baked it with its giblets and chanterelles. Yum! Mourning doves, though tasty, provide mere morsels of breasts. This big bird gave drumsticks as well, enough for a generous meal for two. The flesh was exceedingly delicious, dark and winy, nutty and firm. When I lived in Connecticut I harvested campus acorns, dried and ground them for flour, and made oak-nut pancakes and bread. This kind bird did the work for me, preparing the sweet acorn stuffing, then adding its own generous flesh. A special part of the experience was knowing that this gustatory gift embodied the fruits of the very oaks that Ahlberg planted when our home was his.

Eating the band-tail was illegal but pleasurable. *Columba fasciata* requires mineral licks to help replenish the rich "pigeon milk" both parents regurgitate for the young (a remarkable instance of convergent evolution with mammals). The sediments they need are uncommon, and band-tails are too rare to be hunted any longer, so our native forest pigeon has been removed from the list of legal game birds. Even for allowable game, one needs a license to take it with the state's sanction. But I wasn't about to miss the opportunity to consume this fine creature. The very next day we just missed a sumptuous follow-up, as our silver tabby, Virga, charged a ring-necked pheasant lured by the acorns. *That* would have been a catch.

I hunt insects chiefly, and most of those are catch-and-release. Yet I gratefully dine on larger quarry that has been fairly taken from the land by hunters I respect. Every old family here hunts deer and elk, and it is a rare autumn when some sausages, steaks, or fillets do not find their way to us from generous friends. Fishers bring salmon, sturgeon, and crab, and bird hunters feed us duck and dove and pheasant. But drawing directly upon the food chain oneself is even more real and rewarding. Last spring in eastern Washington, Thea and I foraged for morels and wild asparagus, coming up with just enough of each to garnish one meal. The main course came when, sadly, I clipped a beautiful cock California quail with the truck's bumper. Once in Austria I hit a Hungarian partridge and failed to claim it, and I have rued it ever since. This time I collected the quail and took it home with the morels and asparagus. Prepared and consumed together that night, with Shiraz and equal parts gratitude and gusto, they were sublime.

One day in the spring, as I walked to the compost, I disturbed a patter of feet in the salal and huckleberries off to my right by the Broken Oak. The mother's mewling and her chicks' tweets told me it was a single-parent family of ruffed grouse. A few days later, returning from her run, Thea surprised the big babies grubbing the driveway. Now, in early fall, I watch two ruffed grouse poking through the undergrowth above Loop Road and know they are probably the survivors of that family. Only once has the other local species of forest chicken, the blue grouse, appeared at Swede Park. After a week's absence, we returned to find one that had crashed through the living room window and lay dead on the floor. Aged meat is one thing, but this bird had gone too far for the pot. The grouse are safe here from hunters' guns. For my own part, I'd always rather watch a bird than shoot it. But if a coyote were to drop one and leave it for me, I wouldn't turn down the gift.

IT IS THE birds of passage that most mark the seasons by their alternating presence and absence. They have so many ways of coming and going. A hermit thrush makes a momentary cameo in the back garden on its way to higher country. A flock of western meadowlarks or mourning doves, temporarily lost on the wrong side of the Cascades, give voice where they are least expected. Ten snipe and seven swans materialize at Larson's pond. Two or three dozen hooded mergansers dive cleanly in the silver meadows, and a pied-billed grebe sinks in the Lily Pond like an aquatic elevator. Double-crested cormorants, visiting from their massive colonies on the sand islands of the Columbia, fish up the river, their throat pouches flashing the color of the afternoon school bus. A green heron is profiled by the moonlight on the long arch of a dead oak bough over the road or as a slow dark form rising up from the river with a catlike shriek. The great blue heron sounds a dyspeptic *kronk* as its pale bulk lofts toward a roost in a hemlock grove far up Phelps Road. The white, mild-winter monuments of cattle egrets hang out with the Burkhalters' herd, and the great egret, like a bleached great blue, stalks voles beside the ED SEZ — LBJ FOR THE USA shed, where sandhill cranes sometimes descend. Usually the cranes pass on high, one day in spring and another in the fall: we hear their eerie, chummy hoots, then run outside to see them circling away on high thermals. Many local people call the herons cranes, but certain farmers will call to tell us when real cranes have landed.

Not all the landings are happy ones. I've found a red-throated loon and a red-necked grebe that had crash-landed on rainy roads during migration, having mistaken them for water. The grebe didn't live. But the loon stood, defiant, on the asphalt below the Peaceful Hill Cemetery. I pulled the car over, climbed out, and approached the big bird with my raincoat unfurled. I managed to catch it, and it seemed unhurt. But then I had to get it to the Naselle River landing, almost a mile away. It's bad enough to drive with a scratchy cat, but a frightened loon is a whole other matter. I had to hold it firmly in my right arm and drive with my left, acutely aware of that long, sharp bill deployed too close to my eyes. We made it to the landing. I hauled the loon down the ramp to water's edge and flung it toward the river. It splash-landed, turned around, took one look, and dove.

We go downriver to the estuary to see the tundra swans in passage, looking like great bundles of foam clustered on Gray's Bay, or all the way to the coastal swamps for the small icebergs of wintering trumpeters. Of geese, only Canadas stitch their way through, dropping by the thousands to graze among the elk over by Skamokawa, the few duskies dwarfed by the big, pale commons. Ducks of many kinds find their way up the valley, followed by shotguns booming. At dusk in the willow swamp by the Valley Bible Church, I listen for the duck-call mimicry of the mallards, the quail-call falsetto of American widgeons, all but drowning out the low rumbling croaks of the red-legged frogs. By day, on

Durrah's Pond, even at a distance I can tell the drakes of the two species apart by their different emerald crowns, by mallard's chestnut breast compared to widgeon's plum; I distinguish the inky black butts of gadwall and pintail by the latter's sharp, stiff stern. Every year I'm surprised anew by the elegance of the pintail's lapping secondaries, striated sides, silky white neck sickled to its marten-pelt crown: a bird made entirely of curves.

When I witnessed the exodus of all the swallows that September day, I felt as if I were seeing off a loved one—or thousands of them—at the airport. More often we see them gathering for days or weeks, staging for mass departure, but miss the actual event. When Sally Hughes lived here, she once counted more than seven hundred swallows on lines near the Lily Pond. The next day she saw maybe thirty milling high over the covered bridge. "This is the third time I've seen the swallows 'visiting' this part of the valley before going on," she wrote in our notebook. "Almost like they were checking out old nesting places to make sure no bird was left behind." I like that thought. But in the end, when the birds go, it is we who are left behind. No wonder that when they vacate the valley, whether they were summer breeders or just callers on a winter's afternoon, they leave a hole in the heart.

The memory of all those departers echoes in the vacuum of their absence. When the swallows and thrushes leave, I feel less deserted than bereft. And from the birds that stay behind—the kingfishers, chickadees, and kinglets, the wrens, towhees, fox and song sparrows—along with the occasional frog awake in the winter, the crenelated cascara moths that hibernate in the house, and the perpetual evergreens, I feel a silly, solipsistic sense of what I can only call loyalty. Of course their staying has nothing to do with us, except maybe when we fill the feeders or leave the windows open. It is really just their own adaptation, their willingness to stay put, and their ability to tough out the chilly wintergreen rains to come. Much like our own peculiar persistence.

10 ⋅ Chinooks and Chanterelles

Oh, lovely, lovely river,
Bathed in the moon's soft beams;
Again and again you come to haunt
Your sons' and daughters' dreams.

— HARRIET ALTA MESERVE, "Grays River Beautiful"

Comes the fall, and big creatures return to the valley even as the smaller are departing. The herds of Roosevelt elk that have haunted the hills all summer long drift down the muddy slopes and swales to crop the pastures, to bugle through the fogs, to rut. We'll look out over the fields one day and see forty or fifty large lumps lounging or lunging in the damp grass. Not the usual cattle, but the black-necked, fawn-bodied, white-assed masses that mean elk. Yesterday they were in Schmand's field, today Fittses', tomorrow maybe Linquist's. We watch as they slowly drift upvalley on skinny legs, so many logs balanced on sticks. Cows and calves greatly outnumber spikes and bulls, a ratio that will soon become even more weighted toward the female side.

For next month means elk season, the time of guns and thunder, when hunting camps and rigs materialize like forest fungi. Of the many who buy elk tags, some proportion actually emerge from the woods with a dead animal. When you see the successful hunters at Rosburg Store with big antlers poking awkwardly out of their pickup beds, their smiles shade from satisfied entitlement to outright surprise. Gloria Clark, the youngest of the Gray's River Swanson sisters, runs the liquor agency in Naselle. In fall her cold locker fills with red-and-white-striped carcasses hanging from hooks in the ceiling and with their off-sweet smell.

A farmer who can show economic loss caused by the depredations of wapiti on his pastures may obtain an "elk damage permit" from the state, which allows him to shoot one or more of the offending animals. Some landowners with more cupidity than conscience have been known to exploit these permits to get free meat without having to buy an elk tag, and some have even tried to sell the meat. But people here take their elk hunting seriously and are vigilant about damage to the herd.

Thea and I are also experienced hunters, of different prey, stationary yet also elusive. For elk season is also mushroom season. "Midnight mushrumps," as Shakespeare called them, have their center of diversity in the maritime Northwest: some three thousand fruiting species. The fungus burst in our overlogged Willapa Hills is subtler than what you'd find in the Cascades or Olympics, but it's enough for us. Thea and I met in a mushroom class almost forty years ago, and we hunt them still. Just as local youths catch "deer fever" in the fall, which cuts school attendance in half during the season's opening week, Thea comes down with fungus fever. On one anniversary spent in a spot thick with chanterelles above the Oregon coast, Thea announced, "I am *very* happy." And she is very good: I would not want to be a chanterelle in the same woods with her. She finds her favored fungus from July into December, but mid- to late fall is best, depending on the rains. Her birthday falls near Labor Day, and she often opts to celebrate by hunting mushrooms close to home; this year we returned from our hunt with thirteen pounds of perfect chanterelles and one big, pristine *Sparassis,* or cauliflower mushroom. I love to watch Thea comb the woods, creeping among the ferns, spying and bending and cutting and plucking the bright golden prize.

Thousands of acres of second-growth hemlock, perfect chanterelle nurseries, used to cover these hills. Recent logging has
taken almost all of them; only a scrap or two of prime habitat remains among the baby third-growth within walking distance of
our house. But as other woods mature toward the ripe old age for
pulp crops of thirty years or so, we find new chanterelle fields
not so very far away. These succulent, broad-gilled apricot flutes
can easily desiccate, waterlog, or fail to show, but at their best
they are golden horns of plenty. Even their scientific name is sat-
isfying to speak: *Cantharellus cibarius.* Pursuing them, we also
come across red and maroon russulas, sulphurs, pastel corals,
and the Day-Glo crimson crust of lobster mushrooms, which are
the big white funnels of *Russula brevipes* transfigured by a sec-
ondary fungus. Strange spiky hydnums, turkeytail shelves, or-
ange-peel cups called *Pezizes,* witches' nipples, and elfin saddles
all appear at our feet, and sometimes the most beautiful of all,
the deep purple velvet *Cortinaria violacea.*

For eating, we stick mostly to chanterelles. Safety lies in consuming what you know best, and it hasn't been many seasons
since a local teen succumbed to poisonous little brown mushrooms he thought were psychedelic liberty caps. We won't turn
up our noses at a fresh cauliflower mushroom, fine for fritters;
sunset-colored chicken-of-the-woods, if it's really fresh; ditto for
big puffballs; bulky, succulent, scaly *Lepiota rachodes,* which
come up reliably in the compost; a mess of shaggymanes or oyster mushrooms; or meadow mushrooms from Larson's fields, the
same species you buy at the store, but as superior to them as Diane's free-range eggs are to the pallid supermarket version. But
why bother with anything else when you have chanterelles?

The one big exception, and I mean big, is the king bolete. *Bo-
letus edulis* is known in Germany as *Steinpilz* and in France as
cep, and everywhere it is prized. Right here at Swede Park,
they pop up almost every fall in the ivy beneath the Tall Oak,
alongside fly agarics—those glorious, white-warted scarlet cliché
gnome's toadstools that people of some cultures, willing to put

up with a very bad bellyache for a high, have eaten to elicit visions. We make our rituals instead with boletes or chanterelles: sautéed in butter, cooked in soup, filling an omelet, pickled for Christmas, lining a rare elk steak. Or skip the elk and slice succulent fillets from the great honey-brown caps of the *Steinpilz,* all the sweeter for having arisen in our very ground.

ABOUT THE TIME the king boletes peek from last year's oak leaves, the king salmon arrive in the rivers. We hear them flopping under the bridge at night, so loud they sound like cows clumping across the stream: kings can make as much commotion as kine. These are the fall chinooks, also called kings (*Oncorhynchus tshawytscha),* the greatest of the anadromous salmonids. Summer chinooks, which used to reach a hundred pounds or more, were known as "June hogs." Now most members of the autumn runs are hatchery-bred and released, though some wild salmon still come up. The smaller silver, or coho, salmon (*O. kisutch*) escort them like knights in chain mail.

I have fished for both species in the ocean and in the zoolike Buoy 10 fishing frenzy on the Columbia River. In years when the salmon return allows, this brief opening sees thousands of sport fishers crammed into a narrow zone below the Astoria Bridge, a great unruly gauntlet, and trying not to bump into one another. One time I went with Dan Penttila, a fisheries biologist who is crazy about fishing. I hooked a large chinook, the only one that any of our poles "had on" that day. "It must be forty pounds!" shouted Dan, and he coached me for minute after straining minute. "Let a little line out! Keep the tip up! Not too fast! Reel in the slack!"

When the king finally maneuvered around to the back of the boat and broke my line on the motor, Dan's parents, Harte and Dorothy, just said, "Aw, too bad." But Dan's disgust knew no bounds, and it took me a long time to live down my screwup. Still, I took home three cohos, enough to fillet and grill for weeks to come. Thea and I love good, fresh, wild-caught salmon as much as any meal. Yet when we consider the state of the fishery overall, we eat the succulent pink meat with some compunction as well as pleasure.

The sheer number and mass of chinook, coho, chum, pink, and sockeye in various runs staggered Lewis and Clark when they came; they found whole cultures based on salmon. After the Indians were mostly extirpated by disease, the natural profligacy of the fish inspired a commercial frenzy. Everyone around here knows stories from the time when canneries, fish wheels, and fishing boats crammed the Columbia with life and commerce, all driven by salmon. All the old-timers say you could walk across the creeks on the backs of the spawners. As the fishery evolved, the practical and beautiful butterfly fleet—dories named for their widespread sails—gave way to more prosaic but still handsome diesel sternpickers and bowpickers. Fish wheels were banned, and the salmon runs held up for a while.

Then came the many hydroelectric dams on the Columbia and its tributaries, frustrating the upriver migration for many would-be spawners and, for those that make it past the ladders, grinding their offspring, the ocean-bound smolts, in their turbines. Giant oceangoing drift-net trawlers appeared offshore, far hungrier than the river-based gillnetters. In recent years mariculture based on Atlantic salmon has arisen in Pacific waters. Escapees from fish farms interfere with locally adapted gene pools even more than hatchery releases already have. Farmed salmon beat out the fishing fleet at the market with inferior, artificially dyed carcasses, inspiring bumper stickers reading FRIENDS DON'T LET FRIENDS EAT FARMED SALMON. Fouling of the Columbia by radionucleides, dioxins, PCBs, trichloroethylene, and other chlorinated hydrocarbons became routine. As if these challenges weren't enough, seals and sea lions have increased in the Columbia, lying in wait for roe-rich bellies near the fish ladders, and dredge-spoil islands near the river mouth have lured a large part of the world's population of Caspian terns, with their hunky orange bills, and a great many double-crested cormorants, all feeding chiefly on salmon smolts racing for the relative safety of the sea.

As a final blow, steep-slope logging bared our ridges so that the rain, ten feet of it per year, washed mountains' worth of silt down onto the spawning gravels. Salmon literally bit the dust, to the point that the Northwest fishing industry fled largely to Alaska, and eleven Columbia and Snake salmonids were federally listed as threatened or endangered, including four runs in Gray's River. Because of all these trends, salmon recovery measures, quixotic or not, dominate much of the regional agenda today: culvert replacements, siltation arrest structures, and pollution abatement among them. The 2004–05 season saw bumper runs again, due to abundant hatchery fish returns and favorable, no-Niño conditions in the Pacific Ocean. But the improvement proved temporary and illusory. The early 2006 returns were so low that even much of the offshore fishery was closed for the first time. Overall, the fishin' just ain't what it used to be.

Even an infrequent fisherman such as I can't help but register the losses. I have floated on Gray's River in a graceful wooden drift boat built for catching steelhead with friends who wonder why I don't fish almost out my front door for this most jealously (and zealously) sought-after of Northwest fish: *Oncorhynchus mykiss irideus,* also known as oceangoing rainbow trout. It seems to me that if the steelhead get this far after such a journey, I ought to leave them to it; even if I were willing to trade my warm bed for the cold river before dawn, the fish I caught might be the one that carried the crucial eggs or milt for the next generation. These days wild steelhead must be released, and even those from the hatchery, known by their clipped dorsal fins, are fewer than in former times. Dedicated steelheaders, who used to crowd the banks by the covered bridge on early mornings after winter rains, have thinned out dramatically.

The splashing beneath the bridge on warm autumn evenings is likely to be suckers now instead of the kings we used to hear struggling upriver to spawn. And fisher friends like Kent and Irene Martin are free with their bitter knowledge of why the combined spring and fall fishing seasons on the river now amount to just a few days per year. With the wiping out of an old and sustainable culture on the lower river, the Martins and others now rely on fishing in Alaska to make a living. I've been reeling in a sense of what fish are all about here, but it wasn't until I held a record king salmon in a slimy bear hug that I took this fish truly to heart.

One autumn I worked three nights a week as a Fish Culturist I (Security)—night watchman—at the Naselle Salmon Hatchery. Each night I made eleven rounds, thirty-three in a week, totaling 13.2 miles, keeping the precious incoming hen salmon safe from roe thieves. Mostly I encountered raccoons along the riverbanks, their eyes like green spotlights, and geometer moths and giant stoneflies at the office windows. One night a great blue heron rose through the fog. Another midnight it flew along a catwalk, looking very much like a man running away, making my heart race. Cats and bats were the rest of my company. And every night thousands of cross-spider webs hung on the fences, outlined by droplets of mist.

The fish splashed on the stones of the river, shimmered in the attraction channel, thumped in the races, leaped in the ladders, and made shadows and ripples in the pools. Fry skittered in their concrete ponds as I passed. The shifting sounds and smells of the hatchery sat well with a nocturnal animal such as I. The pipes and pumps sounded like hippos at their bath, then went silent when I rounded to a different vantage. But as the numbers of arriving chinooks and cohos increased into the hundreds, they got noisier, splashing and gliding and jumping, sometimes flopping out of their pools. One night a dead coho lay in the spawning area, a huge leap out of the coho pond. I was led to it by a little orange cat, who was trying to figure out how to deal with a fish bigger than she was without getting her paws wet. I thought of the time I caught Bokis on the kitchen counter, one paw on a huge baked salmon. Many of these fish had a white fungus on their eyes, gill covers, and fins, sometimes nearly all over. They shoved through the algae at the edge of the asphalted ponds as if trying to rub off the fungus. But this one on the concrete was bright. I left it for the morning workers to deal with.

Then one night, after watching two large salmon resting in the eddy around the corner from the fish-ladder entrance, I walked past the adult holding ponds and had nearly reached the spawning shed when I heard a terrific *splash!* and *flop!* and knew that a fish must have leapt out of the holding pond—a prodigious leap, which only three bright cohos of ten pounds or so and one tiny jack or cutthroat had managed on my watch. Only the jack, six inches or so and a few ounces, was alive for me to throw back when I came upon it. But the fish I found on the spawning-shed floor was a huge chinook weighing thirty pounds or more. I had great difficulty subduing it, as it flapped around with all the power of its migratory muscle, soaking my feet and pants legs with weighty slaps. Ed Maxwell, the manager, told me that such monsters had knocked him windless and shoeless with their tails, and he had showed me how to hold the narrowing between the tail and caudal fin with thumb and fingers. I tried, but I couldn't close my fingers around even that slenderest part. Twice I lifted the fish, only to drop it. Finally, on the third breathless try, I lofted the huge salmon on my left arm, balanced its mass against my chest, its tail in my right hand. Before it could lurch from my tenuous grasp again, I *heaved* it up toward the fence top, three feet away and three feet up from where I stood. The great beast sailed over the fence and splashed into the water.

Never before, even when landing a twenty-six-pound chinook, had I sensed the sheer power that drives a massive anadromous fish up current, river, rapid, and waterfall. I understood then how they could make the leaps required to get to the spawning grounds—leaps, indeed, like the one that had gotten this fish into big trouble. Lucky for the fish that I was there, though it hadn't long to live in any case, since spawning salmon die at the end of their race. I hurried up to the manager's house to share the encounter with Ed and Cathy. I wondered why they backed away a bit, until I noticed that my down parka was generously smeared with fish slime. No wonder those who work in a cannery call it "the slime line." Maybe I'd earned my salary that night. But when I returned to my rounds, I realized that in my excitement I'd tossed the big king salmon into the coho pond.

At least, since it was stranded among the smaller silvers, my chinook was easy to identify. It turned out to weigh forty-three pounds, the largest fish ever to have returned to the Naselle Hatchery in its ten years of operation. Ed froze it, and I was later able to visit my big fish in the walk-in freezer and heft it again. Somehow, it wasn't the same.

THIS YEAR, after an early flood, several chum salmon (*Oncorhynchus keta*) were stranded in pasture ponds. Their dorsal fins cut the surface like small sharks as they cruised the underwater grasses. A few days later, two chum lay dead in the receding pond between the blackberry bank and the old King apple tree in the pasture below the house. One was already melting into the mud. The other lay on his side, half covered in silt, his recurved bill hidden in the drowned straw. His lateral and pectoral fins stuck up, all veined and stiff, looking like butterfly wings of a nacreous, muddy mauve. Only the pale pink sunset of once blood-red streaks along his side gave the fish away as the endangered chum.

The flood receded, leaving strange decorations of fish skins several feet up in trees along Satterlund Road, but the rain fell for several more days. When the sun came out the day after Thanksgiving, we walked to the bridge. There, in a pond on the other side of Covered Bridge Road, ripples across the quiet surface betrayed another salmon. For more than a week he had been stuck in the field puddle and was still swirling back and forth. I thought of trying to catch him in a net and carry him to the river a few yards away, in case he might still manage to spawn. After all, I've heard of people tossing them into their trucks right along Loop Road. But he was probably too exhausted to fight the heavy flow coming down the Gray's. Besides, the spawning channel for Gray's River's small chum run had been taken out by a recent flood. As we walked away, the fish's scales shone gold in the sun, his sanguine chum marks showed beneath the water line, and his frayed dorsal fin stood still.

AS THE SALMON, the chanterelles, the elk become scarcer, those who have long harvested them grow more fervid. So it is with razor clams. In recent years a clam parasite that produces domoic acid, a nerve agent that can cause memory loss, has damaged the clamming season on Washington beaches more than the clams themselves. If the acid level in the population drops to an acceptable level and the season can thus open normally, the many devotees of the large and delectable bivalves take to the beaches in great digging packs. If one is on Long Beach Peninsula (forty miles west of here) for a low tide at night, the damp strand glitters for miles with lantern light. When the opening of razor clam season coincides with a propitious tide, fair weather, and a weekend, we really notice the highway. As we do on any bright summer weekend when the beaches beckon or during any of the calendar's run of tourist events that keep the beach towns ticking—the Cranberry, Kite, Sand Castle, and Garlic festivals, the World's Longest Garage Sale, and, worst of all, the Rod Run to the End of the World.

As soon as I came to live at Swede Park—only on weekends for the first few months—I discovered one major flaw in the rural idyll: State Route 4, which forms the northern border of our land. Also known as the Ocean Beach Highway, SR4 originates in Longview, where the Columbia makes its final turn westerly to the sea, and terminates at Johnson's Landing on the Naselle River estuary. U.S. 101 subsumes SR4's route from there to Long Beach Peninsula beyond Naselle. But by whatever name or number, this road connects the lowland trough at the base of the Cascades (Interstate 5) with the coast. I am aware of it each time a logging truck lumbers around our curve with its air brakes bleating, or a chip truck whooshes by in the depths of the night, or a stream of autos, trucks, motor homes, and Harleys blasts past on a sunny Saturday, beachbound.

In its early years, the village of Gray's River was reached only by water. Packet steamers from Astoria, linking with ships from San Francisco and river boats from Portland, brought people, mail, and goods to the head of tidewater. Many settlers, including those at Swede Park, lived well upstream, where the river was too shallow for navigation, so a system of trails and cart roads developed throughout the valley. If you wanted to go to the village for a Grange meeting, a dance, a church service, or to visit Meserve's Store or the post office, it meant a muddy trek of two or three miles by rutted track or sodden footpath. The railroad never penetrated these parts, except for short lines belonging to local logging companies. One such railroad came down from K-M Mountain, extended by the Portland Logging Company downriver to the landing and the shingle mill in the village. I find it difficult to imagine locomotives and flatcars, each carrying a single log, running right through the valley, but Bobby Larson and Marie Fauver remember them. These logging trains did little to improve basic transportation for the residents, but they did lay down routes for future roads.

As citizens came to desire an easier way out of their isolated region, pressure grew for an overland route to link the southwestern part of the state with Portland, Oregon, and points north in Washington. There was a rough way that followed old Indian trade routes across the Gray's River Divide and thence along the Columbia. But the shoreline was too rugged to build an affordable road, so a route over the hills, in part following the logging railways, was chosen. Landowners (never imagining the invention of semitrailers with decompression brakes—known throughout logging-land as jake brakes) gladly gave rights of way for a new route and turned out in volunteer parties to move earth by hand and horse.

K-M Mountain was finally rounded. As the *Oregonian* reported on August 26, 1932,

> Things are happening in south western Washington. People are going calling on each other. Farmers and loggers of Grays River and Deep River are getting better acquainted with fishermen of Skamokawa and Cathlamet . . . Why? All because the Ocean Beach Highway has finally been connected for all-year travel between Kelso and Longview and beach resorts, traversing the three counties of Cowlitz, Wahkiakum, and Pacific, all fronting the Columbia River.

The road was designated State Route 830 back then. It crossed the river near Fossil Creek, then ran below our house along what is now Loop Road and on into Gray's River village. The current gradient, above and behind us, was engineered in 1938 and the road renamed Route 4. Ed Sorenson told me that the realignment of the road disturbed the slope and spring-lines, mucking up the well in summer and flooding much of our back yard in winter but also lifting the increasing traffic out of our front yard.

The road proved a mixed blessing to the community. Some local businesses collapsed because the highway furnished an easy way out as well as in, while others capitalized on the new tourist trade. Gray's River would never be the same, and the river traffic dwindled from daily arrivals to none in a few years. For those along the right of way, the challenge changed from living in practical isolation to living beside a highway. For my part, the road both brought me here and gave me the single greatest reason—larger than a house fire, divorce, relative poverty, or the rain—to consider leaving. There have been times, on sunny Sundays with heavy beach traffic or after the tenth jake-brake salute of the morning from a logging truck, when I've sworn I would move. I know I would never choose another home so close to a main road. But I hate the thought of moving. And where would we go? How could we ever find a place we could afford that offers the view, the life, the relative peace that this one does? We just don't *want* to leave. So we live with the road.

In the early years I sketched elaborate plans for walls made of free concrete cylinders, cast to test the mix and then discarded, piled thirty feet or more, to block the thoroughfare from our sight and hearing. I never built them. The cottonwoods I planted along the bank failed. Had I planted western red cedars twenty years ago, they would now be a tall, thick screen. But at least there is a scrim of oaks and other hardwoods, and the mammoth Port Orford cedar that blocks off a good stretch of the eastern roadway still stands. Horrified, I watched three of its four crowns break off during the Inauguration Day storm in 1993, but the tallest, and its generous lower skirt, remained intact.

Then there are the wrecks. At least half a dozen times since I've been here, a vehicle has left the road or two have collided above Swede Park, and I am no longer surprised at night when I hear that sickening *whump!* A bad curve just east of us has contributed to the toll, as have weather, speed, and alcohol. Two county commissioners went over the edge and down the hill because of ice on the road. I've helped move people off the road who, not wearing a seatbelt, exited via the windshield with unintended nose jobs, and I've gathered people's rain-dampened belongings strewn down our slope. Most of the accidents have been relatively minor. One drunk seemed proud of how his Pontiac had graded and scraped the slope at our eastern approach; I rescued the turfed out spruces and replanted them. Thankfully, we were away at the time of a head-on that was fatal to a neighbor and an immigrant family. But one day when we were home, I felt as much as heard a heavy concussion nearby and told Thea I thought a truck had left the road around the bend. We ran to look and found the log truck upside down, its wheels still spinning, the cab crushed by the load of logs. The volunteer EMTs answered our call in minutes, and the driver, though critically injured, remarkably lived.

But in fact the highway isn't as bad as I thought it would be.

Most of the time it is quiet here, or at least other sounds are more noticeable than road noise. This afternoon I poked my nose out to hear the tinkle and buzz of a feeding flock of autumn birds. The butterfly bushes, maples, and oaks were full of flickering wings. Chestnut-backed and black-capped chickadees, ruby-crowned and golden-crowned kinglets, and bright black-and-yellow Townsend's warblers all worked the late vegetation, searching for every edible creature and seed. A chestnut-backed chickadee in the snowball bush, its rich russet mantle and coral-washed sides arrayed against the last red leaves, speaking its name in sweet, nasal syllables, goes a long way toward stilling any number of logging trucks.

I've come to see that there is something engaging about mobile human life passing by—the Schwan's frozen food truck visiting the neighbors, the ambulance or trooper's siren and concern for what it might imply, the unknown stories inside each lighted car that whispers by in the night, the surflike *swoosh!* of the red Puget Sound chip trucks on their way to the paper mill in Longview. More and more, I've tried to emulate this familiar poem by Sam Walter Foss:

> There are hermit souls that live withdrawn
> In the place of their self-content . . .
> But let me live in a house by the side of the road
> And be a friend to man.

Twice I have found this poem posted outside homes situated hard by roadways. At a cottage opposite a pub in Grantchester, England, outside Cambridge, the poem appeared on a wooden sign in the narrow cottage garden. And next to a hand-built stone house along the Chehalis River north of here, the closing stanza of the poem is inscribed on a slab of Willapa basalt. The tranquility of both idyllic dwellings no doubt suffered from the brewers' drays and log trucks, hot rods and step vans passing by. But their residents both chose to see the road as a window on the world. Since I have no desire to uproot and will probably never build a wall, that attitude makes sense to me. And it might not be too late to plant those cedars.

I LOVE THE propitious juxtapositions of color out-of-doors, like the ruby foreheads of redpolls among rosehips in a white winter scene. The propitious part is in the noticing. Most natural hues neither match nor clash, but their interplay gives coherence to the random landscape. One afternoon not long after Thanksgiving, the sun slides out of its envelope and lights the treetops. We take a walk on Kandoll Road, where the short arm called Seal Slough curves out of Gray's River and almost back again. The soggy bottomlands are nearly depopulated now, the farms for sale, most houses empty. The land, having seen its century of human occupation, is going piece by piece to spike rushes, called tussocks around here, and to the Columbia Land Trust for fish and wildlife habitat. Flood wrack decorates the lane, the dike, and the hedges of osier and ninebark. Artifacts of the old abandoned homesteads—a headlamp from a '38 DeSoto, an iron bowl from a cattle stanchion, chunks of clear-grain Douglas-fir molding, a handmade wooden toolbox—lie among the drift. We beachcomb floodwater fence lines.

Spotting a sun-struck lump in the top of an alder, I resolve it into a sharp-shinned hawk, enjoying the last of the sun before a shower arrives. The rufous streaks down its breast look like more of the alder catkins hanging all around the bird. Then Thea spies a red-tailed hawk a little farther on and higher up in a spruce, its back to us, plumage spread to the southwestern sun. Its tail, that signature foxy vane, reflects the exact shade of the abundant Sitka spruce cones. Both hawks fly, flap-flap-flap, flap-flap-glide, like a Lorquin's admiral, to even lonelier and loftier perches. They seem to leave their rusty reds behind in the sides of two towhees cracking old ninebark flowers for their seeds beside the slough. In these short days of contracting prospects for color, such notes stand out in the valley's complexion.

To break up the dark green smear of the conifers, colors don't have to be bright. Had there been no Captain Robert Gray, the name of the river could well have come from its splendid palette of gray tones. Our living room retains the last of the house's wallpaper from long ago: white fern fronds against a ground of deep gray. The wallpaper backs a pair of local artworks that capture the essence of skies and waters here. One is a small acrylic painting by the late Dodson Benedec, who made his studio for a few years in the old Gray's River Creamery building. Its many layers of ash, charcoal, slate, smoke, and lead equally suggest cloud or wave. Below it hangs an image in subtlest shadings, photographed over the Columbia River by David Lee Myers, who worked for thirty years out of nearby Eden Valley. Titled *A Gray Day on Gray's Bay,* it could be a travel poster for a place where no one goes. A gray day is often spoken of in negative terms, as a mere stand-in for sun. But here, conditioned by clouds and wrapped in rain, I rejoice in grays, such as the lichened silver of the alder trunks, which paint whole hillsides with fresh putty stripes.

I appreciate the outlandish tints of tanagers and such bright creatures, but I know few more handsome animals than the great gray slug. *Limax maximus,* its considerable hide spotted and streaked in dove and charcoal, is also called the leopard slug. As elegant as they are in their morning-suit grays, leopards are alien European mollusks that don't belong here. They are even harder on garden plants than the voracious brown garden slugs. Thea regularly reminds me that I had a chance to arrest the leopards' colonization early on. Some fifteen years ago I found a courting pair, the first I'd ever seen. Recalling what I'd read about their astonishing sexual behavior, I placed the pair in a terrarium and watched. But they escaped postcoitus, and our place has been populated with their insatiable descendants ever since.

Recently I came upon another pair already mating. I had real compunction about dispatching them in the depth of their passion. Utterly merged, they were stunning. Like other slugs, the species is hermaphroditic. Each adult both receives and donates sperm. But great grays do not gather in knots of two or three individuals to fuse gonads among the leaf litter, as the brown garden slug does. Nor do they engage in mutual penetration, as our indigenous banana slugs do. This spring Thea found a banana slug with its mammoth penis erect, shaped and capped uncannily like that of a horse. Great grays' parts are something else again, and the species has contrived a copulatory routine so bizarre as to raise the most jaded eyebrows. "Raise" is an apt verb, for these slugs begin their union by climbing high up a tree trunk or a wall, then circling for an hour or more, mutually caressing with their tentacles and secreting copious gummy mucus. Then, gluing a sticky launching pad to the surface they're on, they drop into the abyss on a shared bungee cord of congealed slime. There they dangle, two climbers moved to merge in mid-belay.

To the cats' apparent disgust, slugs come to cat food more faithfully than to any slug bait but beer. But the two leopards were sliding up the wall of the house above the cat-food dish, more intent on sex than kibbles. A few minutes later they were already slung and linked, their cable pasted to the clapboard wall, their embrace suspended just above the dish. Firkin the cat, munching, was oblivious to the sex play unfurling inches above her head.

The strand hung three feet, roping the lovers upside down. They wrapped around each other in a double helix, so intertwined that we stiff bony vertebrates could only regard their full-body wrap with envy and awe. They dangled and spun, first this way, then that, as their soft exertions spiraled their gyre. And all the while their milky penis sacs—half their total length—pushed out behind their heads and mingled in a clot of blending zygotes. First palmlike, then feathery, these creneled genitals pulsated and throbbed like sea jellies swimming together: stroking, dancing, fanning, swelling, finally forming a modest and sheltering parasol as climax overcame them.

I'd love to have left them in peace, but I remembered the result of the last time I'd watched and the ensuing years of heavy plant predation and censure. So I took the copulating leopards by their magical harness, laid them gently in a bread bag, and placed them in the freezer alongside a few dozen *Arion ater,* also aliens. Later they enriched the compost, and their magnificence returned to the garden, whence it came. We make our choices: *Limax* or lettuce. I consoled myself with the thought that there are worse ways to enter the Big Sleep than in a state of utter rapture.

Once in a while on these late fall nights, another big beautiful gray animal comes: *Catocala relicta,* the white underwing moth. Only three times since I've been here has this impressive insect arrived at our porch light, always in October or November. I found the latest one hunkered by the doorjamb, a big gray delta nearly two inches on a side. Fox-gray fur, the pile deepest on the thorax, lightened into a silvery pelt knitted with black and white bars, spots, and zigzags across the wings. The stippled scales suggested a thickness appropriate to a dweller of northern places. A prominent white spot like a snowflake graced the center of each forewing. The moth had fine, threadlike antennae, checkered palpi, thick-clad legs like woolen leg warmers. Drawn down into a triangle, the forewings hid the sooty hind wings, with their dramatic white median band. Pleated white margins peeked out like petticoat hems. Though the thorax bulged with strong flight muscles, the moth was logy, maybe just waking to the night.

It was a male. I brought him inside for a close look. Underwing moths are strongly drawn to fruity substances, so I mashed a bit of banana and placed it before him. As soon as his front feet touched the mush, the robust, three-quarter-inch proboscis shot out and began probing the softest, wettest part. His head, with its rabbit-fur ruff, moved up and down as he punched his tongue into the banana's flesh. The undersides of the palpi, legs, thorax, and abdomen were clad in snowy ermine fur. Although the caterpillar's host plants are willows and poplars, the forsaken underwing (as it is also called) is known to rest on birches, whose bark its pattern is built to match. No native birches occur here, but the Swedes planted *Betula pendula* all around, and tall ones grow right outside my study.

Sated, the moth stirred. I put him out the window, but he got fouled in a spider web. I retrieved him, cleaned off the web, and walked him out to a birch, where he climbed the black-and-white trunk in light rain. The native white-lichened alders would work just as well as a cryptic daytime resting place, but I was excited to see *relicta* where it had evolved to be seen—or, rather, remain unseen. I looked away and then, looking back, had to peer hard to pick him out again. The next morning, one of golden birch leaves, I could not find him at all. He must have flown off into the rain-beaten black of night.

Several kinds of geometer moths also haunt the cooling nights. *Ennomos magnaria,* the most robust of the autumn inchworms, is also known as the maple spanworm or the October thorn. Often on Halloween night its heavy body bangs against a window pane, scattering powder from its scalloped yellow wings speckled with grape must. Finally, the flimsy but pretty winter moth (*Operophtera bruccata),* colored either charcoal or oatmeal, appears at otherwise deserted windows.

This Halloween, as usual, I carve two pumpkins with leering grins—one with a Mick Jagger tongue, the other a cat's face—and place them on the sawhorse by the back door to let potential trick or treaters know we are open for business. After the last of the children (this year also the first), I carry the jack-o'-lanterns around to the front of the house and place them on the rail of the porch. Then at midnight I walk down to the covered bridge. Back when Bridgette lived at the bridge, if the night was foul, I'd feel her nudge my ankle in the dark. Then I would take her up under my jacket and lean against a beam for a while, looking out at the rain and scratching her ears. When I returned home, Bokis got his turn, but he wondered why in hell I had another cat's lipstick on my collar.

Now, crossing the river, I look for Old Greenface, the covered bridge's resident haunt, according to the Larsons. I haven't seen him yet, but I keep looking. In the flow beneath the timbers, the last of the fall chinooks breast the current. Casting my eyes across the silky flow of the river, the fields, the slope, up to the dark house, I make out bright glimmers from the pumpkins' grins, chanterelle-orange.

11 ⋆ Tree Time

> . . . there has never been
> A critical tree—about the nature of things.
>
> —HOWARD NEMEROV, "Trees"

Ed Sorenson's grandfather planted many of Swede Park's trees. When I bought the place, Ed offered to take five thousand off the selling price if I would agree not to cut the old trees. I tried to look as if I was thinking it over before agreeing. The task of raking the millions of leaves those trees would produce did not occur to me then. As I have learned since, those leaves are the gift of exercise and compost that never stops giving—at least not until the trees themselves fall. And then comes their other gift: their very bodies, sunlight made manifest in wood.

The trees of the Willapa Hills were once among the largest in the world, redwoods aside. But within a single century, the giant Douglas-firs, western hemlocks, Sitka spruces, and western red cedars nearly all vanished. Logging has shifted from what once seemed a cornucopia of timber from Very Big Trees to a fluctuating trickle of pulp from conifers that could be mistaken for slightly overgrown Christmas trees. Looking out from here into the surrounding mountains, I see evergreens from one to thirty years old. A few seventy-fivers or so remain among the alders on slopes of Elk Mountain that somehow escaped industrial replanting. Although we have managed to protect a few small but important remnants of original forest here and there in the hills, the concept of "big tree" is essentially foreign to Willapa today.

Swede Park is often called "that place with the big old trees." H. P. Ahlberg began planting hardwoods native to Europe and eastern North America a hundred and thirty years ago. There is the Lincoln Oak on the front lawn, and up the slope stands the Broken Oak, another ponderous *Quercus rubra,* which broke in half one February; the easternmost of the twin trunks fell directly between the house and the studio, pulverizing the root cellar. And the massive, ferny trunk of the Tall Oak, also a red, rises beside our entrance drive. At more than 130 feet, it is the tallest ornamental tree recorded in the entire state, excluding redwoods. Along with these three, two other enormous red oaks mount the eastern and western skylines of this sliver of the maritime Northwest, more than a thousand miles from their native range.

A few years ago, when the University of Washington published Robert van Pelt's compilation of the state's champion trees, scored by a point system based on girth, spread, and height, it included five examples from this old farmstead: the #1 and #3 red oak, the #1 European hornbeam, the #1 American basswood, and the #3 tulip tree. And Swede Park has other big trees: English oak, pin oak, black walnut, European beech and birch, Port Orford cedar, Scots pine, and sugar maple, and many other species of lesser proportions.

Few of the trees visible from our house are native. Even the line of heroic Oregon white oaks that Ahlberg planted along the river are thirty miles west of the nearest native examples of this species, *Quercus garryana,* the sole oak indigenous to Washington. Most of the Midwestern and European trees introduced by Ahlberg have reproduced, so that Swede Park now hosts a strange mongrel ecosystem of Old World oaks, beeches, birches, rowans, hornbeams, and maples thriving among Illinois bass-woods and butternuts, oaks and walnuts, and native northwest-ern hemlocks, spruces, cedars, firs, hazels, and alders. One im-pressive Douglas-fir somehow escaped the saw, and the land is graced by a handful of fair-to-middling western hemlocks and Sitka spruces. But most of the really big trees are the orna-mentals favored by the Swede, which have grown bigger and faster than they would have in their native range. Expanding vig-orously in the high rainfall of the Willapa, they become too heavy for their tensile strength and thus often break. We have paid high-climbing tree surgeons to prune large branches that might otherwise fall onto the house. The Lincoln Oak, which has twice dropped massive limbs the size of trees elsewhere, works hard to restore its form after both cuts and breaks. Though I have kept my promise to Ed not to cut the trees, plenty of wood comes down on its own. While others around here burn hemlock and alder, we burn oak.

In fact, we haven't been able to use all the wood. Some re-mains on the ground, providing homes to the many organisms I dislodge in the splitting. Some we give to friends. And one re-cent fall we were able to send a couple of cords of oak across the Columbia to the anagama kiln in Clatsop County, Oregon. This dragon-shaped kiln consumes great quantities of wood in firings that last several days and nights to bake masses of pots at very high temperatures. When I heard that fuel was needed for the next firing, I volunteered to furnish a heap of good oak if I could get some help with the splitting.

So it was that I spent a week in August in company with my peavey. It is amazing how much weight one can shift, Archime-des-like, with a peavey. It is still more amazing that I escaped that week without a crushed limb, as I levered and rolled the re-maining twenty or so three- to four-foot rounds of the Lincoln Oak's latest fallen branch downslope to the splitting stump on the mail path above Loop Road. It was high time that chore was done if the wood was to be saved: already the bark and the outer woody layer had rotted into ur-soil. Never have I destroyed so many worlds as I did in moving these. But I got them all down, with only one round rolling onto the county road, and that when no one was driving by.

A week or two later, Barry Lopez, who has written a memorable portrait of the anagama kiln, arrived from the east with his stepdaughter, Amanda, and a hydraulic splitter. Richard Rowland, the kiln's founder, pulled in from the west in his worn pickup along with one of the potters, Ben Steffl. For the next several hours we peaveyed, rolled, man- and woman-handled, split, tossed, and stacked the tangy, heavy oakwood, breaking only for Thea's welcome lunch. Each of us was lost in the trance of good work in the out-of-doors. Richard was a master with a maul, a wedge, and a chain saw, and Barry knew his splitter the way a blacksmith knows his forge. We silverbacks had nothing on slender young Ben and Amanda in shifting fiber by the ton. At day's end we shared a weary satisfaction as two low-riding truckloads of seasoned oak rolled off toward Astoria.

The following New Year's Day, Thea, Dory, and I drove across the Megler Bridge over the Columbia into Oregon, and out the valley of the Lewis and Clark River. After a number of turns and lanes, we came to a clearing in the second-growth woods where the anagama crouched beneath a wooden shed. A nearby open barn contained stacks and shelves of pots and heaps of shards. Richard welcomed us and led us into the shed, where various kinds of lumber and logs were stacked, ready to feed the insatiable firebox. An ancient Japanese form of firing, the anagama kiln brings together a community of potters, all of whom work together in shifts for several days and nights to satisfy the flames. The kiln itself, broad and sinuous, like the well-fed dragon it emulates, runs uphill at a low angle for ten yards or more. Before the bricks are placed to make the dragon's body and seal off the air, the riblike racks within are stacked with dozens of pots of many shapes, thrown by members of the community and ready to fire. The only openings left were the fueling port, the flues, and the stack from the head to vent the dragon's breath.

In the shed Ben and a few of the other potters were moving wood and feeding the fire. Each shift has a designated fire boss, who decides when to put in more wood and how to manage the flues to maintain the critical range of temperature, above 2,000 degrees F. Heat flowed from the brown brick hide of the beast, steaming my glasses as I came in from the January dusk. We were invited to toss a few splits of our own oak into the roaring orange furnace, where they immediately joined in combustion. We watched the hypnotic blaze and the smooth motions of its servants, content like travelers before a strange campfire. Then Richard called us to come outside and see the dragon belch a magenta fire into the winter dusk through its glowing chimney.

Thea was seriously ill for much of that year. The following autumn, three heavy bowls arrived at our door from Oregon. They were glazed in the warm, earthy colors of pelage, mineral, and wood. Ben explained that they were healing bowls, full of the love of community and reverence for wood and clay and fire and life. The Swede's tree was coming home from the anagama to help the current Swede in residence. Hearty soups of squash and chanterelles fired those bowls again. One more autumn on, Thea is well and the Lincoln Oak turns as red as the dragon kiln's breath.

I LOVE THE crazy carpet of colors all over the ground from late September until deep winter, but if the leaves are allowed to stay, they will act just like black plastic to kill the underlying vegetation. So we rake and rake. One year we decided to have a leaf-raking party—we provided beer and rakes. We raked, and our guests mostly drank beer.

One Indian summer day when the children were young, Dory was sunbathing on the lawn and reading *Grimm's Fairy Tales* for the third time. Tom was snip-snip-snipping and machete-slashing at brambles. Thea was pickling chanterelles, and Bokis was rolling in the dust of the driveway. Tom and I took off to net orange sulphur butterflies in a red clover field and returned to find Dory playing with her friend Tracy. Seeing my chance, I dragooned them all to rake. The three kids rabidly raked the sugar maple leaves into a huge pile that held all the oranges, reds, and yellows of a sixty-four-crayon box of Crayolas. Then they got cart rides to the compost heap, with only their laughing faces, hands, and skinny legs sticking out. Thea and Bokis joined us, and, beginning with the semireluctant pussycat, we took turns hurling one another or ourselves into the huge leaf pile. Each got to be completely buried, tickled, and scarecrow-stuffed with leaves. How peaceful, to be entirely immersed in forest-fragrant sugar maple leaves—until it was my turn to be tickled. Bokis went in a few more times and finally got into the spirit of things, having sat apart and watched for a while. Thus began a tradition that continues today with resident cats, visiting dogs, and grandchildren on the rare Thanksgiving that happens to be dry.

The great domes of three American elms planted beside the river many years ago by Farmer Jack Swenden always blazed their best yellow at election time. I used to bicycle down to the Grange Hall for elections when the precinct voted there. I flew down SR4, coasting fast and helmetless past the wonky shake cabin with moose antlers hung on the side built by Farmer Jack, a locally famous boxer who sparred with Gene Tunney and had a Montana governor for a brother. As I crossed Hull Creek and neared his elms, their mingled boughs blazed like a tall, cool bonfire above the village.

Today the elms are two, though Norman Anderson planted a scion of the third, now rapidly growing, when the big one went down in a storm. The elms stand in the Grange's little Meserve Park, established twenty years ago on the site of the old Meserve Store in the village. Until the 1950s, the big wooden building stood beside the river, the better to serve the steamer trade, and so suffered occasional flooding. F. N. Meserve ran the store, and his wife, Alta, published the *Grays River Builder*. In the manner of many grand mercantiles of the time, the Meserve Store had a ballroom upstairs. We like to say that the Oregon Shakespeare Festival got its start there because its founder, Angus Bowmer, once taught here and put on plays in the Meserve hall. He would hold a boxing match one weekend to underwrite a play the next. Some people here can still remember acting in *Seven Keys to Baldpate*.

After the 1996 flood, our polling place moved to Rosburg Hall, several miles west. This year on Election Day, when we parked by the boat ramp on the river where the Rosburg Store and landing used to be, we found only one other car in the lot. Within the hall the three ladies who womaned the polls for each election greeted us with banter, candy, and maybe a little relief that someone had actually come in. "At least you two always vote," said Glenrose Hedlund, but in fact the turnout is usually pretty good in a town where voting gives you somewhere to go. Once we got our ballots, numbers 25 and 26 for Gray's River, and our pencils, and set to work making our marks, two of the ladies resumed a spirited Scrabble game. Afterward Mrs. Rangila handed us the goodie basket and a sticker that read I VOTED TODAY.

Oregon went vote-by-mail some years ago, and our legislature recently authorized Washington's counties to do the same. I dearly hoped we would never see such a change. But the county clerk argued that more than half of the voters already sent in absentee ballots and that a postal vote would save money. I don't understand why anyone would choose an absentee ballot if he weren't going to be away or would want to mail off a ballot as if it were a bill. For me the annual visit to the polling place is a cherished rite of the year passing and as close as I get to feeling the democracy in Democrat. And with all the fuss in recent years over hanging chads, touch-screen voting with no paper trail, and so on, why doesn't everyone just X a piece of paper, as we always have in Gray's River? Such ballots surely couldn't take any longer to count than the human years put into resolving disputes arising from all the vastly more complicated and expensive systems. And I find there is no more direct expression of hope than making that mark with a real pencil beside your chosen candidate's name in the old hall beside the river, where the people come to make their wishes known.

But now the change has come to pass. As the red, blue, and white postcard announced, "Wahkiakum County is now entirely VOTE BY MAIL." Maybe the taxpayers will save a buck. But taxes won't go down on that account, and I believe something real and substantial has been lost from the fabric of this rural remnant.

At least Candidates' Night continues at the Grange. The more or less compulsory confabs give us a chance to meet and grill the candidates for county office, the state house and senate, and sometimes Congress, even if only a handful of citizens attend. No one dresses up, including the aspirants, who may feel stark naked before we finish with them. Not that we aren't polite, but we don't pussyfoot in asking how the office seekers feel about the issues on our minds.

Candidates' Night can also be fun, as it was the night Arlie challenged a young aide representing our Republican congresswoman, Linda Smith. The traditionally Democratic Third Congressional District is a tough one to represent, for it includes both Olympia greenies and Aberdeen loggers, and between gerrymandering and sprawl, the rural population has lost ground to the suburban bloat of Vancouver in conservative Clark County. After a long reign of effective Democratic representatives, including Don Bonker and Jolene Unsoeld, the ultraconservative Smith swept, or crept, into office in Newt Gingrich's "Republican revolution." The honeymoon was definitely over, and Rep. Smith's wacky record was on the line. She had sent the young aide, clean-cut and soaking wet behind the ears, in her place to placate the few voters out in deepest Wahkiakum. Like a lamb to the slaughter. He hadn't a clue about most of the issues and little ammunition for defending some of his employer's least popular votes and positions.

Then Arlie stood up. Arlie and her pal Dolly, a pair of sweet-and-salty pistols who loved their fun and brokered no fools, ran the Gray's River Cafe at the time. Those two filled the place with bygones, peppery talk, and Arlie's occasional outbreak on honkytonk piano. Now she fixed the fresh-faced young Republican with her sharp eyes and said, "I want to know what your boss is going to do about that Viagra deal."

"Excuse me, ma'am?" he stuttered.

"Well, we heard there's a move afoot for the VA to give Viagra to the veterans in the old soldiers' home."

"I don't know anything about that," said the young man, already red and squirming. "Do you have a message for me to take to the Representative?"

"You bet I do!" returned Arlie. "Tell her it's a terrible idea! We can't imagine anything more disgusting than a bunch of old farts running around with hard-ons."

The hall erupted. Whether the aide's mortification had anything to do with Linda Smith's drubbing by the Democratic candidate, Brian Baird, in the subsequent election I can't say.

THOUGH MILD COMPARED to winters where the word has teeth, this can be a bleak season for outdoor creatures. Even after the hunters' blasts have stilled, elk and deer continue to die in the year-round season of roadkill. The heavy fogs and slick roads of December, together with the lack of food in the sometimes snowy highlands, seem to make this an exceptionally tough time for roadside foragers. So it was that two weeks before the solstice, Thea came in with the disturbing news that a deer lay dead in our garage.

He was a young buck, probably last summer's fawn, with a short, juvenile face and no sign of antler buds. Situated as we are between two roads, we have not had much deer traffic in my time here. But in recent years a doe has discovered our little sanctuary and set up shop, producing twins most years. This may have been one of her previous year's offspring. He was a pitiful sight, lying beside a Garden Way cart full of hay salvaged from the road for mulch, his head tossed back over his shoulder. All four legs bore compound fractures. Both forelegs were snapped right across the radius and ulna. The left hind leg was completely disarticulated at the knee joint. The right hind leg, folded under the torso, was snapped across the femur. There was very little blood.

One of the forelegs was caught, though not bound, in a loose loop of baling twine from the hay. Thea conjectured that he went into the crowded garage attracted by the hay, got trapped by the twine, and, in his panic, jumped around (things were in disarray) and managed to break his legs on the concrete floor. She has kept goats and has seen their panic when they think they are trapped and the damage they can do to themselves. An alternative explanation was that the deer had been hit on the highway and tossed down the bank, and then had clambered into the shelter of the garage, where he died. Searching the highway, we spotted one possible blood stain in the rain. Disturbed leaves between the road and the garage could have been towhee or jay work as easily as sign from a scrambling deer, but then I spotted a sliver of rain-washed bone under the cedar. Later I consulted with my friend Richard Nelson, a great deer authority. He agreed that it must have been hit. "Somehow," wrote Nels, "perhaps propelled by adrenaline, the deer must have dragged itself to the garage." On four broken legs! We all hoped that his suffering had been brief after that ordeal.

We carted the poor deer down to the pasture below our house and placed it among winter-blooming buttercups, between a hornbeam and an elder, near the banks of Gray's River. Nearby lay the more or less deflated carcasses of four chum salmon, three cocks and a hen, stranded by the recent flood. I laid open the deer's side to give the scavengers access. His belly was full of fresh green fodder.

The first crow appeared the next morning at nine. Six more followed through the day. An immature gull wheeled overhead several times, but I never saw it land. The next day the crows attended again. That night the coyotes must have come, for in the morning the rib cage was exposed, and a crow sat atop a haunch some way away. That afternoon a red-tailed hawk was perched on the rib cage, tucking in energetically. Next time I looked, it was a pair of ravens. Night fell on a much reduced carcass. The third morning, what was left had been carried thirty yards farther from the river. Two ravens again claimed the vestige, as sixty-six elk, across the river in one of Chamberlain's fields, chewed their cud like so many reindeer. And soon the little deer was all gone.

Our doe is still with us, accompanied by a single fawn this fall, more welcome when they browse the English ivy rather than prune the Asian pear. I'll step out on the porch late at night to visit the cat, hear a rustle, and spot them a few feet away, stepping lightly across the lawn. Telepathically, I urge them away from the garden—and the highway.

ALONG WITH RISING and falling water, winter is the province of wind. When the sea-breath and mountain-roar bend the hemlocks of these hills, the birds hang on as best they can. I could never understand how the eagles' nest in the brittle cottonwood top stayed put in winds that snapped whole trees in half—and then one storm it didn't. And when the air stills and hunkered flocks of chickadees and kinglets reappear, I fail to grasp how these tits, not much heavier than feathers, make it through the winds at all.

On the day after Christmas, a winter wren was hanging about the tall salal by the back porch. In former times in Britain, the wren was hunted by wassailing bands of boys on St. Stephen's (or Boxing) Day. Nowadays a sharp-shinned hawk or a cat is more likely to be its downfall. We wished it the safety of the season as well, as leaves swirled in great rising wind-hurls. And when a string of deep frosts set in, we found two winter wrens bundling for the night in an old barn-swallow nest in the garage.

In the new year a great storm came up one evening while I was away. When I returned, Thea told me she had a ruby-crowned kinglet in a shoebox. I assumed it was a victim of a Bad Cat, but that wasn't the case. This, Thea explained, was the male kinglet that had spent the past couple of winters fluttering around our windows preying upon spiders, their egg sacs, and insects in their webs. At any window we might see his minute packet of gray and yellowish fluff hovering, his white-ringed eyes darting about and his blackthorn bill striking the casements, moldings, and sashes. Or he would be combing a wild mass of wisteria, where he roosted some nights. Sometimes his crimson pileus popped out like a mohawk, though he seemed oblivious to our movements.

Thea explained that as the howling wind gathered and struck, rattling the rippled glass of the sashes, she heard something scratching at the window in the dark, but took it for a wind-tossed leaf. The sound continued, and when she went to look, she saw the kinglet flying up and down at the window. Clearly he was looking into the well-lit dining room—and, she realized, just as clearly importuning for shelter from the storm. Thea raised the sash. The bird settled on the sill. She put out her hand and gently picked it up, then closed the window against the gale. Whether relieved or just delirious from the wind, the kinglet remained still in her palm. She placed it in a shoebox with a soft cloth.

In the morning she brought the box into the bedroom so I could see the bird. As soon as she raised the lid, the kinglet shot up toward the ceiling and then to the sunlit window, where he settled on the sill. Thea took him up with one hand as she raised the sash with the other. Then, bang! he was gone. And it wasn't long before that kinglet was foraging for spiders around our windows again. We always watch for him when the wind comes up, but he hasn't asked for entry again.

AFTER THE FALLING of the foliage, the array of local squirrels becomes visible. Swede Park has always been graced by flying squirrels, though their nocturnal habits conceal them, except for the occasional owl-dropped tail in the morning; by Townsend's chipmunks, piping from a woodpile, racing up the driveway ahead of us, or maybe teetering in hot late summer under a pitiful burden of botflies; and by the native Douglas squirrels, or chickarees, which often sit on a black walnut bough, gnawing a thick-ridged husk to get at the small, sweet meat inside. And that's all the squirrels there should be. We live well west of the oak habitat of the big, beautifully plumed western gray squirrel, now endangered in Washington State. Introduced eastern grays, the squirrels of my Denver childhood, abound in Longview and Long Beach, forty miles to the east and the west, but have not been reported in between. And introduced eastern fox squirrels, present but far less common in Seattle than eastern grays, aren't known to occur anywhere near here.

So I was surprised one early spring day when Thea called me to see a squirrel on the side of our big Port Orford cedar; it was twice the size of a chickaree, with a reddish yellow belly—hallmarks of the eastern fox squirrel! I doubted that ID, but the subsequent occasional spotting of it in one big tree or another—most commonly the Lincoln Oak, whose hollow had been occupied by flying squirrels and common mergansers—confirmed it. Then one day before the trees leafed out, I followed the beast's progress west through the bare deciduous boughs and into the wood until it dropped into an evergreen cherry laurel. When I got my glass on it, I saw that it wasn't at all the color of an eastern fox. It was reddish gray as opposed to reddish brown, and white-bellied, with big ears as opposed to the fox's small ones. It was an eastern gray! But wait, what's this—a second big squirrel lurking in the laurel! Both rodents climbed a tall Scots pine, where I had another look at them before they vaulted off somewhere. One definitely appeared to be a fox, the other a gray.

Still I was dubious, in spite of what I'd seen. Could the "fox" have been just a big Douglas, which also has a yellow belly? Weeks went by with no sightings. One day I was reading on the porch, listening absentmindedly to the slow *whams!* of a pileated woodpecker in the Broken Oak and soft thuds as the great slabs of wood it dislodged hit the ground. Then a loud alto whistle, chuckle, and *churr* issued from the Lincoln Oak behind me. I almost thought it could be some unfamiliar part of a pileated's considerable repertory, but it also recalled a chickaree slowed down to $33^{1}/_{3}$ rpm. Thea came out and we saw that it was indeed a squirrel. Its big head peeked out around the trunk as we approached, then tucked back in, as it continued to call. Then it began its upper-story ambulation westerly. We followed on the ground. As I glassed its movements, my gaze fell on a squirrel on the sugar maple trunk: an eastern gray. It stayed put as the other squirrel sky-hopped past the pine and into the horse chestnut, where I saw it well: an eastern fox for sure, with a rather tatty tail. Had the incursion of the gray elicited its territorial outburst? Again the next day Thea heard it calling from the Lincoln Oak.

So it's true: we have both an eastern gray and an eastern fox squirrel, the first of each recorded for Wahkiakum County as far as I know. A good naturalist friend was horrified: fearing that they could be the thin edge of the wedge, she urged us to shoot them immediately, an understandable reaction to two more exotic species invading new territory. But I am not yet overly concerned. They both seem to be singletons, explorers without mates. With only one of each in residence, I think we're okay, unless they turn parthenogenetic. Besides, my little Daisy BB gun wouldn't faze them.

However they arrived, these arboreal rodents have no doubt settled into Swede Park because its mix of Midwestern and European broadleafs reminds them of their native eastern deciduous forest. In Great Britain the decline of indigenous red squirrels, which are related to our chickarees, has commonly been blamed on the rise of adventive American gray squirrels, but in fact human changes have rendered the countryside amenable to the invaders and hostile to the natives. The coniferous habitat hereabouts is hostile to *Sciurus niger* and *S. carolinensis* (foxes and grays) yet eminently suitable for our native *Tamiasciurus douglasii*.

Not long after the most recent sighting of the fox squirrel, we heard a wheezy barking from a low limb of the Lincoln Oak; it was the biggest, fattest Townsend's chipmunk I have ever seen. Three of her young cavorted around the trunk. When the colder nights arrived, a chickaree moved into the smithy off the garage. Every time we go out to fetch firewood we hear it scritching behind the stack, gnawing on a butternut from the leaning tree outside. On an old homestead of already jumbled ecologies, the interlopers just add diversity. Counting flying squirrels and chipmunks, Swede Park may host more kinds of tree squirrels than any other place in the state.

IN ITS MOST recent appearance, the eastern gray squirrel hunkered on a low spruce bough, its tail wrapped over its back like a pelted punctuation mark. Overhead arched the massive limb of a big black walnut that grows by the site of the former barn. The limb extends right over Loop Road into the lower treetops on our side of the road, a perfect overpass for arboreal beasts. As if to prove the point, a few days later a soft burr of a voice gave away the chickaree, twitching nervously, upside-down on the black walnut's trunk. Its belly the color of the beech leaves below, the squirrel hopped all over the tree, shot along the limb to oaks across the road, raced down to the ground, and disappeared into the brush. This limb, at forty-five degrees, and another branching off it almost horizontally, erupt from a fern-furred crotch of the graceful black walnut. Licorice-ferned at every bend, the walnut and its offshoots lend the road here a distinctly bowered feel. We have feared that the gravity-defying bough will fall or be cut by order of some overly cautious official.

A knock at the back door one day turned out to be Roy Herrold. Roy is a member of an oystering family from the Naselle estuary on Willapa Bay. His daughter, Amber, was a cheerleader when our boy, Tom, was a runner at Naselle High School. "Bob, did you know there's a big snake at the bottom of Fairview Road?" he asked. Roy had been driving through the valley when he spotted the snake, lethargic in the cool damp. I suggested it might be an unusually large garter snake, almost the only native serpent in our area. We were used to seeing them, but not at this season. "No, I'm pretty sure it's not a garter, and it really is *big*," said Roy, holding his hands three or four feet apart. "I think it's still alive. I don't want to see it run over, but I also didn't want to pick it up."

We walked down together, and sure enough, there was a three-and-a-half-foot snake, as thick as a wrist and speckled bright yellow on glossy black. It was torpid but fine. I gathered it up, put it in a box, and brought it home. Before he left, Roy mentioned the black walnut limb arching over the road. "Is it true that you want that branch to come down?" he asked me.

"Hell, no," I said. "I'd fight for it." It seemed that a message I'd once given to the county engineer, that if he ever wanted to remove the branch, please speak with me first, had morphed into an assumption of acquiescence and then desire—exactly the opposite of my true wishes. Roy had been visiting our neighbor Mark Linquist, a former logger who was planning to run for county commissioner and who also liked the limb, and Mark had passed on to Roy that misimpression. Thanks to the snake, Roy had a chance to ask me about it. It turned out that the engineer had indeed ordered the limb's removal, in response to complaints from a couple of valley residents who had bumped their heavy equipment on it. I called Mark and asked him to speak to the engineer on behalf of all us limb-lovers.

The snake turned out to be a king. The nearest native king snakes occur in southern Oregon's Siskiyous, but this one's pattern of lemon-yellow spots, neither random nor solidly banded, suggested a subspecies found in Louisiana. Presumably it had escaped from a bridge visitor or been dropped off by some irresponsible idiot tired of caring for it, the way all of our cats have come to us over the years. I knew that Gavin Maxwell had a good terrarium and was looking for a good snake to put in it. So there it lives today, contentedly feeding on mice and molting now and then. Since Gavin went to work for the Herrolds in the oyster beds, Roy hears frequent reports on the well-being of the snake he rescued. The limb lives on too, spreading over a nice new yellow-diamond sign installed by the county crew. The sign reads LOW LIMB CLEARANCE: 12 FEET. That is called saving the world one limb, one snake, at a time.

BEYOND MY STUDY window in mid-November, a wall of yellow and chartreuse spreads across the broad boughs of hornbeams; behind them is the mellower gold of birches. The Lincoln Oak reddens on the left, and the russet of the Broken Oak, already turned, shines between the bright foliar curtains. Sycamore maples are slender yellow torches; huckleberries, deep pink wands spiked by scarlet berries. Along the highway vine maples, which began turning in August, are at peak now in their paintbox spatters of red, yellow, orange, and green. The black walnuts beside Loop Road go lemony, the Illinois oaks candy-apple and caramel, the beeches butterscotch. In the hills, cherry and cascara leaves hang down like the flags of unknown countries on a still day. Firewood, shade, and their very presence aside, the trees' greatest gift is this strung-out season of brilliance. Scots pine wrapped in yellow-green wisteria; Japanese maple's last sheaf, never more fiery; English oaks glowing molten against the cooler flames of hornbeams. When the sun breaks through some late afternoons, actual ignition seems imminent, especially in that windblown, red-spattered yellow wall outside my window as I work.

As life members of the Washington Native Plant Society, we sometimes wonder if we shouldn't nudge this old homestead back toward a more indigenous flora. Among the relatively few native hardwoods, just one vine maple, one big-leaf maple, and one hazel grace the premises, along with lots of alders, cascaras, and cherries; yet we are extravagantly rich in European sycamore maples and English oaks. In fact, there are so many that Bobby Larson suggested we sell descendants of Ahlberg's historic trees at the Grange centennial celebration as Doug, Bobby, and I dug up saplings in the rain, potted them, hung them with fancy lables giving their pedigree and Pete Ahlberg's portrait, peddled them—and made hundreds for the Grange building fund.

November gold becomes December dun. Good weather for the kitchen. Thea pickles meadow mushroom buttons—eight pints—and sautés and freezes many more. I shell chestnuts from spiny rinds; we stole more than fifty from the jays this year and will roast them on the blue wood stove in the evening to have with the sweet *eislese* grapes I spied high on a wild vine and plucked this afternoon. December approaches on bullet-mold skies and lead-pellet rain. But tints of fall, in rags and fragments, will last deep into winter. And when the colors finally bleach out in the rain, the first saturated greens of Indian plum are just weeks away. "Alles ist Blatt," Goethe was fond of saying; "the leaf is everything." Living beneath the big trees of Swede Park, I understand.

12 ✦ The Time of Rising Water

The earth, in her childlike prophetic sleep,
Keeps dreaming of the bath of a storm . . .

— ROBINSON JEFFERS, "November Surf"

One late autumn night I witnessed a phenomenon I had never seen before and may never see again. As a heavenly spectacle, it rivaled a first-rate meteor shower or comet. My search for Halley's one cold night on K-M Mountain had been a bust, but when Comet Hale-Bopp showed up, its blue tail seemed to spring right out of vermilion Mars at its closest approach to Earth. This marvel was just as stunning, but of a wholly different nature.

A remarkably dry fall had given us salmon sunsets and cloudless nights far beyond the usual measure; for weeks the stars and planets advanced across the night skies in full view. Driving home from Seattle, I found it hard to tell Venus on the western skyline from incoming flights to Sea-Tac; to the south, beyond the urban glare, the sky filled with more and more heavenly bodies. By the time we reached Gray's River, Jupiter, Saturn, Aldebaran, and the Pleiades straddled the ecliptic in descending brightness, and the starry triplet of Orion's belt replaced that of Scorpio's thorax from six months before.

Back home that night I watched the moon rise absolutely full through the baring limbs of the Eastern Oak. When I next went outside, it was straight overhead, with Jupiter and Saturn extending in a line to the south, like moons of the moon. All around loomed a corona, and exactly tangent to the huge circle a contrail shot from some high flight. Soon the vapor trail had taken on the same width and color as the corona and stretched across the moon in a perfect diagonal, making the halo into one of those slash-circle signs admonishing no this or no that — "no mooning," for example. But that wasn't the part I remember most.

Just before bed I went out into the sharp cold once more. My slippers stuck to the wooden steps as frost gripped their soles. Stepping out from under the porch and looking up, I saw a sky painted in two different colors. A light mist had risen, obscuring everything except the moon itself and its sidekick, Jupiter, behind a pearly scrim. The ring around the moon shone as bright as a full-spectrum rainbow, and the space within the corona was inky blue, with the milky moon in the middle. No sounds, except the river's gurgling and the whinnies of waterbirds too agitated for sleep. Even the coyotes, which had surrounded the house in full throat a few nights before, were silent beneath the immense areola in the night sky.

Summer moons are romantic, but autumn moons are famous for their bright yellow color, like one recent "blue moon" (which means the second full moon in a month), the first in decades that was also a harvest moon, and another blue moon (actually amber) that fell on Halloween. Winter moons here are always surprising, in part because you rarely see them at all in a season usually ceiled with cloud. But when nights are clear, the absence of foliage allows that broad silver disk, inscribed by black winter twigs, to shine through the trees. The full moon before Yule is called the Long Night Moon, and it rides higher in the sky than any other luna ultima, just when the sun cruises across at its lowest and briefest.

The closest and largest full moon in our lifetimes, as the

newspapers described it, arrived shortly before the vaunted millennium. On solstice night and the next, Thea and I walked out to watch it rise over Gray's River and the covered bridge, its roof pewtered by the shine. Both nights a lone blue heron stood on shallow river shingle in the middle of the massive moonglade. The heron's icepick bill and swizzle-stick legs stood out distinctly against the night: cast in silver on the first night, then, on the second, with the moon lower, molded in gold. At home on the porch after midnight, I found I could read by moonglow alone, John Burroughs going on in fine print about the earth and "its long steeping in the sea of sidereal influences." Fully steeped in sidereal influences myself, I went to bed thinking of the moon's constant companionship, whether we see it or not.

THE MOON BRINGS and takes away the tides. The tide doesn't reach the covered bridge, but the water beneath it does rise and fall just the same—not every six hours but every six months or so, and several times per rainy season. Not salt but fresh, this rising water flows from the sky and the hills as well as the ground, from the creeks and rills and rivers and swamps. It is a seasonal tide, the earth's angle to the sun taking the place of the moon's pull to elicit high water.

The winter of the Millennial Moon was exceptional in producing not a single flood. Most years here we recorded two or three valleywide floods between October and March, and it is not unusual to see half a dozen major inundations. The year 2000 quickly began to make up for the previous year's dearth by giving us a freshet in *June*—something never seen before by the old-timers, let alone me. The next arrived in mid-November. As our late postmaster Jean Calhoun had instructed me, "freshet" here means a big flow that comes on a warm west wind in conjunction with a super-high tide, just as the June flood had done. No matter how many times I see it, the river's metamorphosis never ceases to surprise. I can go to bed beside a still river no wider than a telephone pole is long and awaken to a fast-shoot-ing sheet of molten pewter a quarter mile wide; sometimes we watch the river expand tenfold between dawn and dusk.

When it rains for days and days here, Gray's River shows a muddy hide that ripples with a fatter and fatter flow. Big logs appear, riding high on the crest of a river that can scarcely float a canoe in late summer. When the water system's old intake was still in place under the river, we knew that our water would soon turn silty and we would receive a "boil water" notice from the Public Utility District. If the river continues to rise and jumps its banks, it covers the valley floor and rampages downstream, threatening the few still-occupied households on the floodplain. A few winters back the river rose, broke Gorley's dike, cut a new course, and took out a house as well as the riverbed well for the whole Western Wahkiakum water system. The PUD's water wizard, Bill Chamberlain, ingeniously slung together an improbable wormworks of PVC pipes suspended from poles and trees to get our water past the reorganized river course. This wonderfully jerry-built system was no doubt the longest, if not the only, public water line of its kind, and it has since been copied elsewhere. The charitable lack of floods the following winter allowed the water to keep flowing through the Rube Goldberg lines until a new wellhead and pumping station came on line in a field downstream. So no more boil-water notices. Yet even the new water plant in Larson's meadow is within the river's conceivable reach.

After that winter, as Gray's River tossed and turned in its silted-up bed deciding where it wanted to go next, the people of the valley gathered in rowdy conclave at the Rosburg School to blame and to vent. Almost no one dared mention that big floods and a shifty river are the price we pay now for the logging that paid the bills here for decades. They would rather see as the villain the Army Corps of Engineers, which wants to dredge the Columbia shipping channel deeper to accommodate bigger ships and the ports upstream, such as Portland, but refuses to dredge Gray's River, whose outflow is admittedly impeded by Corps-built sand islands. Or they blame the habitat biologist of the state Department of Fish and Wildlife, whom they see as an obstructionist when he does his job of holding the line on hydrology projects that threaten fish habitat. Or they dream old dreams of a Gray's River dam that will quell floods while providing cheap energy forever, a dam that will never be built.

There is no doubt that our little river used to run deeper and carry the water away more efficiently. In the days when the packet steamers *Eclipse* and *Wenona* from Astoria docked beside Meserve's Store in the tidal basin, the Gray's ran maybe ten feet deep at mean high tide. Recently when the experienced rivermen Sam McKinney and Robin Cody came to see us in their beautiful little handcrafted boats, which draw almost no water, they anchored at high tide and returned at low only to find their boats beached in midchannel; they had no idea that the Gray's had become so constricted. Yards of silt have collected in the river's groove over the decades. Masses of gravel used to be taken from the river for building highways, but now, with almost no river traffic and little population in the area, the Corps sees no compelling reason to dredge, even if state fisheries regulations allowed it. And dredging would not truly end the floods. The river has indeed become an inefficient conduit, but the same plaque that plugs this artery used to hold back the flow when it was soil in the hills. Now the land just bleeds when it rains.

When the tree canopy and tree roots in steep terrain are disturbed, soil washes away in storms—especially after the roots die, about seven years after logging. Fatal landslides have occurred in Oregon in recent years, and in Longview, just east of here, whole houses are going over the brink of crumbling siltstone slopes. Still nearer, a thousand feet of SR4 collapsed a few years ago, costing millions to replace and harming businesses on this side of the Columbia in the 541 days it was closed. Locals drove around the slide on what they called the Ho Chi Minh Trail, but few connected the hated detour to its likely cause. Upslope logging is the culprit in many of these slides.

As an environmentalist in this land of loggers, I have been

fairly well tolerated. Most know that my beef is with decisions that hurt the people of the woods as well as the woods themselves. But at a town meeting a few years ago, I felt way out of sync with the prevailing mood. The occasion was a rally at Rosburg Community Hall calling for a boycott of the state's rumored offer to buy bottomland for habitat conservation. Some folks felt threatened by the plan, which they saw as an attack on the future of the community. "They want to turn the whole damn place into a park for ducks, and the hell with the people," one speaker summed up. She urged that everyone present a united front against the state and refuse to sell their land to them. It seemed to me that the program would be one way for some landowners to get paid for their property on the floodplain, where farming was no longer profitable and development ill advised. But the organizers were opposed on principle as much as anything: "taking" once productive land and "giving it back to the swamp," never mind that this was a matter of willing sellers and buyer, and eminent domain was not involved.

Several speakers pressed for dredging Gray's River and its bay, and Fossil Creek as well, old plaints that had fallen on deaf or unresponsive ears in the Army Corps of Engineers and the state agencies. When I finally spoke, I suggested a different way of looking at the problem. "The river has its own mind," I said, "and some communities are finding that they have more success trying to work with their rivers instead of against them. I can't see how, without stopping erosion from the timberlands, that we'll ever get the old channel back, even if the Corps would dredge, which is unlikely." Maybe I should have quit there, but I went on. "After all, restoring habitat doesn't have to be anti-people; maybe it's the best use of floodplain, where we shouldn't be developing anyway. Look at the old houses built beside the river by the pioneers—most of them have been abandoned. I think the best thing we can do is to prevent future development in the river's way instead of always trying to control the river." I felt a collective chill more frigid than if I had spoken out against logging. My message wasn't what people wanted to hear, especially those who already lived in the way of the floodwaters.

For a while, the antistate fervor grew. The agencies' resistance to dredging Fossil Creek, on grounds of protecting fish, incurred a powerful state senator's wrath. Heads rolled as responsible wildlife officials—in both senses—were transferred. Legislators bowed to local pressure, overruling the biologists and procuring a permit for a berm to force the river away from Fossil Creek; when the flood inevitably came, it was diverted right across the farm of the former chair of the Water Conservation District, who had predicted just such an effect. The Army Corps did not agree to dredge the river, but it did permit the removal of a large gravel bar, thus shunting the current past one area of concern for the time being. This took the steam off, and attitudes softened for a while.

The Department of Fish and Wildlife backed off their plan to purchase habitat in this apparently hostile valley. The Columbia Land Trust, however, proceeded to acquire a number of low-lying tracts along Deep and Gray's rivers and Seal Slough, from willing sellers, and to build community trust. Although as a private nonprofit organization CLT is not required to hold public meetings or pay property taxes on their holdings, it volunteered to do both. The group also worked hard to remove invasive plants and cooperated with Ducks Unlimited to breach unneeded dikes and replace tide gates with culverts in order to restore wetlands, which are crucial as nurseries for young salmon. But then, in the winter of 2005–06, record rainfall conspired with high winds and tides to produce extraordinary flooding. Dikes failed and property was inundated. A woman who had bought a floodplain holding between Gray's River and Seal Slough suffered serious losses. She became convinced that CLT's dike work had exacerbated, if not caused, her crisis; never mind that flooding was extreme all over the Lower Columbia drainage. Another meeting was held. Although Ian Sinks of CLT explained the group's intentions yet again and offered to take responsibility for any damage that could be shown to be the fault of their engineering, the trust was cast as a greedy agent of ruination out to take over the watershed, if not the world. The people had a new scapegoat for their frustrations with the river.

In the end the river will go where it wants, and the floods will only get bigger. We are thankful that H. P. Ahlberg built well above the banks of the river. His original cabin, on the next bench down, would have been lapped at or worse most winters. As Alta Meserve's daughter Imogene recalled, "When these freshets occurred, the whole valley was covered with water. People were marooned in their homes unless they had a skiff. We would watch the trash and logs come down the swirling muddy water, and sometimes there would be a logger dressed in tin pants with calk shoes and a long pike pole riding a big log down the river." We still see logs go by, though the riders are gone, along with the houses built on the lowest ground. Everyone agrees that the floods are more frequent and more severe than ever.

It may be that the floods will actually save this valley. After the county approved Covered Bridge Estates, an alliance of local citizens—truck farmers, retirees, firefighters, cattle raisers, writers, and others—joined together under the bland but truthful moniker Citizens for Responsible Development. The best part of the ordeal that followed was how it drew neighbors together. We held dances, rummage sales, bake sales, and plant sales to raise money for the best land-use lawyer we could find. At the dances, churchgoing families who didn't dance nonetheless brought and served refreshments, and jigged around a bit with their children.

The Citizens sued both the developer and the county in Superior Court. The judge took months to reach his decision, even journeying out here from Vancouver to see the valley. In the end he ruled against the developer and the county—but not because the plat would mean instant sprawl beside a registered historic site and insinuate a score of new septic systems near a Class I river bearing four listed salmonids. Instead, he cited the fact that floods would isolate new residents from fire and ambulance protection for a number of days each year, infractions of the weak county subdivision ordinance, and violation of the spirit of the even feebler county comprehensive plan. Noting a serious misreading of the state's Environmental Policy Act, he threw out the county's Determination of Nonsignificance as specious and stipulated an environmental impact statement for any future proposal. An EIS would be expensive to conduct and difficult to defend. So the ill-advised scheme was defeated by collective action of local residents in concert with the rain, the river, and the tides—which will be the final rulers in such matters. As if underscoring the judge's decision, the floodwaters rose overnight that fall, inundating several of the platted home sites.

EVEN AS THE developer's dream failed to ruin a perfectly good green valley by plunking homes for the unsuspecting in the path of rising waters, the life of the place went on. After great floods, the sun slipped out of cloud just before setting, turning the sky 1950s pink-and-gray. The haze of a slash burn across the valley atop Elk Mountain slid down the slanting beams, turning late light into old gold that poured over the last oak and beech leaves outside the window. Soon they would go cold amber.

At the riverside Duffy's Pub installed the longest septic line any of us had ever seen, hundreds of yards to a distant field, to get the recycled beer and burgers out of the river at last. Al Salazar turned the scabrous old Valley Tavern, deep in decay, into a place described by an Astoria paper as "quaint and appealing in a ramshackle sort of way." You can get red beans and rice, fresh oysters, homemade pie, and a Guinness on the deck over the river, beside Ramona's Garden, featuring fairy lights and a jumbo Mickey Mouse. Across the highway, a fish-and-chips annex has just opened next to a restored boat. There Salazar and his creative workman have gentrified an old house and a couple of cabins into a gingerbread cluster radically different from anything ever seen in old Gray's River. The tavern caters especially to bikers, beachgoers, and after-work loggers—unlike a previous owner who, disapproving of both beer and logging, cut off her customers after a brew or two.

The shingled Covered Bridge Cafe, the only other business in town, has been everything from a Mexican import store to a grocery featuring fine wines that no one here could afford to a rough and quarrelsome tavern. According to a friend, the last barkeeper, when asked by a woman at the bar to stop serving a cantankerous drunk, told her to go perform an anatomically impossible act. She promptly produced her ID as a member of the State Liquor Control Board and shut the place down on the spot.

The current owners, Dave Henderson and Colleen Haley, leased pasture to a bison rancher for a few seasons. Bison were among the experimental animals that have come and usually gone around here, like the ostriches that loomed out of the valley rain one notably un-African summer, the somewhat more successful emus over in Eden Valley, or Bill Coons's camels on Puget Sound. The big brown bison made a striking presence and liked the grass, though it was greener on the other side, and they had a way of crossing the river to where they weren't wanted and laying waste to fences. One of my genuine regrets is that I never had a Gray's River buffalo burger at the cafe while they were still available.

Finishing a writers' lunch with Pastor Barbara Bate at the cafe recently, I wanted to get home for *A Prairie Home Companion* on the radio. But I couldn't leave without a visit with the Andersons, a good word with the Gudmundsens, a story from Jenny Pearson and Glenrose Hedlund. Then I realized, Why hurry? I live in Lake Wobegon. Or someplace just as engaging, and every bit as Nordic, but with rain instead of snow.

For a while in the eighties you could buy gasoline at three different places in Gray's River: Appelo's Shopping Center, Axmaker's service station, and the cafe all had pumps. But they were close to the river, and between tougher state containment standards and minimal trade, all three dried up. Now it seems remarkable that we can get a cup of coffee, a bowl of stew, or a BLT in two separate spots in this past-its-prime hamlet. Gas is available at Mike's Store, three miles west of here in Rosburg. When I fetched up there on one of my earliest days in town, car out of gas down the road, Mike Swanson handed me a gas can and his truck keys, even though he had never met me before. When I stop in for milk or a box of tangerines, Rosalie or Kathy or Vicki asks, "Put it down, Bob?" Fifteen miles farther on, Naselle has the library, the bank, the grocer, and the liquor store, all staffed by familiar faces. We find less and less reason to leave the watershed, happily getting by with only occasional trips to Astoria, Long Beach, or Longview and even less frequent outings to Portland and Seattle, with their traffic and tempo.

As Gray's River Grange, the oldest surviving institution in town, approached its centennial, a plan was floated to lift the hall above the creeping floodwaters that muddied its floor several times a winter. Some thought razing might be more suitable than raising, but the building's historical value prevailed. Meanwhile, with the parking lot sodden and the floor still slimy from incoming floods, we held the annual Grange Christmas party in the more commodious Rosburg Community Hall, which had already been jacked up. Later our grange hall was indeed lifted above the waters.

The rain was bucketing down when Bobby Larson called and asked me to check on a couple of bicyclists who were tenting in his field beside the bridge. "And invite them to the Christmas party," he added. I walked over and found the small tent attended by a trio of Holsteins, as if it were a crèche. The campers were huddled in their tent, and I heard German softly spoken within. So as not to alarm them, I called out "Guten abend!" A surprised face poked out. I took the young couple home for a hot drink and a warm-up. Then Gunter and Iris went to Grange for their first, and likely still their only, American potluck Christmas party. Both Christmas trees were resplendent: the maple outside hung by nature with tinsel of the long, pale lichen called *Usnea longissima,* and the Douglas-fir on the stage inside brilliant with colored lights.

The young Germans gamely sampled the intimidating pot-luck, with its many meatball, macaroni, casserole, bean, po-tato, chicken, salmon, and Jell-O renditions, then confronted the soda bread, pumpkin and berry pies, and Christmas cookies. After the tables were largely relieved of their burden, Steve Puddicombe and Joel Fitts with his guitar led a lively "Twelve Days of Christmas," with the partridge and lords a-leaping and the rest assigned to groups around the hall; the best sopranos got the five gold rings. Myrtle Anderson read the Nativity story from Luke, making sure to stop just before the circumcision.

My interactive "Night Before Christmas" followed. The fluo-rescent lights were turned off as I settled into an armchair and gathered the young ones around my feet in a pool of light from a floor lamp as old as the Grange Hall. Recruited to supply the sound effects, the small boys and girls reveled in their roles as mice, cats, dogs, and the patter of reindeer hooves on the roof. We deconstructed the mysteries of the text together, such as Santa's enigmatic command to "dash way, dash away, dash away all" when the reindeer have just landed on the roof, what became of Rudolph, and the strange concepts of sugarplums, sleeping caps, and kerchiefs. The script deviated with the unpredictable ad-libs of kids already wound up from lots of sugar and anticipa-tion of Santa's imminent arrival.

My white beard confused the little ones until, to the sound of jingling bells, Santa himself entered the hall. Shaking every-one's hand, hugging the ladies (especially Ila Mae Larson), and dispensing candy canes, Santa went around the room trying to keep his pillow above his belt. Finally, after the children danced in a circle with Santa to "Jingle Bells," came the gifts. "Man number nine," Esther called, and "woman number twelve," as everyone hoped for the almond roca instead of the screwdriver, the chocolate-covered cherries instead of the tea towels. Only the kids got some item they'd asked for, which amazed the small ones. Carlton Appelo filmed the whole party, as he has for decades.

Children grew tired in the anticlimax of torn paper and opened presents. Sheran Parker warbled "Silver Bells" by the piano. Finally, everyone formed a circle with lighted candles in hand and sang "Silent Night." A boy who insisted he was big enough to hold a candle cried when he burned his hand with melted wax, but we made it through the third verse, whose words no one could remember. Then Iris and Gunter sang a verse of "Heilige Nacht." For that little while, it was possible to believe that we were not Americans and Germans, loggers and enviros, old-timers and newcomers, rural and urban, D. and R., for and against dams, dredging, or subdivisions. We knew that we really were a community, one that would persist, rising waters or not.

Iris and Gunter survived their night in the cow pasture, better fed than they'd ever imagined. And in the morning, they came up to our house for breakfast and a hot shower before continuing their soggy winter bike tour of the Northwest.

ONE SUNDAY not long ago we laid Berenice Appelo to rest in Gray's River Cemetery. A business graduate of UC Berkeley and a San Francisco Opera aficionado, Berenice came to Deep River half a century ago to marry Carlton. She managed the family's three general stores and the insurance agency so Carlton could concentrate on running the telephone company, which his father had founded, and pursuing his lifelong devotion to local history. The two traveled far and wide to telephone conventions. Carlton made sure Berenice never missed a local event. She was ninety-four when she died.

Carlton sat with other Appelos and elders beneath a green canopy, while friends and Grangers stood about beneath umbrellas and billed caps under a sky of leaky putty. Rain guttered onto the clipped, heathery hilltop. The names of valley families mumbled out of the moss and lichen of old stones: Barr, Durrah,

Larson, Sorenson, Schmand. Berenice's memorial service had been held in Naselle on a sunny Saturday; this was the simple Grange inurnment rite. Norman Anderson, Bobby Larson, and Carlton wore jackets and ties in spite of the cold and rain. Nylon, flannel, and wool were the order of the day for the rest of us. Grange Master Esther Gregg, whose husband, Dave, had been buried here to bagpipe strains, presided. Chaplain Ila Mae Larson read the Patrons of Husbandry prayers that have rung quietly here these hundred years, and everyone said "Amen."

Each of us in turn passed by the spot where the handsome urn would go, marked with an orange X on the grass by Penttila's Chapel by the Sea. Each of us laid a flower on the spot—red carnation, white chrysanthemum, red dahlia, white alstroemeria, until finally Carlton set down his one red rose for the woman he called his "brown-eyed beauty." And then we raced the rain back to our cars and drove to the cafe for sandwiches, cakes, and coffee. Tables were lined up to fit us all, with the casual diners shunted to the dripping-window tables. We toasted Berenice's memory, lifting our glasses of the one beverage that said it all: good, cold Gray's River water.

Back home I braved the rain again to get the mail. As I rounded the house, I noticed that Bokis's path was fading away. Down the steps, under the dripping boughs of rhododendron and ragged oaks, I paused at the plum grove where Bokis now lies. I thought of his own passing and burial, almost twenty years after he came to me out of another heavy rain. Bokis had been diabetic for years, but pills kept him in good shape for hunting voles, jumping in the leaves, and white-lining it for the mail. The steel plate in his leg clearly pained him, especially in the cold; it slowed him down and gave him a crooked run but never kept him from hiking, hunting, or leaping up onto my lap.

As Bokis weakened, I hated to leave him. One June weekend we boarded him at Oceanside Animal Clinic while we were in Seattle. When we returned, his vet of many years, whom we knew as Saint Katherine, told us tearfully that Bokis had died.

He had spent so many hours in my arms on the Dog Chair that I'd pictured him passing like that, and he might have, had he lasted just one day longer.

My eyes streaming like a Gray's River freshet, I carried him down to the plum grove, where he often waited when he didn't feel like joining me on a walk. I wrapped him in a favorite T-shirt with a mountain lion on it and laid him in a grave dressed with fresh catnip, kibbles, and his collection of mammal tails. Lots of flowers went on top. I said some words, and at the head of the fresh tump I set a big black chunk of local basalt.

The small Bilak Bokis of 1977 had become a big Black Box by the time he died on June 9, 1996. He had a broad white belly, which he loved to turn up to the sun or an available rub by lying flat on his back on the lawn or the rough concrete of the front stoop. I have a photograph of him in this position, his wonky hindleg stretched as best it could, his forepaws straight out, lying in utter vulnerability, trust, and expectation. People viewing this snap often ask if he is dead. Far from it! Several lives to go, and many voles. But now he really was gone. I had no intention of getting a new cat any time soon, but of course it wasn't long before Firkin and Virga were dropped off.

Now when I go for the post, sword ferns, white bleeding hearts, and sweet fringe-cups hang over Bilak Bokis's tomb in the plum grove. Often I pause to think of Bokis and to place some seasonal flowers in a beer bottle by his grave or lay a bright leaf, a ripe plum, or a black walnut on the stone, maybe holly or barberry in winter. On fine days Firkin follows. She leaps onto a fallen mossy plum trunk I call the Bokis-log, pays her obeisance to the King of Cats, and waits for me there while I get the mail.

THE HIGHEST FRESHET anyone could remember—a perfect storm of super-high tide, heavy rain, and wind—came up lickety-split in 1996, isolating the Larsons' house in an inland seascape of broad waters. I called Bobby to make sure his family was all right. "We had the driest October," he said, "and then we had the flood and we had the mud and so nobody could get goin', so she just went by the wayside." "She," I understood, was everything Bob intended to get done before the rains.

I recalled an earlier inundation, when Bob Torppa told me that his son Brandon had seen a big salmon swimming right down the middle of Loop Road and that several of his cows were stranded by the rising river. "In the morning," he said, "the water was up to the cows' necks—and the calves were standing on the cows' backs!" None were washed away, as sometimes happens. During one recent high-water event the new river course cut off Doug Larson's cows from a means of escape. For a while they held their own against the current, but when the waters dropped, six were gone. A high tide after endless rain this winter took six sheep and two horses when Deep River surged over its dike.

Smaller animals take the rising waters hard. One December Thea and I walked out Loop Road as far as we could until the water lapped at our feet. Farther on it covered the hood of a Dodge left for months in an adjacent field. As we watched the great flow, we were joined by a wildlife official and a couple of neighbors. We all noticed small brown forms paddling through the current toward shore. As they reached the high water line, they clambered into the low boughs of an apple seedling, where they crowded, shivering. They were Townsend's voles, which our cats so enjoy. One that I found, drowned, weighed in at a full three ounces; its stomach was full of meadow vegetation that looked like green baby food.

As their tunnels flooded, the voles were flushed out and had to swim for dry land. And good swimmers they were—why not? After all, Ratty, the consummate waterman in *The Wind in the Willows,* was a water vole (*Arvicola amphibius*). But these animals, chilled and tired, looked miserable stuck in the apple selvage. The wildlife agent—for once helping actual animals instead of battling citizens over regulations—scooped up the voles and moved them to higher ground. Noticing hungry garter snakes too at the water's edge, we joined in the cross-road vole evacuation effort. As for Mole, Ratty's boon companion? We saw no moles. I suspect that those in the bottomlands simply drowned and that moles from protected upland places like Swede Park recolonize the valley each spring. As Thoreau wrote of water in *Walden,* "It may rise this year higher than man has ever known it, and flood the parched uplands; even this may be the eventful year, which will drown out all our muskrats."

Even the beavers can be flooded out. Our Gray's River beavers are mostly bank burrowers instead of lodge builders. When the torrent descends, they can be swept away. During one such episode, Kate O'Neal found an apparently orphaned animal I'd never expected to see—a baby beaver. Alone, cold, and hungry, it was the height of cute but also pathetic. We were about to leave town, and no one we contacted knew how to rear an unweaned beaver nor wanted to try. At the wildlife agent's advice, we took it to the mouth of our creek when the water dropped and released it on the bank. We had hopes, but few illusions, that the parents might yet find it. More likely it would be coyotes.

No one can understand this place without knowing its water, and no one knows that better than Bobby Larson. Any number of watershed studies have been carried out in recent years, measuring all manner of variables. The scientists and technicians who take the measurements possess tools and training that inform their findings with a certain kind of sophistication. Some of it may actually help the river and its fish in the long run. But I doubt that any of the experts would be capable of rendering the subtle judgment of an experienced farmer like Bobby when it comes to H_2O.

I was watching Bob baling hay in Lenore's field below Swede Park. When he stopped to take a drink from a cooler of water brought by Doug, I went down to tell him how happy it made me to see his progress. He alighted from the once-red Farmall, with a Vise-Grip for a steering wheel and an old sofa cushion perched on the seat, and removed his big floppy sun hat to wipe away his sweat. "The baler's holding up good," he said. "Doug'll be happy that I've only busted the twine on two bales." Doug laughed; he'd have to heft those bales, and a broken one is no fun. "But I was doing Norman's field yesterday, and it was a whole different deal." I asked how so. "I had to let off the tension on the baler," he said. "The deal was, it was only four-thirty, but I felt my tire, and it was wet. I tell ya', I've never seen that before in Gray's River, never once in all these years."

In that one gesture—stroking his old tractor tire with his practiced fingers—Bobby sensed all he needed to know about relative humidity, the dew point, and condensation. And he knew—just as the phase of the moon told him when to cut and bale the hay—that if he didn't slack off the tension, the swelling hay would burst the string on the bales. So it is one kind of knowledge when a hydrologist profiles the river and its gradient; another when Theodore Roethke says, "The chill is gone from the moon / Only the woods are alive." But the dew on the tractor tire, and what it means in concert with the moon, the woods, the river, and the fields, may be the knowledge that still counts the most out here.

FOR ALL THAT the floods have intensified since H. P. Ahlberg's time, we know that the real time of rising waters lies ahead, and perhaps not so very far ahead at that. First, the sea level will surely rise with global warming, and with it the frequency and severity of riparian flooding. This very day the *Chinook Observer*, a weekly newspaper published in Long Beach, arrived bearing these headlines: " 'What you would see here would be a hell of a mess'—local leaders have no illusions about severity of threat if water level rises" and "Rising waters place county's villages at risk—modest rise in ocean level could inundate 20 square miles of land here." Although these stories refer to Pacific County, Wahkiakum is the next county in from the coast and just as susceptible to water-level shifts on the lower Columbia and its tributaries, such as Gray's River.

Second, we live on the Cascadia Subduction Zone, where the Juan de Fuca Plate makes its gradual (but in some places sudden) plunge beneath the overriding continental mass. Geologists Brian Atwater, David Yamaguchi, and colleagues have studied dropped shorelines and flooded forests of rot-resistant cedars and have shown that seven great earthquakes have occurred over the past thirty-five hundred years, from two hundred to a thousand years apart, averaging five hundred years. These quakes result from the Juan de Fuca Plate slipping against the North American Plate. This long tectonic slam dance, for the most part slow and smooth, then takes a radical and violent step. Major tsunamis inevitably follow.

It's been more than three hundred years since the last big slippage occurred, on January 26, 1700. Registering between 8.7 and 9.2 on the Richter scale, it sent a serious tsunami to Japan and dropped the Washington shoreline five feet. The next could come tomorrow, next week, or next century—anytime really. Brian Atwater gives a one-in-ten chance of a subduction quake occurring in the next fifty years and cautions that it might attain magnitude 9. When our last substantial earthquake struck, I left my computer screen doing the hula and scrambled outside so a large tree could fall on me instead of the roof. I was pretty sure the big one had come, but it hasn't yet. When the subduction event really does occur, the Long Beach Peninsula will be in for it—yet a long-standing debate about building new houses and condos in the dunes inexplicably continues. The terrible events in the Indian Ocean of December 26, 2004, suggest how bad it could be for residents—not to mention for the liquefied natural gas terminals currently, and idiotically, proposed for the lower Columbia River. All of the estuaries will back up in a major saline bore. We haven't seen anything like the violence that will be unleashed since Mount St. Helens went off, and her wrath was pointed the other way.

I like to think that Swede Park, some fifty feet above sea level—or is it thirty?—will be out of the flood zone, though bookcases will surely tremble and fall. Gray's River finally may get the blowout that most folks seem to think is due. But however it happens, I'm pretty sure that most of our issues with the river will seem minor when the big water rises for real.

Aftertimes

Throwing the Cat on the Compost

It's one of those dreams of innocence, this place.

— JOHN GARDNER, *Freddie's Book*

The coyotes called long and loud and very near in the night. Their recital began with one plaintive whine, then rose through an elaborate run of yips and riffs into a full-blown, multitrack jam. I worried about Firkin, curled in her rush igloo on the porch, nice plump toad-in-the-hole for hungry canines. But the next day she was basking in the sun, as always when we are gifted with that precious commodity, which is as likely to happen in winter as summer, and there was no coyote sign anywhere near.

Now that warmer nights had arrived, I opened the outdoor faucet once more; surely the spider I'd flushed out of the spigot twice would have left by now. But there she was, flailing in the chamber pot again. Before I could put her back on the pipe post, she fell onto the ivy at the base. We did have a light frost that night, and I hoped she had found her way back to the post and up to the spigot. My concern was unnecessary. My arachnologist friend Rod Crawford identified her as a false black widow, which lives for years, not months like the winter-perishing orb weavers. She could take care of herself. Many times since then I've found other kinds of spiders in the flush; spiders just have a thing about spouts.

What is the sky to a spider? Or to a cat? Do animals whose vision is focused on flies and voles perceive the heavens as we do? Sometimes, of an especially starry or moony night, I have held Bokis or Firkin up to see, and they've always seemed unimpressed. Humans, on the other hand, are seldom indifferent to the ceiling when out-of-doors. We look up, if only to see if we're likely to be rained on. The sky calls attention to itself, whether scored by herons, cranes, or wires; illumined by sunsets, Perseids, or ballparks; broken up by the twigwork of oaks or maples, painted in rainbows, or just primed in the pale gray of my '52 Ford. If we are truthful, the sky is never neutral.

LAST DECEMBER, walking for the mail on a summery day, I heard tap-tap-tapping from the valley down below. Bobby, Doug, and Brian Larson were dismantling a barn that had been theirs and was given back to them by the woman to whom they had sold the land. The Larsons planned to move it in pieces and reassemble it on their land downvalley. I'm happy to see any barn conserved, even if it's a seventies red-and-white aluminum sheet-and-pole structure.

The old barns are almost all gone or going. Ed pulled down the one that H. P. Ahlberg built on this place, concerned about lawsuits by trespassing bridge visitors; it was so well built that his nephews had quite a time taking it apart, and I knew he was sorry to see it go. So was I, as were its barn swallows and barn owls, though its removal opened a south slope to sun, now mostly birches and brambles. The old Larson barn burned long ago. Chamberlains' lovely old arched barn was lost when a new owner, against Veryl's advice, overloaded it with green bales, spavined its center beam, then burned it down. Cap Schmand's immense barn in Gray's River, lathe-and-plastered for two stories and so grand that the governor attended its opening many decades ago, rotted under an old roof until the cupolas fell in, then it burned too. Another giant barn, built by Ahlberg's pal Chris Sorensen for the Pond Lilly Dairy, was razed long before my time, but I know it from old photographs. Now, following the Larsons' progress with my binoculars, I notice for the first time that the corner of Linquist's broad-roofed, Norwegian-style barn is collapsing. Since it has outlived its function and is beyond repair, Mark and Bonnie are planning to offer the barn boards on eBay. Otherwise, only Klint's, Torppa's, Fitts's, and Zimmerman's barns still stand in our part of the valley, and just a handful more between K-M Mountain and Rosburg. These are the castles in a land of mostly modest homes and few structures of outstanding architectural consequence. As the barns go, so goes the first farmers' hold on the land.

Our house commands a view of this small inland valley. My days, my moods, are tempered by the subtle changes reflected in the landscape as winter passes into spring, as the light shifts from east to west across the fields. But this spot on the earth hasn't always seen great expanses of grass and fence and dairy herds. The valley has always been green, and for many centuries a river has defined it. But this pastureland was hard-wrought; some hundred to a hundred and thirty years ago it was a tangle of spruce and cedar and willow and cottonwood dominating a lowland swamp. Beaver, wind, and water were the forces that decided which trees would survive to maturity, which bars would emerge as small islands in the river's meanders, wreathed by skunk cabbage and creek dogwood.

The heirs of those pungent clumps of skunk cabbage, by hue if not genetics, were the daffodils brought by the settlers who cleared the cottonwoods. Besides the barns, the pastures, and the naturalized yellow smear of the daffodils, the pioneers left other, subtler relics. The moles bring them to light, or Thea turfs them up while weeding the garden. A whole collection of beautiful buttons and baubles have come to light this way: ceramic with carnelian-inlay flower, blue cut glass, tin and copper filigree, jet (as if from a mourning dress and necklace), and brass with a decorated star in the middle and P E L L E thrice around the button's rim. A round steel horse-tack ornament with a glassy jewel in the middle. Bright striped and swirled marbles. Shards of china finely painted with orange, pink, and purple petals and green vinework. Square nails. The century of occupation by Ahlbergs and Sorensons left its sign in the much-worked clay and, in the attic, painted metal chandeliers and fancy garments reworked by moth and mouse. In the cellar, two big cottonwood bowls said to have been carved by some of the last local Indians. And the outbuildings hold hand-carved ladder-racks, an anvil block, some implements I still haven't figured out, and the old P O N D   L I L L Y   D A I R Y sign.

The Lily Pond is still there, but except at highest water, Larson's Pond has shrunk through ditching and the invasion of reed canary grass. The agate beach is gone from our side of the river, accreted on the other shore, and with it the pink S of river at sunset has shimmied into a backward J. Thoreau wrote, "It was not always dry land where we dwell. I see far inland the banks which the stream anciently washed, before science began to record its freshets." We occupy one such bank, for now. When Ed Sorenson left Gray's River, he said, "You know, Bob, we don't really own the land. We take care of it for a while, and then pass it on to the next fellow." We too will leave our brilliants in the soil, and one day they may be unearthed—by the next fellow hoeing soil, by the river risen again, or by the eternal moles.

F R O M   M Y   S T U D Y window I see the mound of the nearer compost heap beneath the bare maples and oaks. Old leaves, grapefruit rinds, eggshells, and other detritus fly up as a plump varied thrush scratches with great energy for beetles and worms. She was there yesterday and has returned today in the expectation of finding something luscious in the steaming heap of rotting goods. Above her the compact flock of golden-crowned kinglets that has been working the birches and oaks all winter long flips past in a loose clump. Their buttery crown stripes flash between black and white side bars, and I can hear their brittle high piping through the glass. They scatter over the lichens on a hoary limb, trying once more to find morsels they missed last time.

It occurs to me that I write by methods similar to those employed by the winter-foraging birds. I go back and forth over the same stuff, the stuff of the lichens and the bark and the day after day, picking for what's new, for what I missed before. I toss garbage right and left over my head, poke my beak into the sodden stink, the holy reek, and sniff deeply. When I am lucky, I find a fat worm. I grasp it; it slithers and twists, trying its best to keep from getting pinned down. I keep at it. Then I go back in for more bits and pieces to round out the meal.

As spring warms up, the varied thrushes will move uphill into the cooler conifer forests to nest. Swainson's thrushes will take their place, whistling querulously in the hornbeams behind the compost at dusk, fluting their eight- or ten-note ascending songs from the hemlocks. Then other feeders will take over at the compost heap. Possums come at night, rooting for unfinished ears of corn, the earthworms that multiply exponentially within, and huge fat brown slugs. The garden slugs, in turn, gorge on apple cores and old lettuce and cannibalize the deliquescing carcasses of their own kind that we have frozen and composted. Thus they become, in John Hay's words, "part of the brown soil, in a state that was neither life nor death but a mysterious merging of both."

My daily walk to the compost heap is the closest thing I know to sacrament. The pile grows out of a round brick pit that once served as an ornamental fishpond. After trying to restore the pond, I realized I could never persuade its broken bottom to hold water, so I embraced Thea's idea: why not make it the place where all the goodness goes, between life and more life, during that great long limbo called rot? Now I love to watch the succession of organic sediment through the months: the zucchini we're never going to eat in January, the first sweet grass clippings of

April, the remains of fresh lettuce in June, the blown flower heads in September, the caved-in pumpkins in November, all punctuated by citrus peels, eggshells, and the stalks and bracts of Brussels sprouts and artichokes. Coffee grounds and tea bags. Now and then a sprout from a big, shiny avocado seed sends up tender leaves until the first frost. A second heap farther out toward the woods receives shredded brush and bushels of raked leaves for longer-term rotting. They too take part in Darwin's "formation of vegetable mould"—making mulch, the potting soil of life.

Around the spring equinox, another yearling deer was hit on the highway, and we barrowed it down to the river field. By the last day of the year, nothing remained but a felt of fur on the matted grass. The next flood washed even that away. When the water pulled back, there was no sign that this particular deer had ever walked the Willapa Hills. Yet even as it reentered the flow, it helped dozens of other creatures make it through the winter. Every road-killed or winter-killed creature, if returned to the fields or woods, gives back life.

Which is how it was with Bokis when I planted him down in the plum grove. High ferns, salmonberry, and Indian plum were all nourished by his considerable bulk. Firkin has her own relationship with the compost, though she hasn't yet entered its stream. I've long played with the cats while raking leaves, and one day it occurred to me that we didn't have to wait for fall: there was a perfectly good leaf pile on the compost. So I carried Firkin out there and tossed her on top of the heap. She seemed to enjoy it. Now whenever there is a layer of dry leaves or fresh-mown grass on one of the mounds (as opposed to sodden veg or kitchen scraps), I plop Firkin onto my shoulder, head out to the compost, deposit my offering, and then fly the cat. She purrs all the way. We have a regular launch sequence, and at blast-off I hurl her toward the summit, which might be six or eight feet high. Usually she makes a four-point landing right on top, surveys the scene, then runs or rolls down the other side before taking off into the woods on errands of her own. As all rituals tend to do, my three rites of taking out the compost, visiting Bokis, and flying the cat glue me to this place. And if someday I too should be tossed on the compost pile, I could think of no better end.

RIGHT AROUND CHRISTMAS this year, two new birds appeared on the same day: a white-throated sparrow and a mountain chickadee. Both species occur rarely in the maritime Northwest; the former is chiefly eastern, and the latter a bird of higher elevations. No one knows why so many of the montane tits descended into western Washington lowlands this mild winter, but they stuck around, hanging out with black-capped and chestnut-backed chickadees, while the white-throat scratched for seeds with towhees and fox sparrows beneath the feeders. A third novelty for our list, a red-breasted nuthatch, later joined them. Like the Persius duskywing butterfly that showed up in the bleeding hearts on the back porch last Easter, these three new birds, each with its black-and-white eye stripes, showed how novelty still arises here. I could attend in earnest to the natural history of Swede Park for the rest of my life—ten years for flies, twenty for beetles, the rest for millipedes and moths—and never exhaust the daily discoveries.

Old, reliable friends can be as rewarding as discoveries. On New Year's Day, taking advantage of mild weather to work outdoors, I was relieving trees of ivy when a red-bellied sapsucker appeared, drilling Braille messages up and down a hickory trunk a few feet away. Its cherry headdress was the high point against a western sky distilling into bands of rose, salmon, mauve, and rust against a backdrop of olive green. Days later, as we took our Christmas tree down, the frog chorus swelled, though still nowhere near its March crescendo. Coyotes called high, piercing, and briefly in the middle of the night, drowning out the frogs, which kept on in fields only moderately flooded. The morning was brilliant—sixty-five degrees, with snowdrops, crocuses, and dwarf iris all about to bloom, and blood currant and Indian plum buds swelled toward bursting. Skunk cabbages already poked up five or six inches along the creek. The sixth of January, at 46+ degrees N latitude, and the bees were out on the heather.

I have little doubt we are seeing the advance signs of climate change. Already wood nymphs have moved west into our longitude with the warming summers. A ravine fronting the Columbia showed fresh growth of corydalis months early. And this February we spotted an American painted lady at coltsfoot nectar beside Gray's Bay, the first ever recorded as wintering in Washington. The phenology of this place—the very calendar of the land—is changing. We could acquire a Mediterranean climate, much like Mendocino's. Winters are expected to be wetter as well as warmer. Thank goodness—if they were to go drier and warmer, we wouldn't have a chance against the developers. Only the rain has kept this place "underpopulated." It always comes down to the rain.

At a recent public meeting to discuss the county's comprehensive plan, people were asked to indicate what they like about the area here. Everyone likes it rural, but most dislike government agencies and regulations that help keep things as they are. This doublethink is an old enigma in the Republic of Ruralia, one that eventually overwhelms many bucolic communities, as naive desires to have it both ways are defeated by outside money. So which is preferable—being overrun from outside or dwindling through attrition to a ghost town? In between is best, we would all say: to be able to leave the freeway at Kelso and breathe deeply, knowing that we'll see only half a dozen cars between Longview and home, and also to know that the EMTs and the ambulance, Mike's Store and the post office, the sheriff and the linemen are all there when we need them.

We're just about at critical mass: fewer than four thousand people and no traffic lights in the whole county, about a thousand in greater Gray's River and Rosburg, yet with adequate to excellent services still intact. The Lower Columbia area offers a great community radio station, a fine string quartet, and lots of homegrown art, drama, and literature, all of which spill over into Wahkiakum. Yet we're on the edge, and we know it; the remaining two schools have declining populations, and the county is cutting more than corners. There is very little work here, and yet property tax assessments, formerly low, have just doubled or tripled because lots with Columbia River views are being bought at inflated prices by outsiders with more money than time to actually spend here. For the rest of us, what Donald Hall wrote about his New Hampshire outpost applies just as well to Gray's River: "There's no reason to live here except for love."

AT GRANGE ELECTIONS last fall, I asked Bobby Larson how his move was going. He had promised Ila Mae that he would get her well above the winter floods, and they were about to move to a mobile home on a knoll on their downvalley land. Bobby had just completed a handsome, rainproof shingled canopy for the trailer. "The bid for the septic tank came in too high," he said, "so the deal is, we're looking for another. These days, seven thousand dollars isn't that easy to come up with." The fact is, it has never been easy for the Larsons to come up with that much, any more than it has for us. Bobby told me how his mother had come as a two-month-old from Michigan, when her father settled up above Fossil Creek. His parents lived at the populous logging camp on the summit of K-M Hill, where his brothers, Harry and Norman, were born. The family came down to the valley floor in the twenties, and Larsons have lived here ever since. Bobby has spent his entire life in Gray's River except for a posting in the Aleutians in World War II.

The Larsons made it out of the flood zone and into their new place at last. But the extended rains the following spring and summer came down just the same, and when prime time for haying came and went with no hay cut, Bobby was fit to be tied. He'd been having dizzy spells, and he finally figured out that they were touched off by frustration when he couldn't get his work done. After a Grange meeting we talked by the river in that particular kind of gloaming that settles on Gray's River on damp summer nights. He was worried about getting the grass cut before it was too far gone and before the bridge's birthday party. "When the last of your brothers goes before you," he said, "you start to feel your age." That age was seventy-eight. But he'd gotten his tractor fixed, and he knew that if he could get the weather to do the job, he'd feel fine. The next day the clouds cleared, the meadows steamed, and he began the cut. One more day, and the sun was hot and full. I watched Bobby and his tractor go around and around the fields by the bridge, shredding his cares along with the grass that flew from the flail. He got it done, and when Bald Eagle Days arrived in Cathlamet, he felt he could take time off to go. The bridge centennial float, signed T H E W A Y W E W E R E , rolled into view in the parade, on its way to the first-place trophy. There on Burkhalter's hay wagon was Marilyn Gudmundsen, knitting in a rocker; Ila Mae Larson, churning butter; and Bobby on the back, slinging hay with a pitchfork. Ila Mae took ill and died the next winter, but not before enjoying life above the flood at last. We miss her immeasurably.

Doug will stay on at the old place with his cows for a while, keeping the faith with Marie Fauver, Virginia Wendelin, and her daughter Bonnie Linquist, among the few members of the valley's original families who carry on. Newcomers and in-betweeners like us will go on making a life here as best we can. We may hope that the cattle, the kale, and the hay will keep this place a little longer in a pastoral state. The valley will persist regardless.

Meanwhile, the cougars are coming back to the hills. In 1936 W. W. Foss caught an eight-foot cougar in a bear trap at a nearby logging camp. It got away but was treed by dogs and shot, which was routine then. I've seen just one puma in my years here, and that for just an instant. But last week a friend called to say she was seeing a mother mountain lion with three kittens on her place by Hull Creek—and no one had tried to kill them. After a long dearth, two little black bears have shown up nearby. Bald eagles have successfully bred in their new nest high in a cottonwood next to the one they were blown out of by last winter's gale. A robin is settling in for a second nesting in an old-growth buddleia. Our doe walked through the yard today, sleek and red, leading a fresh new fawn to a garden she happens to know about. And this much I know myself: the only sure things here are the river, the rain, and the Gray's River sky.

Notes and Acknowledgments

This book, in following a closely observed country year, also pays homage to an old tradition. From Virgil's *Georgics* to Edwin Way Teale's *Nature's Year* and Hal Borland's *Sundial of the Seasons* and on to Edward Abbey's *Desert Solitaire* and Donald Hall's *Seasons at Eagle Pond*, the phenological pastoral, or "personal phenology," as I call it, has a rich history. Some might call it too well trodden. But as no two observers see the seasons the same way, and no two regions are the same, I make no apologies for taking this familiar approach to writing about a particular place. I do wish to note, however, that *Sky Time in Gray's River* is not a straight chronology: it bounces around within a calendrical framework. Nor does it limn a given year, but rather mines the months of the twenty-eight years I have lived here. Some events, sequences, and tenses may thus strike others who have lived them as slightly askew, but they are all true, to the closest approximation I know.

I would also like to point out that while *Sky Time* is informed by local history, it is not a local history of Gray's River. That work remains to be written. The best sources to date are Irene Martin's *Beach of Heaven: A History of Wahkiakum County* (Washington State University Press, 1997); Ruth Busse Allingham's *Wa-*

ter Under the Bridge: Oral Histories from Gray's River Valley (2001); and Carlton A. Appelo's several monographs about nearby villages, published in the telephone books of the company his father founded and over which he still presides, now called Wahkiakum West. To each of these I express my heartfelt thanks and debt.

A note must be made about the apostrophe in Gray's River. Both the U.S. Board on Geographic Names and the U.S. Postal Service have abolished apostrophes in the place names they recognize, so it does not appear on maps, road signs, or our postmark. In fact, Carlton Appelo, our foremost scholar and authority on local history, has assured me that he has not seen the possessive designator on the local postal cancellation of any era. As I explained in my previous book about the area, *Wintergreen: Rambles in a Ravaged Land*, the apostrophe is strictly a matter of my own preference. The name Gray's River, after all, commemorates Captain Robert *Gray's* association with the place, not a plurality of gray tones, though that meaning would be just as suitable. Or maybe the apostrophe, which is used by almost none of the locals, even suggests a different place, ever so slightly unlike the real one with its similar name, thus absolving my portrait of the burden of absolute fidelity.

The acknowledgments in *Wintergreen* rivaled the begats in the Old Testament, and they all apply here as well. A proper "thank you" would extend to all the names in Carlton's phone book and then some. All the folks mentioned in these pages should consider me obliged to them, and to many others who should have been mentioned. Here I must name a few for special kindnesses over the years: Ed and Lenore Sorenson and their offspring; Bobby, Ila Mae, Doug, and Brian Larson; Judy and Merlin Durrah; Norman and Myrtle Anderson; Veryl, Barbara, Bill, and Kay Chamberlain; the Fitts, Matthews, Ervest, and Zimmerman families, among others; Jean Calhoun, Marilyn Gudmundsen, Marie Fauver, Glenrose Hedlund, and Jenny Pearson—I wish I had all their stories; Carlton and Berenice Appelo; Ernie and Selma Wirkkala and Timo Virkkala; Susan and Ted Kafer, Brenda Boardman, Robert van Pelt, Mace Vaughn, Ed and Cathy

Maxwell, Ann Musché and Alan Richards, Elaine and David Lee Myers, Fayette Krause and JoAnne Heron; the Martins, Fletchers, Parkers, and Emlen/Pettersons of Skamokawa; and Neil Johannsen, Bill Leonard, Jeff Eustis, Esther Gregg, Barbara Bate, Krist Novoselic and Darbury Stenderu, Steve Puddicombe, Bob LiaBraaten, Mary Steller, Karen Bertroch, David Shaw, and everyone at Mike's Rosburg Store.

"The Grief of Thrushes" was previously published in *Convolvulus*. Thea Linnaea Pyle's "Reincarnation" was published as a broadside by Ludgate Hill Press. I thank all of the authors of the chapter epigraphs and their estates, and all the other writers I have quoted. The *Wahkiakum County Eagle* and the *Chinook Observer* were essential, as were the Gray's River Computer Center and the Appelo Archive Center and its curators, Linda Amaya, Abbie Laine, Donna Klint, and Maia Wise.

A number of local writers and friends read, critiqued, and commented on early drafts of various sections, including Greg Darms, Brian Harrison, Susan Holway, John Indermark, Brian Pentilla, Pat Staton Thomas, Jenelle Varila, Lorne Wirkkala, and Jane Elder Wulff. Carlton Appelo kindly read the entire manuscript, as did Thea Pyle. I am grateful to Thea for her title-page block print of the covered bridge and to Benj Drummond for the author photo.

The idea for this book came from a suggestion by Clay Harper, as inspired by Donald Hall's ode to home ground, mentioned above. Its realization is owed to the nurturing of Harry Foster, its refinement to the care of Peg Anderson, and its design to Victoria Hartman, all of Houghton Mifflin Company. My ever solicitous, kind, and canny agents, Jenny McDonald and Laura Blake Peterson, saw it through from start to finish. Sally Hughes got this place up and running with me, and Marvyne Betsch made it possible. Thea, Tom, Dory, Bokis, and Firkin have lived it with me, and Thea has made the life here both feasible and wonderful, for which I could not be more lovingly grateful.

Finally: *This is no utopia.* Please don't move here because of this book! Some did as a result of *Wintergreen*, and very few have remained. Believe me on this—*you won't like the rain!* One headline in a local paper this winter read "42 inches in 25 days." An-

other told of beating January's previous sodden record by five inches. Instead of luring you to some idealized bucolic hideout that would almost certainly disappoint in the end or rot your heels, may this little book assist you in finding the heart of your own home, which lies in the lives and the skies of everyplace.

RMP
April 2006